DADDY
SHARPE

DADDY
SHARPE

A Narrative of the Life and Adventures of
Samuel Sharpe
A West Indian Slave
Written by Himself, 1832

BY FRED W. KENNEDY

Ian Randle Publishers
Kingston • Miami

First published in Jamaica, 2008 by
Ian Randle Publishers
11 Cunningham Avenue
Box 686
Kingston 6
www.ianrandlepublishers.com

National Library of Jamaica Cataloguing in Publication Data

Kennedy, Fred
        Daddy Sharpe: a narrative of the life and adventures of Samuel
Sharpe, a West Indian slave written by himself, 1832/Fred Kennedy

        p. : ill., maps: cm

Bibliography: p.

ISBN 978-976-637-354-2 (hbk)
ISBN 978-976-637-343-6 (pbk)

1. Sharpe, Samuel, d. 1832 – Fiction   2. Biographical information

I. Title

813   dc. 22

Cover and Book design by Ian Randle Publishers
Printed in the United States of America

This narrative is dedicated
to my three daughters,

Amanda, Sarah and Julia

I would rather die upon yonder gallows than live in slavery.
Samuel Sharpe, 1832

XL.   Any slave who shall pretend to any supernatural power, in order to affect the health or lives of others, or promote the purposes of rebellion shall upon conviction thereof suffer death, or such other punishment as the court shall think proper to direct.

—Laws for the Government of Negro Slaves,
Jamaica, 1787

Open your eyes
And look within
Are you satisfied
With the life you're living?
We know where we're going
We know where we're from
We're leaving Babylon
We're going to our Father's land.

—from 'Exodus' by Bob Marley

FOREWORD

In December 1831, Jamaica underwent the largest, most significant slave rebellion in its history. The leader of this revolt was Samuel Sharpe, one of Jamaica's seven National Heroes, who was born and who died a slave in the Parish of St James.

The narrative that follows is a fictionalized account of his life, told, as I have been able to imagine it, from his point of view.

In recreating this period of Jamaican history, I have remained as faithful as possible to an accurate portrayal of the major political, social and economic events of the years prior to emancipation. I have described and recreated some of the incidents, characters and places as they are recorded in the chronicles of history, but for others, especially in the years of Sam Sharpe's childhood, where historical details are sparse, I have allowed myself full poetic licence in inventing the narrative.

Sam Sharpe's biographical information is sketchy. The details which we do have are those of his life as a rebel slave. Edward Kamau Brathwaite notes that the information is often contradictory:

> Indeed, there is every indication that neither missionaries nor Government officials knew whether they were dealing with Sam or John Thorp or Tharp or Sharp or Sharpe; and whether they were dealing with a slave from Croydon, Hazelymph, Catadupa or Cooper's Hill and whether his owner was a male

> solicitor or a female then residing at Montego Bay,
> or a man called Gray. (Brathwaite: 1976, p. 23)

For literary purposes, I have exploited these and other examples of incongruities to help weave the narrative of Sam Sharpe's life by blending fact with fiction.

Throughout the text, I have used direct quotations, which are credited in the section on *References* for each chapter. These notes also aim to clarify points of historical significance and to distinguish, where appropriate, factual from fictional information. A glossary of Jamaican words, a list of Bible quotations and a bibliography of primary and secondary sources also appear in the appendices, for readers who may wish to extend their knowledge of this period in Jamaican history.

This work is an artistic interpretation of the life of Sam Sharpe, creative in the sense that I have fictionalized characters and situations but non-fictional in that I have re-told historical facts, wherever possible, from a chronological viewpoint. It is also the story, on a more symbolic level, of a people who fought for freedom and later broke the chains of slavery. I trust that the reader will find the events both informative from a historical perspective and entertaining from a literary one.

Fred W. Kennedy

A Narrative

of

The Life and Adventures

of

Samuel Sharpe,

A West Indian Slave
Written by Himself, 1832

CONTENTS

Part I
Cooper's Hill

*

Part II
The Bay

*

Part III
Croydon Estate

*

Part IV
The Bush

*

Epilogue

Part I
COOPER'S HILL

The Island of Jamaica with Names of Parishes and Towns, 1831

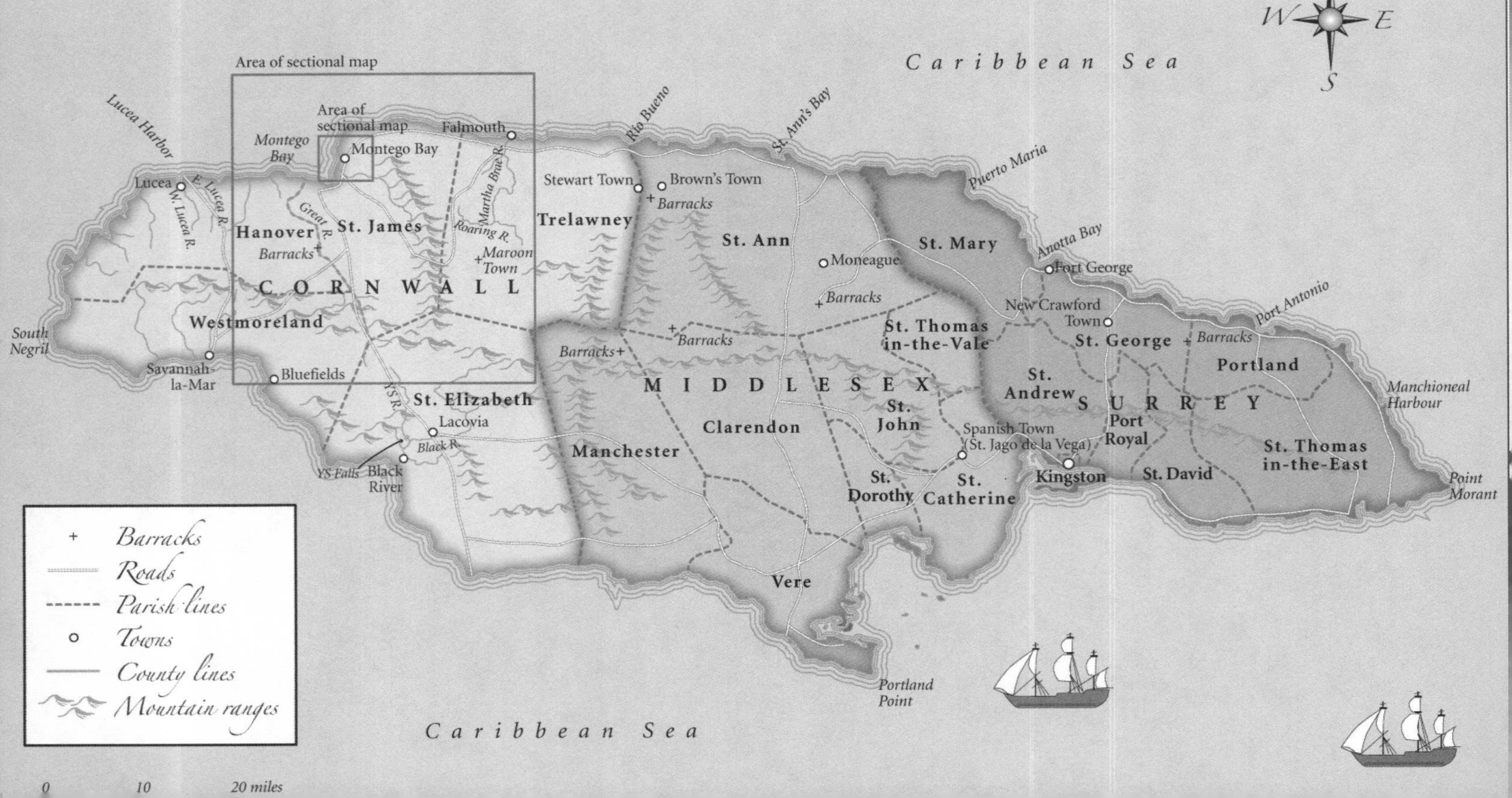

ONE

March 1832

I *was born into slavery on the island of Jamaica about the year 1801. My narrative begins with boyhood memories of my mama and of an old slave named Tacky at Cooper's Hill in the Parish of St James.*

The magistrates of the parish have given permission for the story of my life to be recorded and for Parson Bleby to publish the writings. It seems strange that a slave would write stories, but thanks to the kindness of my master, Samuel Sharpe Esquire, I now possess the ability to read and write and have acquired many other graces of an English gentleman. His wife, Mistress Sharpe, has offered to edit the work and to assist Parson Bleby in the publication of the memoirs. No doubt, these two persons will improve greatly upon the grammar and style of my scripts.

The narrative is dedicated to my fellow slaves who have fought so valiantly with me for the cause of freedom. My intention in writing this is not to condemn my oppressors, but instead, to reveal to you the madness of slavery.

I have faith in God, my Saviour, that freedom will soon come and that my brethren in this sweet land will rejoice and praise the Lord.

1814

One night I was seated in front of the Negro houses in a circle with Tacky, Mama and two of my best friends, Robert Gardner and Thomas Dove. Tacky was the oldest slave on the property and he loved to tell African stories of the famous

3

spider, Anancy. He was an Akan Negro from the Gold Coast, advanced in years but young in spirit. I remember his deep black skin which ran tight all over his muscles and his woolly head of hair silvered with age. When he told us stories, he bent over, leaning on a crooked logwood stick, his eyes shining like fireflies in the night, his voice strong like thunder.

'One day, Tiger swear dat once and for all, him was gwine fi break up 'Nancy bone them. But as you know, 'Nancy always did guard himself gainst Brother Tiger.' Tacky stood upright for a moment and pointed his stick at us. 'One day, unu gwine haffi guard youself same way.'

The night was hot but I felt a cold shiver down my back. I looked over at Mama for her comfort. She was a strong woman, a salt-water Negro brought here to Jamaica on the big ship from Africa. 'Mimba, field labourer, able-bodied' was how the head driver said the Massa wrote it in the stock book. When she first reached Cooper's Hill, they used a hot iron to brand her with the markings 'SS' on both shoulders to show that she belonged to her rightful owner, Samuel Sharpe Esquire. The cattle had the same branding as she. Mama gave me a stern look now, to tell me I should be paying more attention to what Tacky was saying.

'One night, just like dis one, Bro Tiger lie down fi sleep, wrap up in a him sheet. Him tell him wife sey him waan 'Nancy fi believe him is dead, "'Nancy is too much boderation, let me tell you, and de time come now fi finish him off, once and for all." So Bro Tiger, him lie down and wait fi 'Nancy, but 'Nancy nah come. Bro Tiger get vex, vex fi true and him sey to him wife, "Mistress Tiger, what wrong wid dis 'Nancy? Him don't know that Bro Tiger dead?"

'"How is Anancy supposed to know, Brother Tiger?"' she talk in her most proper English.'

Dove looked startled for a second as if he had heard a snake. His instincts were sharp. Dove and Gardner were my age. They had no mamas, at least not living with us anyway. Tacky continued with his story.

'"You is suppose fi tell him. What wrong wid you, woman? Go out into de yard, and start fi bawl, tell all de people sey yuh husband dead, and sey in de loudest voice you have, 'Lawd have mercy pon me soul, me husband dead', loud, loud so that even 'Nancy can hear sey yuh husband dead."'

'By dis time now, Brother Tiger well vex. Him waan fi get back at 'Nancy real bad.'

Tacky stopped suddenly. The patu called out from the cotton tree up by the Great House. The night had been quiet except for the screeching of the bird. I looked up towards the house. The fireflies lit a path all the way up, their yellow light shifting and dancing in different patterns. The house rose up big from the land with its white stone walls bright in the night. I wanted to go into my shelter with Mama, to hide under the cane-trash roof, safe within the wattled walls of mud and bamboo. The bird stopped making noise and all was silent again.

But then the overseer broke the silence of the night, moving down the path, his eyes green like puss, his big belly white like fish. He was wearing no shirt and his trousers hung below his belly button. He was wobbling back and forth, carrying a switch to fight his way through the fireflies. I knew he was coming for Mama.

Mama quickly gathered us up, pushing me and the two other boys into the slave hut. I looked back and saw Mr Crawford's face when he entered the mud clearing, his eyes flaming red like a mad bull. And I smelled the rum.

'Lef de woman alone, Mr Crawford.' Tacky blocked him from Mama.

'You impudent ass, move out of the way.' Mr Crawford grabbed Tacky's logwood stick and beat the old man until he fell to the ground. He raised the cane to hit Mama, who was crouched down near to him. She stood up with her face close to his.

'Don't you f__in lick me with dat stick.'

He grabbed her left hand and pulled her along the dirt path down from the slave huts to the cane piece. I had wanted to break his legs with Tacky's stick and rub his white face in the black dirt, but I was too coward. Mr Crawford was the man we all feared. He was the White man who was put in charge of us all. We called him Busha, the common name we slaves use for the man in charge.

The patu cried out one more time.

I listened for Mama, but could hear only the rats scurrying in the cane piece, which was next to Massa's property. When the rats got fat during crop time, I loved to go into the fields with Gardner and Dove to kill them with a cutlass. They were so big that even the cats were afraid of them. We would bring them to the hut for Mama to cook and we would all have a feast on the sweet meat. The buckra were glad for us to hunt them down because when rats breed plenty they ruin the cane. Cane is of no use once the rats bite it.

Tacky moved slowly from the spot where Mr Crawford had left him, shuffling over to his hut like a lame lizard, pushing his way along the ground on his hands and feet. I wanted to hear the end of the Anancy story but he was too beaten down for that.

I looked around for Dove and Gardner.

I called out for them, but there was no answer. They must have run out into the darkness. In times past, Tacky was one of the strongest slaves on the property. He had been a member of the Great Gang, the group of slaves the massa hired out to dig cane holes on nearby estates. At first, Tacky used to boast he was the healthiest and priciest male slave Massa Sharpe owned, but with time he grew old and could not do his work any more. Now, he cleaned up around the place, weeding the yard and feeding the animals. In the evenings, he enjoyed telling us stories of the times when he was younger, stronger and full of tricks. He had loved a slave woman who lived on Content Estate, past the Montego River, on the other side of the Great River. He told us how he had wanted her very much. On nights not too bright from the moon shine, he would leave Cooper's Hill and walk barefoot, quiet and quick through the bush, down to a special hiding place by the river. Tacky said he always remembered to bring a stick with him because of the snakes.

'You must nebba touch de yellow one, Sam. It grow so tall, sometime all twenty foot in length, so tall dat one man kyaan even budge it. Dem call it de boa. Never touch de yellow one. It will strangle you.'

His sweetheart was the lovely Quasheba. Poor Tacky thought that they were secret lovers but little did he know that with all the susu-susu that went on among the slaves, word spread fast that Tacky and Quasheba were doing a ting down by the river every Saturday night. Besides, it was told that Mr Crawford had his own spy, a slave boy named Roach, who saw Tacky coming back up from the river every Sunday morning.

The head slave was instructed to set Tacky's feet in the bilboes and place him outside in the night without pants or shirt. His hands were chained and a collar with a padlock put around his neck. He told us that the mosquitoes used to bite him so hard that his whole body would swell up and the dews would come down wet, pon his head and give him fever. But he loved his Quasheba so much that when the chains came off, he would make plans to go back down once again to his special hiding place at the river crossing.

The situation grew worse. Tacky disappeared for days, weeks at a time. So finally Mr Crawford ordered the head slave to make a wood frame for the runaway. They fit the frame over Tacky's head and shoulders, and in the top of the box they put a cowbell over his head.

'There was no way me could a escape now. If me did ever try fi run, Mr Crawford would a hear de bell. Everybody would a hear de bell. Poor me.'

But not even the bell stopped Tacky. His love for Quasheba was too strong. One night, he asked his slave friends to gather up leaves from the yard and tief some cloth from the cookhouse. They stuffed the bell so full that Mr Crawford could not hear Tacky when he walked. But when poor Tacky went down to the riverside that last night, Quasheba took one look at him and said there was no way in the whole world she could love a man with a wood box and a bell on top of his head. From that time forward, Tacky's heart was broken.

After Tacky was beaten down by Mr Crawford, he managed to crawl into his hut. I found him lying sideways on the ground with his knees folded up close to his face. I reached down and pulled at his shoulder. 'You all right, Tacky?'

'Mr Crawford too wicked, Sam. If him don't look out, dem gwine obeah him.'

'Don't worry bout dem ting now, Tacky. You mus rest.'

He reached up with his free arm and grabbed me, pulling me down toward him. His grip was still strong. He held my neck-back and pushed his face in mine. I smelled the rum and tobacco. He spoke close to my ear. 'Mr Crawford is a raas.

Him don't like it when anybody stand up to him. And him not treating yuh mother right, Sam. You know what we call him? De name perfect fi him. Mista C is a Raas C. I tell you, Sam, dem boys gwine obeah him, me sure of dat.' He let me go and lay back down on the earth. His voice became fainter. 'You mus go now and tend to yuh mama. You is a man-boy now, Sam, so you mussi strong and mek sure you tek good care of her. Promise me one ting, Sam, before you go. If you should ever see Quasheba, tell her fi me dat me always did love her and dat she will always be me Queen of Sheba.'

I went back to my hut and lay down at the opening to listen for Mama. The earth felt cool on my belly. The rats must have feasted themselves because I could not hear them any more. Instead, the night crickets were now making noise, raucous and mad. I was not sure whether they were fighting or making love but the sound was ringing in my ears. It had rained, so the cockroaches too were plentiful, flying about and crawling out of their holes in the earth. Gardner and Dove and the rest of us boys liked catching them and squeezing them between our toes to see the white blood ooze out. It was the lizards we did not like, the croakers looking down with their evil eye from the thatch roof of the huts.

I did not think I looked different from any of the other slave boys my age, but Mama told me that from when I was little my eyes shine bright, sparkling like the stars in the night and that my hair stand back far on my forehead. My skin is jet black, my nose broad and my lips full like an African. Some say my father was Bigga, the head slave, a stout man with thick arms and legs and shiny black skin. Others say he was the massa because we had the same name, Sam Sharpe, but I was not light enough to be a mulatto and he was very young, too young to be my daddy.

9

Crop-over was the best time of year for us slaves. Towards the middle months of the year, barrels of mackerel, beef and other goods would arrive from town. Mr Sharpe would tell the overseer to share provisions with the slaves to reward us for the months of hard labour. Mr Crawford gave out portions of the salted meats along with bottles of wine, bottoms of sugar and quarts of rum. I think he only shared it out because Mr Sharpe told him to do so.

Mama received her own special gifts. One night she brought me a jacket like the one the White boys wear. For the females, she carried cloths of bright colours for making blouses and petticoats. Other times, her basket was full of oil, red herring and salt beef. Mimba never smiled when she handed out the gifts. She only said, 'De buckra send these things fi unu.' Then her face would go blank.

I followed her one evening when she went out. She left the slave houses just after dark, walking straight through the plantain-walk to Busha's house. As I came closer to the house, I saw her step up to the piazza where Mr Crawford was sitting, catching the night breeze. He did not look surprised when she reached by his chair. He just rose up, grabbed her from behind and stole her away into his stone house. I waited for her the whole night. Close to the first cockcrow, she walked quietly down the steps of the veranda carrying a basket full of gifts.

I finally saw Mama's figure come out from the cane piece like a duppy in the night. It moved closer and closer to me, not making a sound.

'Maami.'

'What you doing out of yuh bed dis time of night?' She folded her arms as if she was cold.

I didn't see Mr Crawford anywhere. I wondered whether he was too drunk to walk or if she had chopped him up with a cutlass.

'Me was waiting fi you, Mama.'

'Get up and go to yuh bed.'

She grabbed me by the shoulders and shook me hard, raising her voice. 'What you think you doing, bwai, staying up so late?'

'Me didn't want him fi hurt you. Me wanted fi you to come back.'

'Don't talk things you don't know, Sam,' she screamed like a mad woman, pushing me inside the hut, slapping me again and again across the face. Then she began to cry. She bent down low, holding her belly as if in pain, pulled up and looked straight at me, holding my shoulders tight. 'Don't trouble yuh head worrying bout me, Sam. My daddy and his daddy, we is a strong people from de coast of Guinea. You will grow like we, you will learn fi guard yuhself like Anancy gainst Brer Tiger. You will fight fi freedom one day like Cudjoe, de brave man who led de slaves in battle. Dem people was Coromantees from de town of Ashantee. We is de same blood. So, don't fret yuhself, Sam. You must take care of yuhself and you musn't worry bout me.'

We were silent after that, gathering up strength from each other. Soon, we slept quietly like the farm animals until the second crow. Then it was time for the shell-blow, the signal for the first spell of the Great Gangs everywhere to head out to harvest the fields.

When cock crow fas fas, day soon light.

TWO

Through the bars of the prison door, I see the guards hauling in two female slaves. They push them up against a wall, tie their feet, and tell them to raise their frocks up above their heads. From behind, the women appear to be naked. The guards begin to laugh. They play with them by touching them. Then they flog them. The females are strong, saying not a word lest they satisfy the lust of their attackers.

I have not had a bath for weeks. I scratch my head and pick white lice from my hair. The cell is filthy. At night, the rats run back and forth through the cell, happy to feed on the urine and human waste.

I expect Parson Bleby will soon come for a visit. He will question me and then report back to the magistrates about my involvement in the slave rebellion. He will want to know whether or not the missionaries played a part in inciting the slaves.

I know that God will judge me and find that I have been righteous and have wanted no evil. I will not change my views, for before I would be a slave I would be buried in my grave and go home to my Lord and be free.

I must go on with my story despite my distractions. Prisoners are wailing in neighbouring cells and my own place smells worse than a pigpen.

1815

Tacky was not able to work any more after Mr Crawford beat him with the stick that night by the slave huts. He could not straighten up his body but needed now to lean all the while on his walking stick. Mama and I took him to the sick-house on the next property up past the cow pasture. Much sturdier than our huts in the village, the hospital stood tall with smooth cut stone and a thatched roof.

I dreaded going up to the yaws house, as we sometimes called it. The smell was renk, a mixture of sweat, medicine and herbs. It held about twenty slaves who came from neighbouring estates. They had many kinds of sickness, some with fever, others with dry bellyache, but the worst was cocobay, better known by Whites as leprosy. The arms and legs became spotted with runny sores and swellings which oozed and smelled bad. After the surgeon made sure that it was cocobay, then the slave was taken away to a special place in the big city they call Kingston. Mr Crawford put Tacky in the stink-house because he was of no use. He was too broken-down to work.

Cooper's Hill is a small property, situated a couple miles up the hill from Montego Bay. The slaves numbered about fifteen at the residence and Mr Sharpe owned more slaves on an adjacent property which he operated as a pen. The strong males and the robust females like Mama were hired out to the big estates as 'jobbers'. Bigga was the driver, the head slave who took orders from Mr Crawford and Mr Sharpe. Life was tough for the slaves when Massa was away because Busha then had full control over us. A few privileged slaves did not work the fields: the carpenter, the pen keeper and the stable boy. Sometimes, Massa would even pay them for their labour. The house slaves also had a more comfortable life than the field slaves. Mr and Mrs Sharpe had two females helping in the big house, an elderly slave who was in charge and a younger girl who assisted her. Sometimes other females were brought in to wash the clothes and help clean the house. Young children from nearby pens did the lighter chores like weeding the yard and feeding the fowl. The lighter skin slaves received more liberties and were given less work. Mama was not one of those favoured ones. She was a salt-water Negro, or sometimes we call them guinea-bird Negro, a true Black African.

The sturdier males, when not hired out, worked the crops and tended to the animals at the pen. Mr Sharpe owned hogs, chickens, cows and oxen which he bred and sold to the larger estates. He also owned his own woodland, fruit trees and provision ground. As I got older, Mr Crawford assigned me to the harder chores of chopping and hauling wood. When we were not working for the massa, we could tend to our own provision grounds where we had foodstuffs like plantains, fruit and ground roots. If Mr Crawford was in a good mood, he would give us every other Saturday to work our own land.

The residence was situated on a rise above the town. At the top of the property by Mr Sharpe's house, I loved to sit on the limestone rock to look down on the roofs of houses in Montego Bay, and beyond that, at the tall ships in the harbour and the sea spreading out in many shades of blue. On the other three sides, behind me and to the left and right, the green mountains rose up from the plain. We did not have much free time but if Mr Crawford and Bigga were otherwise occupied, I sneaked up there. On those occasions, I wondered what it would be like to swim out into the blue or to be one of the big white gulls dipping freely to grab the flying fish. When I felt sad, I wanted to escape with Mama on a big ship sailing out of the Bay, becoming smaller and smaller as we reached the part where the sea met the sky. I wasn't sure where the ships went, whether to Africa or to England, or if they just vanished beyond the horizon.

Since I was a boy, I have sensed a greatness beyond the sea and sky and have wondered about how the bright stars at night came to be. I have always felt there was a spirit bigger than myself. I longed to understand these mysteries, but did not know how to uncover them. My mind was too occupied with the bad things Mr Crawford was doing, and I needed to find a way for Mama to be free of his evil. The man was too wicked.

To one side of Massa Sharpe's house, between it and the Negro houses rose a tall silk-cotton tree, towering three or four times the height of the house. Its top branches touched the sky, the lower ones reaching almost as far as the slave huts. At its base, large thick roots stretched long and smooth on all sides, forming deep crevices where the duppies lived. The ancestral tree always blossomed at crop time, producing clusters of splendid white flowers. There lived the patu which made its calls every evening.

In front of the house, logwood trees lined a cow pasture and fields of guinea grass grew four to five feet tall during the rainy season, around September, October time. The sharply pointed blades always shimmered a light shade of green in the sun-hot. The livestock loved the guinea grass and we Negroes used it for medicine. When I was sick, Mama boiled the leaves to cure high fever. Massa told me that a sea captain long ago brought the seeds to Jamaica to feed his bird, but on the passage the birds died. So when he arrived here he threw the seeds on the ground and up grew fields of green guinea grass. Ever since then, there was no stopping the grass from covering the open fields in Jamaica.

Up to one side, opposite the Negro village, Mr Sharpe kept animals: fowl, hogs and cows. Behind this was his plantain-walk where he grew banana, plantain and mango in plenty, yam, cocoa and other ground provisions. Around the Great House and Mr Crawford's smaller house, large shade trees grew, tamarind, mahogany and flowering ones like Flame of the Forest with bright red and yellow blossoms at the tops of its branches. To salt-water Negroes, the tree spoke of their homeland Africa where they said it grew in abundance. They called it the African Tulip.

On our own grounds, we grew provisions but raised no animals. On the mountainside, we planted yam, yampy, plantain and pineapple. We had our own fruit trees, star apple, sweetsop, ackee, breadfruit and jackfruit. The jackfruit amused me, always green, growing out from the trunk, big and bulbous, heavy like a fat pickaninny. The yellow meat and the roasted seeds tasted nice but Massa always said the fruit had a bad smell, something like cow manure.

Life was good at Cooper's Hill, except for Mr Crawford. Under the silk-cotton tree was his favourite place for beating the slaves. For no apparent reason, he would use the cart whip on the women and the smaller boys whom Mr Sharpe owned. 'Why are you looking at me that way, boy? It's time you get a flogging.' The poor wretch would have to pull down his pants, lie with his face in the dirt, and, with four men holding his arms and legs, take Mr Crawford's punishment. Thirty-nine was the legal limit. Busha never laid hands on me, though. I am not sure why. Maybe it was because of Mama, or maybe Maas Sam told him not to touch me. I never did find out.

One day two of the man-boy slaves and I were given an order to cut a patch of guinea grass. The midday sun was hot. We worked without shirts and this made our black skin burn. Sweat ran off our bodies and the salt stung our eyes. One of the boys made the mistake of taking a break. He moved closer to the roadside where rows of logwood trees provided shade from the sun-hot. He leaned his machete up against the trunk of one of the trees and slid himself down to the ground, leaning his back against the bark.

'Why unu nah come out of de sun-hot? Raas C mussi drinking him rum back inna him house,' he shouted over to us. We called him Half-Pint because he was so small for his age. He never did grow tall.

Suddenly, with no warning, no dust flying, quiet like a thief, Mr Crawford appeared out of nowhere. He and his horse. I do not know how he came upon us without us hearing him. He tied his horse to a lower branch of the logwood tree where Half-Pint was sitting. First, he grabbed the boy's machete and threw it some distance into the field. Then he pulled the slave boy up and tied his hands to another branch of the tree so that his legs were dangling off the ground. Half-Pint did not cry out at the start. When I first heard him cry, I saw the blood, the moment the horsewhip broke his skin. The sweat from his labour mingled with his blood and the salt made the wounds sting even more.

'Who the raas you think you are, resting under a tree?' Mr Crawford pulled Half-Pint's head back and stuck his red face up into the boy's. He was breathing heavy and snorting like a bull. I would never understand why but I think Mr Crawford got pleasure from thrashing the slaves. 'I shall have Bigga fetch you at sundown.' There he left the boy, tied to the tree.

We never knew what to expect. Sometimes we would do bad things like report late to work and Mr Crawford would do nothing to us. Other times, the slaves would get a beating for no reason. He took a dislike to one of the females named Sally, and made up a story that she had stolen a fowl from the coop because he saw feathers in the boiling pot she was using. He told the driver to dig a round hole in the ground so that when she lay down, her pregnant belly would fit in the hole. And then he beat her. Must have been close to forty lashes. The next day, Sally bled so much she lost the baby. It was a Saturday, I remember, her day off. Mama told me she never did tief any fowl. The White boy from the Great House, Master Henry, stole the chicken and gave it to her. If Massa had known how bad Busha treated us, I am sure he would not have had him stay at Cooper's Hill.

That same year, something happened at Cooper's Hill which changed our lives forever. Mama got so vexed with the way Mr Crawford was treating us that she could not take it any more. Busha had ordered her and three other slaves to work at Adelphi Estate where Mr Winn was the proprietor who owned more than 200 slaves. Her job there was to cut the cane. On that particular day, she refused to go to work. Instead, she just stood up in front of the Great House waiting for Mr Sharpe to come home.

A gig came up the main road, a one-horse chaise with a canopy to shelter Massa from the sun. As it turned through the main gate and made its way up the winding road by the cow pasture, the wheels gave off clouds of white dust, marl stones flying in every direction. It seemed that the horse was agitated or that the driver was in a hurry. Bigga, the slave driver, and Mr Crawford had gone down to the Bay to fetch Mr Sharpe, who had been on one of his voyages to England. The slaves were always happy when Massa returned from his journey because Mr Sharpe was kind to us, listened to our complaints, and gave us lots of salt mackerel, oil and foodstuffs.

A few female slaves had gathered in front of the Great House in expectation of our master's return. Their heads were bound in brightly checkered handkerchiefs and they carried flowers which matched their petticoats. Mama stepped out in the middle of the road as if to block the approach of the gig. She was dressed in a one-piece frock made of coarse grey linen called osnaburg, which the male slaves used for their shirts and pants.

As the gig rounded the last curve, it came to a sudden halt, the horse snorting and rising up on its hind legs, almost completely toppling over and nearly spilling Massa and Mr Crawford out onto the limestone road. Mama stood tall and firm, her arms folded in front of her and her legs spread wide. Bigga sat on the rider's seat, frantically trying to control Star, Massa's favourite horse, a black stallion from the Spanish Main. The two White gentlemen remained seated in the rear of the gig, somewhat shaken up. Mr Crawford's face had turned red with the excitement and he was huffing and puffing, squawking like a fowl. Mr Sharpe remained calm as usual. He was a tall, lanky man, his waistcoat and breeches always several sizes too big. He had a long, narrow face and a pointed nose, and his hair was yellow like dried guinea grass. He would have made a good scarecrow for the fields, yet his eyes were kind and his demeanour gentle.

'Maas Sam, me waan talk to you,' Mama hollered so everybody could hear.

Mr Crawford could not contain himself. 'Bigga, get this raas slave out of the road.'

'Maas Sam, me waan talk to you. De busha nah treat we so good.'

'God damn, Bigga, drive this woman out of the road so that we can pass. So help me God, Bigga, if you do not do anything. . .'

Bigga hesitated, then rose up out of his seat, the muscles on his arms bulging with his sudden movement. Holding the reins with his left hand, he drove the horsewhip with the other, lashing Mama on her shoulders. He never licked her that hard but it caused her to fall to one side. Star lunged forward, pulling the gig to the front steps of the Great House. I rushed over to tend to Mama, but she pushed me away, her face twisted in anger and shame.

Mr Sharpe alighted from the small two-wheel carriage. 'Bigga, gather up Mimba, and take care of her. Tell her that I will hear her complaint after my breakfast. I am also expecting a visitor, Mr John Lunan from St Jago de la Vega. Tend to his needs when he arrives. Sam Sharpe, come along with me to the house. Thank you for the ride, Mr Crawford. Everything now seems to be in order. It is always good to be back home.'

I trembled as I climbed for the very first time the large double-sided staircase of the Great House. The piazza, a covered veranda, extended the whole length and both sides of the second floor where Massa normally sat to catch the cool breezes. I followed through the centre door to a large room, the dark boards beneath my feet feeling as cool and smooth as stone. A long table stretched itself out in the middle of the room. On it were large bowls of mangoes, oranges, guava, banana, and foreign foods which I did not recognize. Hanging from the ceiling were candle lights, hidden in sprawling iron lamps which looked like giant Anancy spiders.

Massa led me to the next room, where music was coming from a large brown box. One of the White girls, Anna, was standing up straight with her hands clasped behind her back, singing, 'Rock of Ages. . .' in keeping with the tune from the music box. Anna was a maaga girl, looking pale and sickly. Her skin was so clear it seemed like the light could shine through it. Her hair was blonde like Mr Sharpe's, but much longer, reaching down to her waist. The slaves said that Anna was not Massa's daughter.

She and her brother, Master Henry, came from England after they lost their parents in a shipwreck. Mr Sharpe and the mistress had two pickaninny at that time. Their son, Samuel Sharpe, was two years old and his sister Katherine had just been born.

I stood still, taking my signal from my master, who stopped at the doorway. He watched in silence until the singing and music had ended. I looked around for Anna's brother but did not see him anywhere in the room. He was always roaming about and straying from the property. He probably did not even know that Mr Sharpe had arrived home.

Mistress Sharpe sat on a chair holding the newborn baby asleep in her lap. She did not notice when we came into the room. The Missus would have looked pretty except for the frown fixed across her brow. Her hair was long and black and tied in the back with big red pins. She looked uncomfortable in her tall frock and long sleeves.

Nana was there also, standing attentively by the girl's side. She was the most respected slave at Cooper's Hill. She had suckled and raised most of the slave pickaninnies, as well as the master himself. But now her breasts were too old to give milk. Nana shuffled when she walked, her frock and apron drooping off her sagging belly. She always forced a smile and a pleasant hello even when she was in pain, suffering as she did from fevers and swollen joints. Even in the cool times of the day, she could not stop from sweating. To calm herself, Nana quietly sang hymns which she had learned in the White man's church.

Mr Sharpe finally spoke in a voice loud enough to startle her. 'Hello, Anna.' She turned and then rushed over to embrace him. He gave her a few pats on the head and turned his attention to the mistress. 'Jane, dear. How is everyone? It seems such a long time that I have been away. I trust everything is fine. Mr Crawford reports that our affairs are in order.'

He reached over and squeezed the back of my neck with his bony fingers. 'Here we have a promising young servant, a man-boy whom Nana will surely train to learn the manners befitting a house slave.'

I bowed my head nervously, making sure not to make eye contact with anybody in the room.

'Go along then, boy.' He pushed me toward her. 'Nana, take this vagabond and do your best to make him presentable.'

Nana did as she was told. She took me round the back of the house and made me remove my dirty slave clothes. Then she filled a tub with water and scrubbed me all over with a coarse brush made of dried coconut husks. I had been accustomed to washing in the river, so with this kind of bath, I became frightened that my skin was going to turn white from the scouring. Nana started to laugh after me because I was squirming so much, but I never saw any joke.

She dressed me in scratchy clothes which grabbed me tight all over. Then she put on me a white shirt which was starched stiff. The sleeves were long and buttoned close on the wrists, and the collar was high, pinching me around the neck. My feet were squeezed into a pair of shiny black shoes and a pair of long stockings cramped up my privy parts.

Not long after, she made her presentation to the master.

'All freshen' up now, Massa.' Nana gave a curtsy and left me standing in the great hall.

I felt like a fool, like some John Canoe in wild costume.

'Don't we look dashing in this new finery?' said Mr Sharpe. 'Nana has done a splendid job as usual.'

Massa and a tall gentleman whom I had never seen before sat facing each other in front of the doorway which gave to the piazza. The long table in the middle of the room now held the leftovers of a meal, barbecued pork, pigeons, turtle — more food I saw in one setting than could feed all the slaves on the property for a week.

The visitor spoke a proper English. 'I have no doubt that regardless of the extreme self-interest of the planter, even the least liberally minded of men would concede that there is some semblance of humanity in rescuing the slave from the darkness of heathenism and African spiritualism. I believe our English clergy have a role to play here. Don't you think, Samuel?'

'Yet, John, the preachers with whom I have had some acquaintance are so learned in their teachings that I do believe the slaves would walk away dumbfounded and find their doctrines incomprehensible.' Mr Sharpe shifted his weight in his chair as if he was uncomfortable. 'I think I may have received an injury from the jolting of the horses on the ride in from Falmouth this morning.'

'The roads can be treacherously narrow and rocky.' There was a moment of silence before the visitor spoke again in a low, serious voice. 'Samuel, the conversions of the Negro ought not to be taken frivolously. No doubt it will take some time for the poor wretch to change his habits to be more in keeping with a Christian way of life. Their indulgences must be curbed. That will be a formidable task! To make it worse, the miserable knaves have no one to emulate. I dare say many of their owners act in ways that we would hardly call Christian. The Assembly will soon be appointing curates and it is making provisions in the law for them to pay regular visits to the estates.'

'Would you care for a Cuban cigar, John? The day is still young but I relish the taste of a good tobacco after a meal. Sam, fetch that brown box that you see sitting on the sideboard there and bring it to Mr Lunan.'

I brought the box over to the visitor, not knowing what to do with it. I felt my shirt sticking to my upper body and sweat trickling down my back. The air was still and hot, the sea breeze not yet strong enough to cool the upper rooms of the house. I dared not make eye contact with either of the gentlemen, but I felt their eyes on me.

'A healthy man-boy like this must be worth two or three hundred pounds, Samuel.'

'He's not for sale, John. He still requires training, and, who knows, with a little education, he may even assume some graces of an English gentleman.'

The men lit their cigars and I returned to my post by the door. I wanted to be out in the slave village, even out in the fields cutting guinea grass or in the pens feeding the hogs. Any place but in that room.

'Curious thing, Samuel. I remember these same conversations with your father, sitting in this very room. You are very much alike.'

'I have but childhood memories of him.'

'We shall have to reminisce one day and I shall tell you many stories of your father. What worries me now is that there are many planters on the island, some as young as you are, who believe that the slaves are of too barbarous a nature to be instructed in the Christian faith.' He blew the cigar smoke in a long, straight line. The cigars were different from those Tacky smoked. The buckra ones were firmer, more evenly shaped, and not loosely wrapped the way Tacky rolled them.

'I think it would be more beneficial for the clergy to teach the slaves to read than preach the dictates of the Church. Religion, I am sure, would be better taught if the poor brute had some inkling of the meanings of words.' Mr Sharpe winced as if he was in pain.

'Instruction in reading and writing, Samuel, some believe, would implant in their minds ideas of equality. And you know what that would lead to? It would be a natural precursor to disobedience, and ultimately, to insurrection.'

'That sounds like nonsense.'

'In any event, we are being asked as magistrates to consider granting licences for preachers to visit the estates. I should be able to make arrangements with Custos Barrett in the Bay, if you so wish, for a curate of good repute to start visits to Cooper's Hill. They will have an incentive to pursue their vocation with zeal as the legislature will be paying them a more substantial stipend than has been granted previously to missionaries.'

I began to cough from the cigar smoke which was filling up the room. It was strange to watch the two men sitting opposite each other and breathing the stinky smoke in and out of their mouths.

'That would be fine if something could be arranged. Many planters will be reluctant, though, to give the curates permission to come on to the estates. They are certainly not going to want to give up their Sundays, which are days of work on most of the large properties.'

Mr Crawford appeared at the doorway and motioned for me to step aside so he could pass. He gave me one look — excuse my expression, but his face was uglier than john crow batty. Mr Lunan stood up from his chair as if preparing to retire.

'John, this is Edward Crawford, my bookkeeper and overseer. I do not believe you have met. Edward, this is John Lunan from St Jago de la Vega. He is visiting friends in the western parishes.'

'Very pleased to meet you, Sir.' Mr Crawford greeted him

politely.

'Can I offer you something, Edward? A glass of port perhaps?'

'Thank you, no. I received a message that you called for me, Sir.'

'Do have a seat, gentlemen.' Mr Sharpe motioned to me to bring up another chair.

'Samuel, if you would excuse me, I think I will retire for a bit. Just like my horses, I need some refreshing after the long journey.'

'Sam, show Mr Lunan to his room.'

'No, no, I can manage, thank you. No doubt we will find time to continue our discourse over another fine Cuban cigar.' With that, Mr Lunan left the great hall.

'How are things generally, Mr Crawford? The slaves appeared somewhat restless when I arrived. What seems to be the complaint from Mimba?'

'The issues are of a frivolous nature, Sir.'

'I am sure. They always are. Do you not wish a glass of wine, or perhaps a cigar? Our new houseboy will certainly oblige.' Massa looked over to me and grinned.

'Why, no, thank you, Sir. The day is still young. The complaints never change, Sir. They want more food and less work.'

'I understand that Mimba wishes to bring a case forward to be heard by the magistrates and is asking for me to arrange for such a meeting.'

'It is preposterous, Sir. I would urge you to ignore the request. The grievances which they bring forward are based on false and outrageous pretences.'

'Very well, then. I have been thinking about this and I should like you to arrange for her to be sold and transported off the property within a fortnight. We cannot have this sort of protest going on here. It creates a general feeling of ill-will and uneasiness.'

'Sir, I believe it would be a grave mistake to transport her at this time.'

The massa raised his voice, 'And why would that be, Mr Crawford?'

'She is one of our best jobbers and her labour brings in substantial income. The slave is of a robust nature and of sound health. And the tax we pay to own her is little or nothing.'

'We shall replace her, Mr Crawford. I think it is the only way. I do not want any public shame brought to our family.'

'Business is not good, Sir. The exports of sugar have declined and the demand for livestock and feed has diminished. It may be difficult to replace her at this time. Besides, Sir, I am not sure the other slaves will react favourably to this decision.'

'Enough of this. I am not running a plantation here. We have a small operation. Do as I ask, and report to me if there are any further complications.'

Mr Crawford's face flushed bright red and his eyes turned big in his head. When he was leaving the room, he glared at me with such hatred that I felt he had cast an evil spell upon me.

I remained standing at the door for what seemed a long time. Mr Sharpe was quiet, blowing his cigar smoke in circles into the room. I felt trapped in the silence.

'Massa, may I be excused, Sir?' I said finally.

'You will become my house servant, Sam, and well deserved is this.' He spoke in a joyful way, with a high-pitched voice. 'My mother always had a fondness for you and you very proudly bear my father's name. I shall give you the opportunity to learn to read and write, and in my house you will grow up to be a Christian man. But you must always do as I say and always be an obedient servant to me.'

Thus began a new phase in my life. I was removed from the slave village in the yard. I stopped chopping guinea grass in the fields and started to tend to the needs of my massa in his own house.

THREE

March 1832

Parson Bleby looks down at the Bible on his lap. 'You are familiar with the scriptures as much as I am, Sam. Perhaps you will recall these words of St Paul to the Corinthians. As you know, there were slaves in his time too.

> Let every man abide in the same calling wherein he was called.
> Art thou called being a servant? care not for it:
> but if thou mayest be made free, use it rather.
> For he that is called in the Lord, being a servant, is the Lord's freeman;
> likewise also he that is called, being free, is Christ's servant.

'I have no doubt that Mr Burchell read these verses to you and other slaves who were becoming overly zealous in the quest for freedom.'

'I did everything for the Lord's sake, Minister. If I have done wrong in that, I trust I shall be forgiven; for I cast myself upon the atonement.'*

'You may have had the best of intentions, Sam, but nevertheless many lives were sacrificed.' The reverend frowns, glancing at me as if he is accusing me of a dreadful crime.

'What has happened to the rest of my brothers, Minister?' I feel suddenly weary, not wanting to be with him any more. I wish he would leave me alone so I can say my prayers in private.

'*For rebellion and rebellious conspiracy, Sam, the slaves have been rounded up and executed. You must have seen some of this before your surrender. George Spence, whom you know, was sentenced to hang along with others. There was no substantial evidence that he took part in the rebellion. The only conclusive proof was that he stood with others and watched them burn buildings on the estates. The magistrate wanted to know whether or not Minister Burchell had told him that he and others of the slaves were to be free at Christmas. George told the court that he did not know who the minister was.*'

Parson Bleby sits opposite to me on a rickety wooden chair which the guard has brought into the cell for his visit. On his lap, he holds the Bible, open now and sunken between his legs, supported only by the thick cloth of his long black cassock, which flows gracefully to the floor. The chair leans against the wall beneath the small prison window through which the early morning light casts shadows about the cell. Beads of sweat form on the minister's brow, his face now red from the heat.

He does not tell me why he is here. Perhaps he wants to read my early chapters to make sure I am progressing with my writing. I know for sure that he wants information from me. He is curious about me, always studying me with his beady eyes. Maybe the magistrates have sent him to get a confession from me so they can convict me. Or he could be here to learn about the Baptists' involvement in the rebellion.

Mr Bleby is a Methodist minister, one of those the buckra call sectarians. They are similar to the Baptists, different from the Anglican priests who are sent out from England to be curates of the parishes. The government thinks of them as friends of the slaves and enemies of the planters. That is why he is fearful for his own life. The government blames the missionaries for inciting the slaves to rebellion.

'Hangings are now so commonplace in the public square of Montego Bay, Sam, that bystanders go about their daily chores, barely paying heed to the cries of the desperate prisoners being tied and bound to the gibbet. Bacchus is the name of the Negro who is their executioner. A brutal man. No doubt, many of his victims are insurgents with whom you are acquainted.'

The cell door opens and the guard signals to the reverend. *'It is time now, Minister.'*

'It is estimated that over 100 slaves have been hanged here in the Bay alone. Many have been flogged, each receiving 200 to 300 lashes in the public square.'

'I know this, Minister. The times are desperate. May I ask you some favours?'

'You know I would oblige, Sam.'

'If you come here again to visit me, would you ask the guard if you can bring a book for me?'

'And what book might that be, Sam?'

'The Holy War.'

'As you wish. May I ask why this one in particular?'

'I began to read it years ago and never finished it.'

'You know that it does not put forward orthodox views of Christianity?'

'I want to know how the battle ended. Would you also do me the favour of bringing God's blessings to Mr Sharpe, to the mistress and all their children?'

'I shall make a point of doing so. They are in reasonably good health except for some discomfort that Mr Sharpe suffers.'

'Tell them for me, Minister, that I always loved them and that I always will, and that the things I did were in the name of the Lord. I beg them forgiveness for the wrongs they may have suffered.'

'I will convey these messages to them, Sam.'

'One more thing, Minister.'

'What is that, Sam?'

'If I write a letter to Mr Burchell, would you make sure he receives it?'

'I am not certain there is enough time for this. He will be setting sail for America very soon. I should have to collect it as early as tomorrow if you can have it written by then.'

'I shall. God's blessings go with you, Minister.'

'God's speed, Sam.'

The guard escorts him out of the cell and slams back the iron door.

June 1816

I continued my domestic chores in the service of my master, Samuel Sharpe Esquire. By living in such close quarters with him and others of his household, I came to learn the gentlemanly ways of the English people and because of all the favours I received, I became the envy of the field slaves and of Mr Crawford too.

I never had a chance to say a proper farewell to Mama when it was arranged for her to be sold. Bigga took her away by horse to an estate soon after Maas Sam had decided that she should leave Cooper's Hill.

I did not see her again until she returned for Tacky's burial. He lasted a long time in the sick-house but eventually grew frail and could no longer bear the filth and disease that surrounded him there. I visited him in his last days. His eyes were glazed over and he had a distant look as if he were waiting to travel to his ancestors. Tacky knew me when I was with him but he drew no comfort from me. He wanted to complete his journey on his own. His belly was distended and his breathing laboured, as he heaved and gasped.

He died during a dry time, when the sun is hottest, that period between the rains and the hurricane season. In that year, the sea breezes blew hard against the coastal plains. The salt withered up the vegetation along the shores and the guinea grass pastures turned yellow. The cane was already cut, and the ratoons struggled to make their way in the parched soil. The earth caked up, the clay forming itself into squares, hard as the honeycomb rock. The cattle became sick and maaga with not enough to eat. To seek shelter from the sun-hot, they would gather under the dogwood trees, their heads hanging low. The slaves too were hungry because the provision grounds were dry and supplies short. At night-time, runaway slaves raided estates, stealing sheep, pigs and other livestock. People said that *you must mek sure sey you nah dead during drought time cause de john-crow dem all de bout fi come nyam yu up.* The sea seemed to be the only beautiful part of nature in the dry time. It became brighter, the blue more brilliant and the white caps shinier and more plentiful than in the rainy time.

It was too hot to bury Tacky when the sun was high, so the ritual started in the early morning before the second crow. Two men washed the body — only the front of the body, not the back, starting from the head and working down towards the feet. They made sure not to wipe from the feet to the head, otherwise the duppy of the dead man would mock them. They dressed him in a white frock. Mama had wanted him clad with boots and a knife so that when his duppy rose up he could come out and *get* Mr Crawford. They lifted the corpse up and down several times before it was placed in a wooden box. Two bearers carried the box on their heads through the village, stopping at each hut to make sure that Tacky could take leave from all his relatives and friends. Everyone made sure not to touch or kiss the corpse. Otherwise, their teeth would rot like the dead body.

The box went down into the crusty earth. The gravediggers, six in number, turned their backs to the hole in the ground, and with their legs spread far apart, moved the earth with shovels backwards into the grave through the space between their outstretched legs. Once the grave was completely filled, Bigga removed a white cock from a crocus bag. It made an awful cackling noise. He placed the body of the bird under a water bucket with its neck sticking out from one side of it. With a quick hack of the cutlass, the chicken's neck was severed from its body. When Bigga lifted the bucket, he quickly grabbed the fowl by the feet as it began to scurry, headless, around the grave. He sliced the body several times and squeezed the head, spilling the blood of the fowl as sacrifice over Tacky's grave. At the head of the grave, Mama then placed a calabash containing soup made from the remains of a hog, and at the foot, she put a bottle of rum which Maas Sam had provided for the occasion.

The beating of the goombays, the drums of the Eboes, began. Two men stood hugging the large barrel-shaped drums, using small sharpened sticks to beat the sides and sheep-skin tops. As the beat gained momentum, so did the wailing of the mourners. Slowly the crowd moved in a circle round and round the grave. In tempo with the drums, Bigga began to stomp his feet on the ground and others beat their chests and wailed in unison.

O poor man Tacky

A whe him deh oh
Him a dead and gone.
O poor man Tacky

A whe him deh oh
Him a dead and gone.
We shall meet again
We shall meet again some day
O poor man Tacky.

We shall meet again
We shall meet again some day
O poor man Tacky.

The voices travelled across the mountains, sending back wild and woeful echoes.

Tacky's spirit was restless that night. The horses ran wild around the pasture, refusing to be caught. Mama said it was because Tacky's duppy was riding them. She said that only after forty days would Tacky's spirit depart that place and return to the world of the ancestors. He would go on trial and be found worthy to be admitted to the company of the elders in the land of the Tigris and the Euphrates. There, in the form of a shadow, he would live forever.

Maas Sam offered one of his best hogs to be barbecued the night of Tacky's burial. Close to the slave houses, Bigga drove a stake through the pig, dressed it, then smoked it over a fire in a pit with coals and leaves. Massa also gave us bottles of red rum, which we drank to our delight. Many slaves, old and young, came from faraway estates. I met Quasheba, Tacky's lovely Queen of Sheba, that night at the funeral. I sat next to her in a circle by the grave.

'Him wanted me fi give you a special message.'

'And what is dat?'

She looked just like I imagined a queen to be. Her skin was smooth, her cheekbones high and her eyes as sparkly as the stars. She sat straight up and proud, and her voice was as sweet as the song of a bird. 'Poor Tacky. Me did feel bad fi him. You know, is love did a mek de man tun fool-fool, so much dat it lead him into a whole heap of trouble.' She turned to me as she spoke and started slowly caressing my cheek with her hand. 'Dat was a long time ago, though. But when him was a youth, him was a good boy, but fool-fool all de same.'

'Tacky was a strong and wise man. Him tell me many stories which I will always remember. Him show me how to be smart and to be brave. Him sey me should always beware de yellow snake.' I became uneasy as she continued to stroke my head.

'Dat was good advice him give you, but Tacky was a man, let me tell you, dat nebba have enough sense in him head fi follow him own advice. Me know sey it mussi love mek him gwaan so. But me better shut up me mouth, you hear, otherwise me know sey him duppy gwine get me.' She laughed, which made her eyes light up in the night.

'Me feel bad fi him, though, Miss, when him tell me sey you couldn't love him no more. Him wanted me fi tell you dat, no matter what, you would always be his Queen of Sheba.'

'Thank you, Sam. Dat is sweet and a glad you tell me. Me tell you de truth, though, me heart did go out to him. Dem did beat him so till and him still wouldn't listen. Me could a nebba go on wid him. Life would a too miserable. Tacky you sey was strong but him was stubborn bad, Sam. One thing, though, me always did want him fi meet him pickaninny, me dear Nyame.'

'Him never tell me bout her.'

'Me nebba even think him know bout her. You will haffi meet her someday. She prettier than all de heaven put together. She a young gal now, Sam, but she soon tun big woman.'

Our conversation was interrupted by the merriment and loudness of the crowd by the grave.

'Get up, bwai, and mek Tacky proud and show Quasheba what a man-boy you is.' Bigga pulled me from the ground to join those who were now singing and dancing in a circle. The drums were beating loud. The men and women wore shakas about their wrists and legs. These are rattles made of calabash with stones inside which made rhythmic sounds in time with the beat of the drums. He pushed me and a slave girl called Bessy into the middle of the ring. Bessy was the prettiest woman-child that Massa owned, a mulatto with bronze-coloured skin. She stretched her slender arms out wide and fixed her stare on me. As the drums sounded louder, she moved her lower body faster and faster, whirling and writhing in time with the beat of the goombays. Slowly I started to copy her movements, drawing closer and closer until our bodies touched, shaking and shifting together. The drums beat harder and harder. I felt my sweat and smelled hers too.

There's a brown girl in the ring, Tra la la la la.
There's a brown girl in the ring, Tra la la la la.
There's a brown girl in the ring, Tra la la la la.
For she like sugar and I like plum. *

The crowd started to call out my name, clapping and shouting at the same time. Then someone grabbed my waist from behind. Mama pulled me away from Bessy.

~

Maas Sam eventually arranged for a preacher to visit the property. We could hear the ringing of a bell coming from afar one Sunday morning. The sound became louder and louder until we saw a man approaching on horseback wearing a long black frock. He was being followed by hundreds of slaves beckoned by the sound of his bell. He came to rest on a mount not far from Cooper's Hill. The morning was cool and still, curls of mist still hovering in the valleys and forming a haze where we stood. Below him we gathered, mostly older women and young children. The able-bodied slaves were absent, making preparations to carry baskets of food down to the Bay for Sunday market.

'My name, dear friends, is Reverend Smith. I come to tell you about Jesus Christ who is the Son of God. I come as His priest to minister to you. Today is His day, the day of the Lord. It is called the Sabbath. It is a holy day and on this day, you should pray, you should not toil. He came into this world as a man, born of the Father who is in heaven. He came so that your wrongdoings may be forgiven. He sacrificed His own life so that you too may die and be freed from sin to enjoy eternal life. He shed His blood for us. He is the Lamb of God. My beloved lambs in Christ, I am here to tell you today that if you believe in Jesus Christ, you will turn from your wicked ways. The truth that you shall find in His Spirit will give you eternal peace. You shall be forever happy, for you shall inherit the Kingdom of God.'

I sat with the crowd on the brow of the hill listening to the minister's strange words. The ground was soft and wet with the morning dew. Many started to mumble, trying to make sense of this White man's talk.

'Is wah dis man a talk bout?'
'Is dis Jesus Christ fi we new massa now?'
'Him sey de massa will set we free?'
'Is whe dis Jesus live then?'
'Me tink him sey him faada live inna de sky.'
'Is why dis Massa Jesus a shed him blood fi we?'
'Him sey so we poor wretch can be free.'

'Me nah tink sey de massa gwine mek we free still.'
'Me tink dis preacher should a go back a England.'
'Wah you tink?'
'Iin-hiin, him a chat foolishness.'
'Him all a call me lamb.'
'Iin-hiin, come like we is some sheep fi slaughter.'
'Mek we go, you hear sar.'
'Yes, man, come mek we go.'
'Me raas a get wet wid de dew.'

The older men started to get up to leave, but this did not stop the reverend from preaching. 'No longer will you sit in darkness if you embrace the Word of the Lord Jesus. I have come to bring you out of the darkness into the light, to deliver you from the power of Satan who is the evil one. I am here not for my own sake, not to bring glory to myself, not to gain material things from you or your masters, but I am here instead to carry the Good News of eternal life.

'As I begin my ministry in this island I have knowledge of several thousand souls which have been turned from the power of Satan unto God. No longer will you perish because of ignorance. You will grow to know the true Lord, our Saviour Jesus Christ. I beg those of you who are thinking of leaving to stop for a moment to listen to the words I shall read you from the Good Book.'

He pulled a black book from his cassock and began to read words which he said Massa Jesus spoke:

> *Verily, verily, I say unto you, He that heareth my word, and believeth in him that sent me, hath everlasting life, and shall not come into condemnation; but is passed from death to life.'*
> *Jesus said unto her, 'I am the resurrection, and the*

*life: he that believeth in me, though he were dead,
yet shall he live:
and whosoever liveth and believeth in me shall never die.*

'Those whom he taught, followed Him and preached His Word to convert all who were sinners and heretics. I want to teach you a prayer now. Jesus said we should pray to our Father in heaven. Please repeat after me:

Our Father, which art in heaven.'
Our Father, which art in heaven.
He went on in this fashion, saying one verse at a time and asking us to repeat after him.
'Hallowed be thy name.'
Hallowed be thy name.
'Thy Kingdom come.'
Thy Kingdom come.

We did not know what we were saying, but repeated each verse of the prayer until he was finished. He then looked down at the Book, which seemed to be talking up to him. Out of his mouth came the following words:

*Know ye not that the unrighteous shall not inherit the
kingdom of God?
For this ye know, that no whoremonger, nor unclean
person, nor covetous man, who is an idolater, hath
any inheritance in the Kingston of Christ and of God.
He that believeth and is baptized shall be saved; but he
that believeth not shall be damned.*

'These words I leave with you, my friends, so that you may give up your wicked ways. Your masters have given me permission to preach to you the Gospel of Jesus Christ. They wish for you to be obedient, to be good slaves, for you not to swear, to steal or to fight. Go now and tell others of the Good News which you have heard this morning.'

So we withdrew to our huts, all going our respective ways. We pondered the minister's strange words, our heads hung low in confusion.

The reverend had planted a seed in my soul. I yearned now to know more about Jesus who promised that I would be set free if I believed in His Word. The minister visited a couple more times, much to the disgust of Mr Crawford, who tried to run him off the land. Mr Sharpe had to set him straight on matters of religious instruction of the slaves. He convinced Mr Crawford by telling him that the preacher would teach us discipline and correct our wayward habits.

The minister taught us that there was only one God who was Creator and Father of all things in heaven and on earth. I tried to imagine how this spirit could be greater than the sun and the moon. And I did not understand how He could be my father. The minister told us also that there was another spirit called the devil who was the evil one. He captured those who committed bad acts and made them burn in a place called hell. Reverend Smith said we should pray each day so as not to be tempted by the lure of this evil spirit. He kept reciting the Lord's Prayer over and over again, 'Our Father which art in heaven, Hallowed be thy name,' until all those who listened came to know it by heart. I became curious about all these mysteries and about the black book which contained these secrets.

My cravings became so strong that they led me to do something unlawful for which I would pay dearly. I had seen a black book stacked with other leather-bound volumes in a bookcase in the Great House. I knew it was similar to the one the reverend brought to the meetings. The shapes of the twelve gold letters on the spine of the book were identical: The Holy Bible. One day, I found an opportunity to be alone in the great room. The silence gave me a feeling of power, of control over time and space, and of freedom from Massa's orders.

Pass me one of those Cuban cigars, boy! Fetch me a glass of madeira. Hurry, boy, or I shall send you back to the fields. I thought how wonderful to be a master and not a slave.

I searched for the key in a drawer where I had seen Maas Sam place it. The cabinet door opened with ease. I felt a magic power come into my hands when I pulled the Book from its spot on the shelf. Even though it was wrong to take it, I knew I must have it. It contained answers to secrets which would lead me to greater truths. Next to this book was another with an inscription which later I understood to be *The Holy War* written by John Bunyan. This too I stole, believing it would also lead me to solve the mysteries of life.

In front of the books were personal possessions of my master, white clay pipes, gold and silver coins, quill pens and a penknife. The knife had a casing made of smooth white bone, the colour and texture of pearl. I slipped this into my pocket.

FOUR

Montego Bay gaol house
Thursday, the 14ᵗʰ of March, 1832

My Dear Mr Burchell,
Baptist Minister in the Parish of St James:

I trust that this letter finds you in good health and in the protection of the Lord Jesus. I write to you from the gaol house in Montego Bay where hundreds of captives from the rebellion have been imprisoned. I have received a visit from Parson Bleby who assures me that he will arrange to have this sent to you. He did not tell me of your whereabouts but I have heard the great news that your discharge has been arranged.

Here, my fellow prisoners and I await trial. Some are executed without due process of meeting with the magistrates. I expect that it is the will of the good Lord that I be confined within these prison walls and that I face the ultimate judgement. You did warn me many times that I was too restless in my desire for freedom. Mr Bleby tells me that I should have known my rightful place. You parsons were right and now I must suffer the consequences of my indiscretions. However, the Lord Jesus, I believe, must have a plan, for despite my wrongdoings and the bloodthirsty deeds of my fellow slaves, He will see fit one day in his Providence to set us free from this odious bondage.

I remember the words you taught me from Galatians 5:
'Stand fast therefore in the liberty wherewith Christ hath made us free, and be not entangled again with the yoke of bondage.'

You taught me that liberty is the birthright of every man. We worked long enough, Minister. We worked long enough and have gained nothing.

I was saddened, as you know, by your departure for England last July, but understand that you were in need of a cooler climate to heal your infirmities and that you did not mean to desert your faithful. Many of the poor ones whom you left behind sincerely believed that you would be returning with freedom papers from the King. They heard it said that before the following Christmas, we would be set free. A star would fix itself in the corner of the moon as a sign that we should cease our labour. They waited anxiously but they did not see you. And the time passed and they saw no star appear in the corner of the moon. I should have known better. The King could not have liberated us. We are not his royal subjects, we are but the chattel of our owners. These are troubled times for Jamaica, Minister. Both planter and slave have suffered dreadful losses. The Governor issued proclamations of pardon but yet hundreds of our brethren were rounded up and executed, some for no apparent reason other than that they be slaves.

I knew of your arrival in Jamaica in January and your subsequent arrest under the authorities of martial law. I had been in hiding from the militia until I surrendered two weeks ago, so I was unable to have an interview with you. I am mortified at the behaviour of those who detained you and Reverends Knibb and Gardner. The magistrates and justices of peace who did this to you are the ones who should be convicted of sedition, not you. It is shameful that they should have subjected you and the ministers to confinement, and pure wickedness that our chapel and the property of the mission were demolished.

I want you to know that I do not blame you for any wrongdoing. We heard no evil words come from your pulpit and we took no direction from you to take up arms against our oppressors. I take full responsibility before God for being a prime mover in the rebellion. It is me they should lynch, not you. As God is my witness, you must know, Minister, that despite what everybody says, I did not contemplate the shedding of blood and I did not want the tribulation that has been brought down on the heads of my brethren. I did it for freedom's sake in the name of Christ Jesus.

Minister, if you receive this letter, I hope it finds you in good health and that you will have the time and disposition to send me a reply by way of Parson Bleby. If God wills it and life spares, I hope to see you again in person one day. If this be not the case, then I have faith that Jesus will bless us both in His love.

For I am persuaded, that neither death, nor life, nor
  angels, nor principalities,
nor powers, nor things present, nor things to come,
Nor height, nor depth, nor any other creature,
shall be able to separate us from the love of God,
which is in Christ Jesus our Lord.

Romans 8: 38–39.

My only refuge is in the Lord Jesus.
Yours very truly in Christ,
Samuel Sharpe

1817

Relations between the slaves and Mr Crawford did not improve. Mama especially caused trouble for him. Even though she now belonged to another owner, she managed to create a whole heap of mischief which would eventually drive him from Cooper's Hill.

One way a master can punish a slave is to sell him off, to part with him and never see him again. Yet, in Mama's case, I think Maas Sam did it as a kindness to her so that she would be free of the wickedness of Mr Crawford. Maas Sam was a good man. He was like family to me. He was kind and gentle. But Mr Crawford treated us not even as good as the farm animals. From what I could see, no hog, no cattle, no horse got as much flogging as the slaves did. It must be slavery that hardened his heart that way. It probably was not easy for a White man to be civil with the corruption all about.

Mama would sneak visits to Cooper's Hill at night, and it felt like old times, sitting and chatting with her by the slave huts.

'How dem let you out of de big house, Sam?'

'My chores are done for the night, Mama.'

One night, with a short stick in her hand, she sat and stoked a small fire which had just a few remaining coals. 'If you live a good life, Sam, you will enjoy its sweetness. *Wobo bra-pa a, wote mu dew.* That is how we say it in my language.' Mama did not speak often in her native Ashanti, but when she did, she taught me wise sayings of her ancestors.

'Those words sweet me, Mama. I shall remember them. Say dem one more time fi me.'

'*Wobo bra-pa a, wote mu dew.*'

'*Wobo bra-pa a, wote mu dew.*' I repeated the words after her.

'You learn fas, bwai. Don't look so sad, Sam. Remember what me tell you. You mustn't fret bout me. Me is a big woman and me can tek care of meself. You don't see how me doing good so far?' She patted herself on her arms and legs as if to show me she was still strong. She smiled at me with eyes that were tender and loving.

'You not doing so good, Mama. Dem drive you weh from here.'

Her manner changed. She spoke as if she was vexed and her body stiffened up.

'No matter whe dem send me go, Sam, me figure sey me a slave still. So don't worry bout it. We not free, no way you look pon it, we not free, Sam. And dat go fi me, fi you and fi most of de Black people in disya country. Dat raas man, Mr Crawford, me will tek care o' him. You will see, me will talk wid Bigga and arrange up things. Don't worry yuh head bout dat.'

'What kind of arrangement?'

'He done too much wickedness, Sam, and it's time him pay fi it. But you listen carefully to what me telling you, you mustn't follow in me ways. You hear me, Sam? You have yuh own life fi live. Me waan fi give you something, Sam. It's a long time now since me have it and me been meaning fi hand it to you all dis while. Me faada did give me it before de White man dem did tek me weh from him.'

She opened the palm of her right hand which contained a small object wrapped in a leaf.

'Tek it and open it up.'

I reached for it. The little package was heavier than it looked. Like a weighty piece of metal. I peeled away at the small folds of the leaf.

'It is a lion. It hold de spirit of de ancestors and it will attract to you what you wish for in life. Dat is why me tell you, Sam, dat you must be good and then life in turn will be sweet to you.' Her voice was kind and her spirit strong.

The charm was golden, still shining bright after all those

years. It was as thick as my thumb but only about half its length. The lion had a hump on its back with a long thick mane and jaws wide open as if ready for battle.

'It is beautiful, Mama. Me shouldn't tek it from you, it belong to you, not me.'

I rubbed it in the palm of my hand. It was smooth all over.

'Me waan you fi keep it, Sam. It gwine bring you strength of spirit and de power of healing.'

'And what about you? Don't you need these special gifts?'

'Me tell you aredi not to fret yuhself bout me. We is a strong set of somadi, you know. Some sey we is de first race of people on dis earth, the Akan people.'

'Me will guard it wid me life, Mama.'

'It gwine guard you, Sam, protect you from all danger.'

'Me gwine miss you when you go back, Mama.' I felt weak inside.

'Don't start again wid you foolishness. You mussi strong, bwai, just like de lion. You know me nebba did waan fi call you Sam?'

'Why is dat?'

'Well, you was born pon a Saturday just like me, so me did waan fi call you Kwaame for de sixth day of de week. But then de massa sey dat yuh name must match fi him own.'

'Why you tell me these things?'

''Cause you should know dem.'

Then Bigga called out to her from up the plantain-walk, 'Time fi go now, Mimba.'

'Me will tek care of meself, Mama, and me will ask Maas Sam if me can come visit you.'

'Come and see me when you is a man, when you is big and strong. Then me will know whether or not de lion was good to you and provide fi you in de proper way.'

As she was leaving with Bigga, I handed her a kerchief tied

up in the shape of a ball.

'This is for your journey, Mama.'

In the package I had placed some new sugar, which we call *wet sugar*. It still has the taste of molasses in it. Wet sugar was her favourite.

I did not see Mama again for a long time.

~

Mistress Sharpe was not in the habit of talking to me but one day while her husband was absent, I was cutting open water coconuts when Nana shouted out to me: 'Put dung yuh machete, Sam, and come here. Mek haste, de mistress a call fi you.'

'Wah she waan see me for, Nana?'

'She a call fi you, Sam. She waan you go up in her bedroom.'

'You a joke wid me now, Nana. You see you, you waan fi get me in trouble.'

Nana's tone became serious. 'Get yuhself inna de house, bwai, and go upstairs fi see de Missus. Me nah tell you no lie.'

I was accustomed to attending to her husband, not to her. She had her own slaves to tend to her needs. Mistress Sharpe had been keeping mostly to herself, and when she did show her face, she looked gloomy and sad. Nana said it was because of all the pickaninnies she was having. In the five years since she and Maas Sam were married, she bore three children for him and she was now pregnant with a fourth. She was breeding faster than any slave girl I knew.

I was careful to knock on the door before entering her room. She was alone, seated in an armchair by the window.

'Good morning, Mistress. You called for me, Ma'am?'

'Come in, Sam, and stand here by my side.'

I felt I did not belong there in the room with her. I stood by her for a long time while she remained silent. I did not know what this woman wanted with me.

She spoke at last. 'You know, Sam, that in Jamaica, almost every White man, of every class, has his Black or Brown mistress with whom he lives openly.' She looked off into the distance.

'Yes, Ma'am.' I glanced down at her feet, avoiding her eyes. I was not supposed to look at my mistress when I spoke to her. It was a rule we slaves learned.

'How do you mean, "Yes, Ma'am?"' She was frowning at me.

'I mean I agree with you, Ma'am. Mr Sharpe tells me, Ma'am, that I should not come into your bedroom.'

'He is not here now. So, you shall listen to me. And you know what the punishment is for being disobedient?'

'Yes, Ma'am.'

Her face became flushed. I was always curious about what to expect when I saw a White person's face turn to a different colour. This time I think she was vexed.

'Have you ever received a flogging, Sam?'

'No, Ma'am.'

She paused and then her tone of voice turned softer. 'Then you must be a good slave.'

'Yes, Ma'am.'

She continued with her talk about White men and their slave women. 'Sometimes, even when a White woman is betrothed to be married, she allows the Brown mistress to remain in the master's house and agrees also to raise their children.'

'Yes, Ma'am. This is true.'

'Of course it is true. I would not say things that are false. Many Creoles of my class raise the bastard children of their husbands. To them this seems neither base nor ignoble. This attitude, however, is not prevalent among ladies who are born and educated in England. They despise such a custom.'

She did not look at me when she spoke. She stared off into the horizon, above the bush and housetops to the faroff ocean. The room was dark except for the square of light made by the window frame. Over to one side was a tub which Nana had filled with warm water in preparation for the mistress's morning bath.

She broke the silence, 'I was never sure about Bessy.'

'Bessy is a sweet girl, Ma'am.'

'She is an indolent slave. She thinks herself superior to all the other house slaves.'

'She act sweet to me, Ma'am.'

'I am not asking your opinion of Bessy, Sam. When we assumed ownership of the house, I drove her mother from here. She was intolerably rude. I believe Bessy must have inherited her bad traits. Besides, I was never certain about who Bessy's father was and I wanted no slave of a promiscuous nature living in my home.' She turned her head and looked up at me. 'Take that smirk off your face.'

'I not doin' nothing, Ma'am.'

'Do you know why you bear my husband's name?'

'No, Ma'am.'

'Someone took a fondness for you. So you were christened at birth with that name. His father left you to the family in his will.'

'I grateful for that, Ma'am.'

'And why would that be, Sam?'

'I care for you and Maas Sam like family, Ma'am. He show kindness to me always.'

She stopped talking for the longest time. I just stood there beside her trying my best to be still. I needed her permission before I could leave the room.

'It amazes me.'

'What is that, Ma'am?'

She talked as if I wasn't there, staring outside with a blank look on her face. 'The male follows the fashion of the day. If the female were to do the same, she would certainly fall from grace and civility. She would fall lower than the level of the most common slave.'

She went silent again.

I heard the sound of the coconut brush on the floors of the piazza and I could smell the cleaning mixture of lime and orange. Hercules was at work. He was a young slave who helped twice a week with the more difficult chores around the house. He was one of the master's prizes, as strong as the oxen that drove the cart at Cooper's Hill. The overseer was not pleased with the arrangement to lend his services to the Great House, because Hercules could be better used earning money as a jobber. Hercules was slim, but muscles bulged in every part of his body. He worked quickly and seemingly without effort. He was always courteous, and this pleased Mistress Sharpe.

'Is that Hercules starting his work?'

'I believe so, Ma'am.'

She raised herself from the chair and leaned forward towards the window.

'It's a curious thing.' She was looking out at Hercules.

'What is that, Ma'am?'

'That young slave always does what he's told without the least bit of effort or resentment.'

'He is a good worker, Ma'am.'

'Would that they were all like that. It's strange.'

'He is a good slave, Ma'am.'

'Yes. It's odd. When they are so servile and willing to please, one feels a strange attachment.'

'Would you like me to call Nana to freshen up your bath water, Ma'am?'

'Yes, go now and have her fetch me some hot water. It has sat there too long. You have been good company for me, Sam. Go now and do your chores, and do not spend time with Master Henry. He is far too fond of whiling away the hours with the slaves.

'Yes, Ma'am.' I turned to leave.

'Wait. Tell Nana that when Hercules is finished his work, she should give him a large bowl of pepper-pot soup.'

'Yes, Ma'am.' With that, I made my escape.

~

Master Henry and I climbed a mountainside, not too far from the property, up behind the Negro houses, past the yam hills and fruit trees, up where the limestone rock became jagged and steep. To steady ourselves so we did not fall backwards, we held on to the branches growing out from the rock.

'Look out for the macca bush, Master 'enry, they will juk you.'

I led the way, my bare feet gripping the rock much more securely than Master Henry's shoes.

No sooner had I spoken than he let out a loud cry. The ebony bush had pricked one of his fingers as he grabbed it to balance himself.

'You imbecile, you startled me. Look what you have caused.' He held up his bleeding hand.

I never realized how soft he was. He yelped like a baby from the pain.

'Sorry, Sir. Suck the blood from your finger and you will drain the poison.'

'You are more of a buffoon than I thought.' He wiped his bleeding hand on his trousers and motioned for me to proceed.

Though the path was familiar to him, my companion still laboured up the hillside. His body was lean but not strong. In the sun-hot, his face turned red and his yellow hair became wet from sweat which smelled different from mine, raw like fish mixed with the sweet smell of powders which he used on his body.

The land levelled off in two spots. We did not stop or rest at the first landing because Bag-o-Bones lived there. Bag-o-Bones was an obeah man who dwelled in a deep cavern set in the hillside. I had seen him only once when I was younger. At the opening to the cave, he had stood, leaning to one side on a walking stick, his wrists decorated with silver bangles. He was not too old, maybe the age of Mama or Bigga. His hair was long, knotted in long braids down to his shoulders. One eye looked larger than the other, shiny, as if it was made of glass. At the entrance to the cave, I had seen several items: old rags, bird feathers, a bunch of whitened animal bones. Some said he was called Bag-o-Bones because he carried a bankra, full of bones. Others said it was because he was so maaga and bony looking.

I remembered then what Mama had told me, 'Don't go up into de hillside unless you want de obeah man fi set duppy or work guzu pon you.' The salt-water Negroes, those from the Guinea coast, the Coromantees like Mama, believed in a malevolent spirit, *Obboney*, who pervaded the heaven, the earth and the sea. He was the author of all evil and nothing would appease his anger except human sacrifice. This was a good enough reason for me not to go near Bag-o-Bones.

That day, Master Henry and I did not see him at the entrance to the cave, but we wasted no time lingering there, quickly making our way up to the second plain which was more fertile with larger shade and flower trees. The estate owners, including Maas Sam, used these trees, the fiddlewood and the rosewood, to build barns and sheds. In one of the mahogany trees, maybe ten times the height of a man, Master Henry and I had built our own tree house up in the branches which leaned over a precipice and gave a view of the flat lands below.

With our legs dangling from the makeshift boards of the treehouse, we sat, looking out to the houses of Montego Bay below us and to the ocean beyond. The buckra book, the Holy Bible, lay open on my lap. I remember clearly the magical moment when I turned the pages of the Bible and began to read verses for the first time.

Many times before, Master Henry had shown me the pages where the Lord's Prayer and other familiar verses were written. I had spent many hours reciting these, and came to learn them by rote. The more often I said them aloud, the more beautiful and meaningful they became. I would open the Book to search for common phrases and words I could recognize, like *Jesus* and *heaven,* and eventually with the tutoring of Master Henry, I was able to recognize the shapes of letters and words. Groups of letters became words and words became sounds I could speak from the Book. The Book was no longer dead. It contained meanings, the great secrets of my soul.

Words ran off my lips in a way I could not explain:

> *Blessed are the poor in spirit: for theirs is the kingdom of heaven*
> *Blessed are they that mourn: for they shall be comforted.*
> *Blessed are the meek: for they shall inherit the earth.*

Master Henry looked at me and then at the Book. 'You owe a great deal of gratitude to your brilliant tutor.' He smiled. The sun caught his locks, yellow like the hay we fed to the horses. He continued in his smug manner, 'You know that you would receive thirty-nine lashes and be put in the stocks if Mrs Sharpe ever discovered that you stole the Holy Bible from the great room. She would not like it much either that you have learned to read the scriptures.'

'Mr Sharpe wanted me to learn. He even told your tutor to show me maps of the world and to read to me about kings and queens.'

'Don't be impudent with me, Sam, or you know that I shall flog you myself. Much to the embarrassment of my family and of the White gentry, Mr Sharpe dotes on you in a way that is disgusting, and unbecoming of a master.'

I did not understand why he was speaking about his adopted father in that way. 'You act like me friend, Master 'enry, and I am grateful for this.'

'I wish you would pronounce your God-damned aitches. Say Master H-Henry.'

'Master H-Henry.'

'Good. But it would seem to me, Sam, that you are greatly indebted to me.'

'Tell me how I may repay you, Master 'enry, and I shall oblige.' We were both quiet for a moment. 'Would you care for some sugar cane?' I had stored in the tree house stolen pieces of cane and the penknife I had taken from the Great House. I ran the knife in a circular motion around one of the joints of the cane, at the same time twisting the bottom of it with my left hand. I snapped off a piece, and peeled the skin off in strips.

'I am afraid these pieces are far too large to manage all at once. You need to cut these smaller.'

I cut the cane into narrower strips for Master Henry, but kept the whole and larger pieces for myself. 'It taste sweeter my way, Master 'enry.' Instead of using the knife, I stripped the skin off with my teeth. The cane was soft ribbon-cane with the stripes on it. That was the sweetest kind.

'You will never acquire the manners of a civilized man, Sam. Despite any opportunities of a liberal education that you may receive, it is inconceivable that you shall ever completely learn proper habits, not as long as you have African blood running in your veins.'

He seemed to be chewing incessantly.

'You must spit out the trash, Sir. It's not good for your stomach. After you suck out the juice, you spit out the trash.'

'Damn, you, Sam. You are testing my patience.'

'Or better, Sir, spit the trash in your hand and rub it on your teeth. It keep them white and clean.' I showed him how.

'You look like an orangutan. You're telling me that is why your teeth are white? You're an imbecile, Sam.'

'Or better, Sir, you can mash some coal and tek the pieces to rub all over your teeth. Make them glisten.'

Master Henry ignored me. He removed a pouch of tobacco and one of his father's pipes from a box which he kept hidden in the tree house. He lit the pipe and blew circles of smoke into the fresh air while I read to him more passages from the Bible. For a fleeting moment, it felt as if I could be his companion and no longer his slave.

~

Maas Sam always left a collection of newspapers on two round tables by the door to the upstairs veranda. He loved to sit with his Cuban cigar and pore over these every day after his morning meal. When I was serving him, he read aloud to me articles that interested him about the political issues of the day. It was not long before I could read them fluently myself.

Any opportunity I had to be alone in the great room, I would sneak a look at the newspapers that lay about, making sure that I was not caught by the Missus or reported by Bessy.

I learned a great deal about Jamaica. I discovered that the Parish of St James where I lived was one of many parishes, twenty-one in number, in fact, and that not all the slaves lived on a gentleman's property like I did. Spread around the country were over thirty villages and towns, the biggest being Kingston where over 30,000 persons lived. The newspapers Mr Sharpe read were called the *Jamaica Journal and Kingston Chronicle,* the *Courant* and the *Royal Gazette.*

Many slaves about the country were unhappy. They spoke of a man in foreign by the name of Wilberforce who wanted freedom for the slaves in Jamaica and in other places. The slaves called him King Wilberforce. One night, an overseer in another parish heard his slaves singing this song at a funeral:

> *Oh me good friend, Mr Wilberforce, make me free!*
> *God Almighty, thank ye! God Almighty, thank ye!*
> *God Almighty, make we free!*
> *Buckra in this country no make we free:*
> *What Negro for to do? What Negro for to do?*
> *Take force by force! Take force by force!* *

In one newspaper article that I read, Mr Wilberforce quoted a churchman by the name of John Wesley who said in his *Thoughts on Slavery*: 'Liberty is the right of every human creature as soon as he breathes the vital air. And no human law can deprive him of that right which he derived from a law of nature.'

In Jamaica at that time, I read that there were more than 300,000 slaves and about 20,000 of those had run away from their masters. I saw printed the names of apprehended deserters who were locked up in the Kingston workhouse. The newspaper would give descriptions so that the owner might claim back the slave:

> HENRY JOHNSTON, a creole Negro man, 4 feet TEN inches, marked JJ on his shoulders, has two large scars, one from a scald on the left shoulder, and another from a machete on his forehead. Says he belongs to Miss Brown, a person of colour, Old Harbour.

The situation was making the White people nervous. Major General Marshall, who was in charge of the island forces, with the help of a group called the Maroons, broke up several gangs of runaway slaves and killed many of them. Maroons were runaway slaves themselves, one group of them living in Accompong, not that far from the Sharpe's residence. Any maroon capturing a slave would receive fifty pounds for his bounty. I wondered if Mr Sharpe got more than that when he sold Mama.

~

It was in the month of June that Mr Crawford came down with a terrible fever. Some people thought that it was the same malignant fever that kills White people in this country. Bigga took over the duties of the overseer. He told us that Mr Crawford was suffering from violent headaches, upset stomach, and pain and weakness of the spine. Some were saying that he was making strange noises in the night and going mad with the fever. Many thought that it was not the White man's fever at all but that Bag-o-Bones had set obeah on him. Bigga said he had seen the man from the cave come down one night to collect dirt from Tacky's grave and that he had buried eggs of the sensay fowl and roots of the wangla plant in the open yard in front of the overseer's house. To frighten the poor man out of his wits, the slaves informed Mr Crawford that he was sick because someone had obeahed him and that he should find out who it was. Otherwise, the fever would get worse and worse and he would drop down dead.

One morning, Mr Crawford awakened to find fowl eggs and bird feathers on the piazza of his house. We have a saying in Jamaica that danger is near when you see eggs where no fowl is near. His appearance was dreadful that day. His hair had grown long and unkempt, his face dirty and scrubby, and his eyes wild and red with rage and fear. Even though his features looked drawn down from lack of sleep and food, his rum belly still stuck out, appearing bigger than usual. No one dared to approach his house, where the following words appeared written in blood above the entrance door:

TACKY DUPPY COME FI GET YOU

Mr Crawford became more fearful. He ordered Bigga to have the words removed from his house, but they remained there for a long time. I never found out who painted the words. Maybe the obeah man must have done it.

People said that Bag-o-Bones had come down that night from the mountain to tempt Tacky's shadow out of the grave and that it was he who had set the duppy on Mr Crawford. White people, and especially Mr Crawford, were not supposed to believe in the powers of obeah, but it seemed that Bag-o-Bones's magic was too strong for the overseer to escape. Mr Crawford wanted to know what he should do so that he could sleep at night. He said that he heard terrible noises, loud banging on the roof and the howling of the patu bird through his window. Bigga reported that the poor man was driven near to madness.

Bigga told him that he knew of a special doctor, a myal healer, who could help him get better by providing him with herbal medicines. In return, Mr Crawford would have to give the doctor plenty of foodstuffs, rum and hogsheads of salt pork, and livestock including a hog and a fowl. In addition to taking the medicine, Mr Crawford would have to wash his house with salt water in order to pull Tacky's duppy from there.

But Mr Crawford refused to meet with the doctor or to take any medicine, and his health failed to improve. The man went out of his head. The evil of the obeah drove him mad. He left one day during the rainy season, carrying a crocus bag under his arm, running and screaming down the road to a place nobody knows.

Maas Sam instructed me to wash down and clean out the overseer's house, burning any belongings that were left behind. I did as I was told except that one of his possessions which I found, I kept and did not destroy. That was Mr Crawford's journal.

Many said afterwards that Tacky's shadow no longer lingered about the place and was finally able to depart to the ancestral world.

We were glad to be rid of Mr Crawford, but I knew memories of the overseer would continue to haunt us. Mama especially would not forget.

FIVE

March 16th, 1832

Saying with a loud voice,
Fear God, and give glory to him;
for the hour of his judgment is come:
and worship him that made heaven, and earth,
and the sea, and the fountains of waters.
And there followed another angel,
saying, Babylon is fallen, is fallen.

'Where you from?' *I ask the two inmates who are new to the cell.*

'We come from Unity Hall Estate, de massa there, him name Mr James Galloway. Him residence bon dung and de White people dem a run gone a de Bay.'

The older man is missing two front teeth and has a scar down one side of his chest. Maybe a chop from a machete. He wears no shirt, and his upper body is heavily built, his skin black and rough, the hair on his head, knotty and dirty. He looks as if he is about my age.

'What are your names?' *I am curious if they have news from the outside.*

'Plato, and this is Thorpe.'

Thorpe is younger, a man-boy, and of lighter complexion; sambo, maybe. The two of them look as if they have been living in the bush for a while.

The younger one speaks up, animated, as if he has had a sudden revelation, 'You is Daddy Sharpe, ruler and general of de rebellion.'

Plato is quick to cast blame. 'Yes, Thorpe, but yuh Daddy is now behind bars. Him is no saviour fi de people now.'

I feel shame for the fate of these two men and of others who did not obtain their freedom.

'Things bad out there, Daddy Sharpe. De ting dem don't work out so good fi we slaves. Dem find we inna de bush and bring we in fi trial, dem lick we dung fus and then beat we next.' Thorpe turns to show me his bare back, marked with slashes and welts caused from the cat-o'-nine-tails.

'We tell dem we try fi stop de rebel from bon dung massa great house but dem don't waan listen. Dem round we up and beat we till we sey wah dem waan fi hear.' Plato's voice is rough, and bitter.

Thorpe speaks excitedly with the vigour of youth. 'Me try fi get weh but dem cut me dung. Me cuss some raas and dem beat me some more.'

'Some of de slaves dem a hide up inna de bush and dem a sleep inna de trees a night-time.' Plato's speech becomes slow and deliberate, almost forlorn. 'Others gone back to de plantation cause dem have no food and dem haffi work much harder now since the sugar works and de cane bon dung. Ah tell you, Massa well vex. Him tun enemy pon we.'

The two men are sitting opposite to me in the small cell. The guards have thrown some crocus bags on the floor to serve as their bedding, not too far from the bucket which I use for urine and waste. There is no telling how long they will be here. Sometimes new inmates are tried and executed within days of arriving at prison. Some do not even reach here. They are slaughtered on the estates or wherever they happen to be captured.

I feel saddened by their stories. 'The White men and the King's soldiers betray us, my brothers. This beautiful land is desolate now, but if we trust in God, we can rebuild it and we can gain our freedom.'

Plato raises his voice in anger. 'Don't give me no raas bout freedom, Maas Sam. Dem lock we up in a dis prison cell, and me know sey we nah gwine walk free.'

'They would have put us out at the muzzles of their guns and shot us down like pigeons if we had not stood up for ourselves. It is late, my friends, and we must rest now. Tomorrow we pray to sweet Jesus to deliver us from evil. "And Moses lifted up the serpent in the wilderness, even so must the Son of man be lifted up: That whosoever believeth in him should not perish, but have eternal life."'

Plato looks at me in scorn and kisses his teeth. All is then silent and we curl up on the crocus bags in the stench of the night.

1818

A succession of terrible storms blasted Jamaica over the five or six years prior to 1818. The heavy rains and winds usually started around September month time. Maas Sam knew the signs when a bad storm was approaching. The skies darkened a certain way and the air became still. It was then that all of us slaves had to work hard to board up the windows of the Great House, prepare stocks of food and supplies of water and protect the livestock. Many times we made these preparations and no storm would come, but Massa never took any chances. One year in particular, I recall that the Montego River, which ran close to Cooper's Hill, raged and flooded the lands all around it. The winds were fierce and loud, cutting off the tops of the coconut trees. We could not venture outside because pieces of board and debris were flying about. When the rivers rose up, the winds were so strong they rooted up the sugar cane, and the water was so plentiful, large boulders fell from the hillsides and blocked the roads to the Bay.

After the storm, Massa became concerned about financial affairs. The sugar crop was ruined on many of the large plantations which would normally produce twenty to thirty hogsheads of sugar per season and work hundreds of slaves. Maas Sam was not able to hire out many jobbers, and his own livestock and provisions, which he used to supply to the large estates, were reduced. The roads to neighbouring estates remained blocked for several weeks, making travel by oxen or horse, and transport of slaves, animals and food provisions, impossible. Food supplies such as salted codfish, flour and oil became short. Massa told the mistress that with the scarcity of goods and storekeepers' rising prices, Cooper's Hill was in grave danger of receivership.

In those times, Bigga worked us extra hard. I was returned to outside labour, to repair damaged pens and stables, to clear fallen timber, to re-plough the fields, to replant ground provisions and fruit trees. We had to attend to Massa's property before we could mind our own plantain-walk.

After Mr Crawford was driven from Cooper's Hill, life did improve for us slaves. Maas Sam put Bigga in charge of the field slaves until he could hire a replacement. He vowed not to take so many trips to England without an overseer to look after matters. But Massa didn't really keep his promise. The trips continued and the Mistress was left to tend to the children.

Mistress Sharpe was concerned that the boy Henry had been influenced too much by Mr Crawford and was growing up to be rude and out of order. She wanted Master Henry to go to England like Anna so that he would be educated in the ways of better society. Instead, Master Henry convinced Maas Sam that he should remain in Jamaica and be schooled here. His argument was that he would learn first hand from Mr Sharpe how to manage the business of his property, and that one day he would become an attorney like him. This would give Massa the peace of mind that his affairs were being looked after in a trustworthy way. But the Missus maintained that he would not grow right if he remained in Jamaica, and that he would be a more capable attorney if he was educated in England. She thought that the few hours of instruction per day he received from his tutor were not enough to educate him and to fashion him to be an English gentleman.

Mr Sharpe was easily persuaded by Master Henry's jinalship and probably relieved that he did not have the added expense of educating him in England. So, Mistress Sharpe had to tolerate the situation for now, and keep a watchful eye on him. She did not want Master Henry associating with the slaves, for she thought companionship with a slave would debase his character and lead him into temptation. This presented an unusual situation in the household, because it was the custom for most White children to have their own servants.

As it turned out, Mistress Sharpe's suspicions were well founded. Master Henry had ample opportunity for idle play and amusement, and it was difficult for her to supervise his movements. As a child, he was rambunctious, and as a young man, he found pleasure in being defiant to Mr and Mistress Sharpe. It was perhaps this inclination that led him to want to keep my company every opportunity he had.

He would not let me forget that I owed him several debts, the first of which was keeping the secret of the stolen Bible, and the second, teaching me to read and write. In exchange for these, he made me grant him certain favours. One was to procure for him contraband supplies from the Great House. He enjoyed smoking Mr Sharpe's pipe tobacco and his Cuban cigars. On occasion, he would take a shot of madeira he said Massa brought specially from the Spanish mainland. Much finer, he said, than the rum made in Jamaica.

These objects were not too difficult to obtain because I was so often serving my master alcohol and fetching him tobacco. I was careful to sneak them in small doses lest Massa notice his supplies dwindling. Sometimes, Master Henry asked me to take coffee and tea from the kitchen. This proved more difficult, for Nana kept a watchful eye over all goings-on in the kitchen area. I would have to creep in there early in the morning, and, even that was risky because of Nana's unpredictable movements. I was hopeful, though, that as long as I could keep supplying Master Henry, he would keep his side of the bargain.

Master Henry was as stubborn and difficult as a mule. He would not listen to anything I told him but kept making more and more demands on me. I feel bad about the favours I did for him. I could blame his wayward character for leading me astray, but I must take full responsibility for what I did.

Master Henry took a liking to Bessy. She was mainly Anna's servant, but when Anna was in England, Bessy assisted with light duties about the Great House, baking, serving tea, dusting, and helping Nana attend to the mistress and her children. Other slaves were brought in to do the heavier work like scrubbing the mahogany floors, carrying water or washing the White people clothes. Bessy was a clear-skin gal, with a beautiful, smooth cocoa-coloured skin, the kind that would look sweet to any man, White or Black. She moved with ease and charm, giving the impression to anyone who did not know her that she loved to provoke and seduce men. Mr Sharpe gave her special liberties to attend evening functions in the Bay, and reports were that she loved to dance and be merry. She was fully aware of her own status as a Brown girl, waiting for the day when she would be granted her freedom, but in the meantime, resentful of the labours she had to perform as a house slave. She gave off an air of snobbery, a pride in being once removed from the Negro race, yearning for the day when she would be the mistress of a White man.

The mistress was adamant about keeping Master Henry away from Bessy. He was not to spend time alone with her and was discouraged from giving her any orders. One day, the mistress surprised them in the kitchen. Master Henry was pulling at the back of Bessy's apron and holding her around her waist with his other hand. She, in turn, was calling his name in a vex way and kissing her teeth. 'Master Henry, Master Henry, why you nah stop wid yuh foolishness, man?' For three days following, I was ordered to bring Master Henry his meals in his bedroom, where he was confined day and night.

When he was finally freed, Master Henry ordered me to arrange for Bessy to meet him at the entrance to the plantain-walk, up behind the animal pens. This walk was narrow and private, sheltered by the overhanging leaves of plantain and banana trees. I went to fetch her at the slave quarters at the rear of the Great House, where the domestic servants stayed. I did not mislead her but told her the truth, that Master Henry had ordered for her to meet him at the appointed place. She never did want to go, but I told her the consequences would be great if she did not obey. I accompanied her just as far as the entrance to the walk and from there she found her own way. When I saw that she had met up with him, I quickly retreated. I had done the dirty deed!

I am ashamed to say that I did this favour for Master Henry more than once. He and I did not talk of these encounters except for his instructions about when and where the meetings should take place. He must have threatened her in some bad way for her to have agreed to keep coming back to him. It was not long, though, before Bessy rejected these invitations. Master Henry put more pressure on me to persuade her, but to no avail. Miss Bessy began to take on a sad demeanour.

The gleam in her eyes had vanished, replaced by a look that reminded me of Mama when I would see her returning those nights from Mr Crawford's house. Master Henry became vexed at her refusals and blamed me for breaking our agreement. Everybody began to notice his irritable moods. There was no telling what extremes Master Henry would go to, but I knew he had a malicious nature and would become vindictive in some way. His rage cooled down when Bessy persuaded a young female, a field worker, to take her place, but towards me, he showed nothing but scorn.

~

'Maas Sam sey him waan you fi learn how fi ride horse.' Bigga gave me a broad smile, showing his pearly white teeth.

'I would love that, Bigga.'

'Him is a good massa.'

'Is trut you a tell, Bigga. Him treat me well, yes.' I was always grateful for the kindness Mr Sharpe showed to me. Now this was extra special. Only the more trusted slaves could get permission to ride horses, and a select few to leave the property on their own. The greatest privilege of all was to accompany the massa on his expeditions.

'An so it should go, Sam, cause you is a good bwai.' He hugged me with one of his burly arms, heavy and big like a tree trunk. I wished I would grow strong like he was.

Bigga did not talk to me much but when he did, he showed a kindness I never knew from anyone else. His frame was large and rough, yes, but his manner was tender. I felt he had a special liking for me.

Pebbles was chosen for me. She was magnificent. One of Maas Sam's racehorses from England, she was of a high breed and could fetch a price of some 140 pounds, more value than any of the most treasured field slaves.

Pebbles stayed with the Cuban and local breed horses in the stables, which were situated not too far from the Great House, close to the other livestock, on the opposite side to the slave village. The stables were built with adjoining stalls made of low stone walls and thatch roofs to keep the sun from burning the animals. Even hardier than the slaves, the horses toiled in the Jamaica heat, sweating just like us, but the English ones were like buckra, not able to stand up so well to the sun-hot.

The groom's name was Strap, and he was a young slave no older than me. His job was to care for the horses, to shoe, feed, exercise and ready them for the master. Strap's body was lean yet strong, his movements on the horse limber and smooth, and his back always straight. He seldom wore a shirt or shoes and always rode bareback. He and Pebbles rode as one, as if nobody could separate them.

'If you see Pebbles ear dem tun back, long and slick, you know sey dat she sense danger. You must keep yuh yeye dem peel, looking out for any trouble inna de night, and mek sure she don't get vex. Otherwise, she gwine throw you.' Strap loved his work and took pleasure in teaching me how to ride.

Pebbles was so tall and I so far from the ground that at first I felt strange sitting high up on the horse, but it did not take me long to feel at ease and to learn how to move with her. Strap rode ahead and led Pebbles with a rein. We rode up behind the stables and the Great House, through the plantain-walk of mango and banana trees, and on to the narrow limestone paths which ran through the property. I wanted him to let go the rein so I could learn how to command Pebbles and feel her motion on my own.

We continued with my riding lessons and I was soon able to travel far up the hillside where we exercised the horses on the meadows. The grazing cows did not seem to mind. They just kept that dumb look with their heads hanging down low as we rode around them.

'She love you, Sam. Me can tell dat fi sure. She letting you lead her and soon you can tek her anywhere you want.'

I thought all along that I was in control of the horse, but it was Pebbles who was teaching me. When Strap let me ride out on my own, I felt a rush of excitement inside, a great release as if I was free from the chains of slavery. Pebbles showed me the open fields, the banks of the Great River, the treacherous foot passes, the thick bush and the tall forests. We could go anywhere we wanted. I felt the strength of spirit Mama used to talk about and knew that the lion charm was bringing to me what I longed for.

My friends, Dove and Gardner, also learned to ride with me. They became expert horsemen too. Dove was much shorter than either Gardner or me, his eyes sunken in his forehead, and even though I don't think he meant it, he gave off a sinister appearance, his mouth displaying a disdainful twist of a smile. He showed himself to be crafty, a jinal like Anancy.

Gardner was much taller, more muscular and well proportioned, and by then, possessing the prowess of a man. He spoke good English to the massa, and to everybody, whether White or Black, he always acted boldly. Gardner had a commanding presence, a confidence you usually don't see in a slave. We learned from a young age to act in ways to make the White people vex wid us. Some of us acted fool-fool, others, lazy, and if you were like Dove, crafty. These were our own quiet ways to revolt, to gain control over our situation. But Gardner was different. From the time he was a pickaninny, he acted brave and forward, he worked hard and went on boasy-like. As you can imagine, no buckra would like those traits too much.

We stole off one moonlight night, Gardner on one horse and Dove and me on another, to an old Spanish bridge by the

Great River. The moonshine was bright, creating moving shadows as we rode the narrow limestone paths. The hooves of the horses made loud clicking sounds on the marl. We needed to be careful because we were not supposed to be out and about beyond sundown. Many landowners had spies to check on slaves travelling in the night-time. Mr Crawford had had his own scout, Roach, a cripple with a hunched back, shrivelled up like a dried fruit.

I was also anxious because I had heard stories of duppies travelling in the night. I did not dare look over my left shoulder, lest I see one there. I reminded Dove and Gardner that we were not to talk loud, as the duppy would steal our voice and hurt us bad. While we rode, I sensed sudden bursts of hot air in the night, not sure whether it was my imagination or just my body heat from the exercise. None of us wore shirts and our heads were bare too. Maybe that wasn't good. Mama always said I should cover my head when I go out at night. The dew could make me sick with fever or, worse than that, duppy could give me a hard knock on the pate. Luckily, Pebbles did not seem troubled, her ears not pulled back in the way Strap had described to me.

Gardner knew of less travelled routes through the bush where the thicket was dense and the macca plentiful. It was safer for us to travel this way as we were more hidden from the Spanish dogs and night watchmen who might be searching for us. To reach the river, we rode for a distance up rocky hillsides. On one side lofty rocks rose high, on the other side were steep precipices. At times, we needed to dismount to lead the horses around large boulders which had fallen in the path. The bush in the interior took on a stronger smell at night, wet and spicy, which seemed to drive the insects wild. White flower blossoms gave off sweet smells, attracting the night moths, and the fruit of large fig trees lured hundreds of squeaking rat-bats. The crickets also made noise, buzzing riotously and without end.

We tied the horses to one of the trees by the riverbank. The stones were flat and smooth, plentiful on the black sand that covered each side of the Great River. In one area close to us, some men's trousers and women's shifts were draped on the stones, forgotten by someone who had lain them out to dry. Not too far from where we left the horses, the river took a bend, and an old bridge with two big arches spread its breadth. Below the bridge, the water was still and black, in spots picking up the silver of the moonshine. In both directions, farther up and lower down the river, we could hear the gush of rapids. Gardner was the first to try the water.

'Me dare you, Sam, fi go up deh and jump.'

'You mussi tek me fi some idiot bwai.'

'De water cold but it nah have no rockstone inna it. Come nuh, man, tek off yuh clothes dem and jump.'

'Me kyaan swim good, you know, my friend.'

'Then, what bout you, Dove?' Gardner did not let up easily.

Dove didn't speak a word. He wore a scowl on his face and ignored what Gardner said.

Gardner's voice grew louder. 'Unu too coward.' He climbed out of the river and up the bank to the top of the bridge. He took off his trousers, stood naked on the ledge a few moments, and then jumped, holding his legs up close to his chest, letting out a squeal like a wild hog as he crashed into the water.

A minute later, he rose up out of the river, wiping the water off his face with both hands. 'Me a tell you, unnu too coward. Jump off de raas bridge and come dung here nuh man.'

Neither of us replied. But I wanted to join him, so I climbed down by the riverbank and waded in the shallow parts, hesitant at first to go into the deep water. Dove stared down at us, silent as before, holding his spot at the bridge top.

I felt we had stolen moments of freedom, fleeting as they were. No orders, no massa, no cow-cod whip — just washing in the cool river water and enjoying each other's company.

73

'You gwine haffi jump off de bridge one day, Sam. Me a tell you God truth.' Gardner came over and dunked my head under the water. I wrestled back with him, but he was stronger and pushed me under each time.

He stared at me, no longer playful, but serious and pensive. 'I tink it's time me and Dove move weh fi go somewhere else.'

'Why you say dat?'

'Maas Sam a wuk we too hard wi de Great Gang. To tell you de truth, me waan learn a trade like mason or ironwork, but Maas Sam sey him need me fi wuk as hired hand.'

'De trut is, Gardner, hear me now, me tink him need you fi stay at Cooper's Hill fi breed some pickaninny.'

'All a dat too. Dat me no mine so much still.' He smiled and started to splash the water, beating his chest with both fists. 'De women need fi breed, yes, for him is a poor White and him nah have no money fi buy no more slave.'

'Then we gwine haffi help him out, Maas Sam,' I said jokingly.

'Except poor Dove, him too miserable and cross fi waan any of dat. De women dem woulda scorn him.' Gardner shouted up to the bridge, 'Dove, come dung here nuh man. Duppy gwine start lick you dung wid rockstone.' Gardner paused, then looked up to one side where the riverbank rose as a tall cliff. 'Look up deh, Sam.'

A tall fig tree grew on the edge of the riverbank and a long thick root hung from it, dangling close to the water edge. Gardner was the first to climb the tree. He grabbed on to the fig root by wrapping his legs around it and then carefully pushed himself off from one of branches. He swung back towards the tree trunk, the rope held tight between his legs, and this time, his bare feet against the bark of the fig tree, pushed himself even harder. He gave a cry of freedom as he dropped himself and splashed into the river.

'It feel better if you tek off yuh trousers, Sam.'

We took turns climbing the tree and swinging on the rope, squealing like mad monkeys.

We talked late into the night.

'Tell me, Sam, who am I? Me hab no life but me walking still,' Gardner joked.

'Me nah know. Let me see, mussi duppy.'

'You right, Me is a shadow. How come you so smart, man?'

'Don't tell me you is a duppy now.'

'Just a joke, man. Your turn, Dove. Who am I? The longer it tan, de shorter it get.'

Dove spoke for the first time that evening. 'Me sorry for you, Gardner. Me tink sey you was a real man and you could manage better than dat.'

'You is a raas, you know dat? You nah know de answer, so you a joke round wid me and insult me.'

'Sure me know de answer, is fi yuh woody.'

'Me swear me gwine chop up yuh raas one of these days. De real answer is candle. De longer it tan, de shorter it get.'

'Dat is some fool-fool joke,' Dove shot back at him. 'Me tink sey it was yuh woody get short pon you, the more it tan up.'

'Who trouble you, man? Why you so miserable? If you so smart then, why you nah tell me a better joke?' He waited for a reply, but Dove did not say a word. 'You see dat now. You nah even know one joke, to raas.'

I wanted our time to go on forever but knew there would be trouble if we did not return to Cooper's Hill by daybreak. We gathered up the horses and they led us back safely before the first cockcrow.

~

White people generally did not approve of preachers converting slaves to the Christian way. They hated it even more if the parson was a Black man. A Negro had no place instructing others in the ways of the Lord, and if White folks were the ones he was ministering to, Lawd, that was the worst situation of all.

Gardner told me of a Black preacher who had a congregation up in the hills of St James, not far from Cooper's Hill. The owners were becoming concerned because the minister was attracting huge crowds at night-time. Jamaica had a law that prohibited slave meetings after sundown and before cockcrow.

His name was Mr Moses Baker. He was baptized by a man from the Americas and told to spread the Word of God to all heathen slaves. The planters said that he was preaching nonsense and that his beliefs and practices were not Christian at all. The only White man who welcomed Mr Moses was Mr Winn, who invited him to stay on Flamstead Estate.

People in the surrounding districts told stories of Moses Baker going down to the Great River at night, and there multitudes would gather to witness converts being washed clean in the river water. The newly baptized remained for days and nights in the wilderness, tempted by Satan and ministered by God's angels. When Moses baptized them, they walked out of the Great River, the river Jordan, to behold the heavens open wide and the spirit, like a dove, descending upon them.

Moses was a strict man. He would become vexed with the slaves if they did not follow in the ways of the Lord. The people called him 'The Judge' because he had so many rules. 'Too much wickedness is in the land,' he would say. 'Too much fornication, drunkenness and waywardness.' He said that the Jamaican man, both free and slave alike, go on too bad and cuss too much bad word. He had heard it said that even the massa swear more than the slave. The Bible tell us we must not swear at all, not by heaven nor by earth, and that fornicators and adulterers will come under God's judgement.

And here again, the Jamaica man, massa more than slave, love to have more than one woman. So we all is in plenty trouble. All will be damned who believe not the truth but have pleasure in unrighteousness.

I wanted to meet the man, to go to his prayer meeting on the mountain to listen to the lessons of righteousness. So one night Gardner, Dove and I took the same two horses from Maas Sam's stable and rode the journey to Mr Winn's estate. Hundreds of worshippers gathered under the protective branches of a tall silk-cotton tree. Beneath was a covered altar made from four bamboo sticks and a thatch roof, and on the table, draped with a white cloth, were a book, a basin of water and two lit candles. The short preacher stood with a younger man behind the altar, and in front, a small group formed a semicircle, mostly female slaves dressed with head-ties and long white frocks. The candlelight made the white dresses and head-wear shine like gold but the faces remained black, difficult to see in the night. Others stood apart, outside the circle; and to one side, close to the tree and to the preacher, two men sat with goombay drums.

Moses Baker was a mulatto, a brown skin man, old with white hair and bent-over shoulders, but he had vigour in his voice which reached far and wide across the valley. He spoke in a scolding tone:

'As you all know,
God sent unto the children of Israel
His only begotten Son.
He has commanded us to preach unto the people
to testify that He was the one ordained by God
to be our Judge.
The wages of sin is death, my friends,
And the Lord God said unto the serpent,

"Because thou hast done this,
Thou art cursed above all cattle
and above every beast of the field
upon thy belly shalt thou go
and dust shalt thou eat
all the days of thy life."'

The circle moved, swaying gently before him. The faithful kept chanting, 'Amen, Amen', over and over again, whispering under their breath, humming and saying words I did not understand. Moses went on in his serious tone:

'God judgeth the righteous
and God is angry with the wicked every day.
If he turn not, he will whet his sword.
He hath bent his bow
and made it ready.'

The inner circle spoke as a chorus:
He hath bent his bow
and made it ready.
Amen, Brother Moses.

Moses' voice became louder.
'Paul reminds us in Corinthians:
"Be not deceived:
neither fornicators,
nor idolators,
nor adulterers,
nor effeminate,
nor abusers of themselves with mankind,
Nor thieves,
nor covetous,
nor drunkards,
nor revilers,

nor extortioners,
shall inherit the Kingdom of God."'

The words echoed in my brain, reminding me of the words
Reverend Smith read from his black book on the mount at
Cooper's Hill.

Brother Moses' voice became frail and the younger man
moved closer to hold him, to prevent him from falling:

'Praise the Lord.
Praise the Lord.'

The people spoke out in unison, *Praise the Lord.*
'Praise the Lord, my people. Moses must rest. Daddy Powel
will continue the prayer.'
Praise the Lord, Moses. Praise the Lord.

Two men approached to assist Moses Baker as he departed
from the altar and retreated through the bush.

Daddy Powel took his place as the main preacher. He was
young and strong, his voice full of passion and rhythm.

'Preacher Baker sey, "Praise the Lord."'
The refrain rang out in the night, *Praise the Lord.*
'The Lord has blessed this night. He has come to His people.
He is here in the spirit. Praise the Lord.'
Praise the Lord.

The preacher began to chant his words, his voice reaching a
peak of excitement. He bent low and moved his upper body
back and forth, pointing at those before him and stabbing the
blackness of the night with his finger:

'When you are covered with the blood of Jesus,
When you are covered with His blood,
Jesus is your Saviour.
We are not going to win the battle
unless we are fully covered with His blood.'

The ladies in white repeated his phrases, *Unless we are
fully covered with His blood.*

'Say with me, brothers and sisters
O, Glory to God.
Hallelujah,
Hallelujah.'

Daddy Powel's voice became harsh and scratchy, and it
scared me:

'When you are with Jesus,
the enemy don't like you.
Call the name of Jesus
and you will be healed.
You need to be covered
for you to be saved.
Covered with His blood,
Glory be to God.
Hallelujah,
Praise the Lord,
Hallelujah.
Jesus,
O, Glory to God,
Hallelujah.

Hallelujah.

'O, Jesus is mine,
Jesus is mine.
True deliverance is in Jesus.
Praise the name of Jesus,
Praise the Lord.'

Praise the Lord.

'Jesus is come, Praise the Lord.'

Praise the Lord.

'Is there anyone among you who would like to give testimony? Now is the time to come forward. Is there anybody who had a vision? Is there anybody who had a dream they want to share with the faithful? Is there anybody who wants to witness how Christ has come into their life? Now is the time, my brothers and sisters.'

Women came forward, one by one.

'I am happy in Jesus. Sweet Jesus is my God and Saviour. Praise de Lawd.'

'Me heart full of joy and me feel warm all over me body. De blood of de Saviour cleanse me and now my sins are forgiven. Praise de Lawd. Praise de name of Jesus.'

'I am happy in my soul for I am a slave to Massa Christ. Nobody can trouble me because me open me heart and Jesus enter into it. Praise de Lawd. Praise de name of Jesus.'

'Massa Christ shed him blood pon de cross so dat we can be happy. Praise de Lawd. Praise de name of Jesus.'

The singing started, the drums following in tempo. One of the ladies dressed in white broke from the circle and walked through the crowd shouting out in song:

I hear Thy welcome voice,
That calls me, Lord, to Thee,
For cleansing in Thy precious blood,
That flowed on Calvary.*

The large crowd joined in with the refrain and the goombay drums beat louder and louder in the night.

I am coming, Lord,
Coming now to Thee!
Trusting only in the blood
That flowed on Calvary.

The song finished, but the drums continued beating.

Another woman burst out from the ring to enter the circle. She was about Mama's age, but weaker, maaga, with a wild stare in her eye. She started to dance with her arms outstretched, wheeling round and round in the centre. She breathed heavily, moaning and wailing like a mad woman.

'Faada in Heaven,
Look dung pon me poor soul.
Forgive me, sweet Jesus.'

Daddy Powel remained calm.
'Open yuh mouth, daughter,
and say, "Thank you, Lord."
He was punished,
He shed His blood.
We are healed,
And now you are healed.
Reach out yuh hand, sister,
and touch Him.'

Then the followers in the inner circle stretched out their hands to cover the lady in the ring.

Daddy Powel continued:
'Jesus, Oh Jesus.
Jesus is near.
Jesus,
Hallelujah.'

Jesus,
Hallelujah.

'O, glory to God,
Say to me.'

O, Glory to God,

Hallelujah,
Hallelujah.

Look down upon your daughter,
Dear sweet Jesus.
When you are covered with His blood,
the enemy don't like you.
Call the name
and you will be healed.'

The preacher leaned over and reached into the basin on the altar. He sprinkled the water on the lady in the ring.

'Jesus,
Jesus is my Lord.'

Jesus,
Jesus is my Lord.

'O, Jesus,
O, Glory to God,
Hallelujah.'

The drummers consecrated their drums with white rum and washed their hands and faces with the liquor. They beat their music hard and, as the tempo increased, the people started to dance. Some bowed to the drummers in reverence before they began. They came up into the circle and moved together in pairs, twirling and twirling from left to right, hand in hand, around the altar table. Some of the older ladies jerked their heads in short rapid movements, wiping the sweat that poured down their brows.

Then the spirit took the maaga woman. She spun and she spun until she turned mad. She fell upon the ground, her eyes staring wildly into the darkness, her legs spread and stiff as if she was dead. Her head, with the white tie on top, began to roll slowly back and forth, and then, with a quickening motion, her whole body quivered as if she had a fever. Then one man went into the circle to take hold of her, to control her madness. Others around her hummed and whistled, moaning with the woman's cries, clapping hands and stomping their feet on the ground.

Her eyes rolled in her head, her body jerked and convulsed in a violent rhythm, her arms and legs flailed all about. Unknown words came out of her mouth, sounding like the African language Mama would speak but stranger than that, stranger than even duppy could talk.

The worshippers continued clapping, shouting out praises to the Lord, and the Eboe drums kept in time with their rhythm. One of the women started to chant:

'*Hallelujah,*
Praise Jesus.
O, praise the Lord.'

The mad woman eventually quieted herself, the man still cautiously holding on to her. Then the whole night grew peaceful.

Powel raised his hand:
'I sought the Lord and He heard me,
He delivered me from all my fears,
Praise the Lord.'

Praise the Lord.

'This poor woman she cried out
And the Lord heard her supplication.
He saved her from all her tribulation.
The Lord is mighty,
Praise the Lord.'

Praise the Lord.

Daddy Powel reached out his hand and the woman rose up, praising the name of the Lord. He asked her if she would accept Jesus as her Lord, and when she agreed, he commanded two of his disciples to take her down to the river to be baptized in the name of the Father and of the Son and of the Holy Ghost. 'Can any man forbid water that these should not be baptized, they who have received the Holy Ghost as well as we?'

And so the people left that holy place underneath the cotton tree to descend to the Great River to watch the woman be baptized.

When the crowd began to disperse, I set eyes upon the most beautiful young woman I had ever seen. Her skin was black and smooth like the stones of the riverbank. Her eyes shone bright in the night and her look was as fair as any sweetness I had ever known. I thought of the Queen of Sheba and the way Tacky must have felt when he first glimpsed his love.

'My name is Amelia. I prefer you to call me by my African name Nyame, I come with my mother, Quasheba, who say she know you. You are Samuel Sharpe, the young house slave that can dance so fine.' She was dressed in simple slave clothes, the common frock cut low in the front and a cotton cloth wrapped about her to keep off the night dew. The 'kerchief on her head was tied back in a way to make her face look round and pretty. Her body had slender curves, but she was full-bodied, like a ripened fruit.

'Yes, I am Sam, but I don't dance so good. Your mother told me about you. You live not too far from Cooper's Hill?'

'A ways up by Content, but the massa not so good to me, so I hoping he will send me to a different place.' She looked sideways at me with a glint in her eye.

Even though she spoke of sad things that evening, a smile formed out of the corner of her mouth each time she glanced at me.

'That's not so easy if they don't want to sell or auction

you. But tell me, Nyame. How come you find yuh way to Flamstead tonight, so far from where you stay?'

'Mama want some company fi hear old Moses talk bout baptism and salvation.' She gave me that sweet look again.

'Would you let me come to Content some time to visit you? My massa is good to me. He lets me ride his horse and I can come fetch you one night, one night soon.'

Lawd have mercy pon my soul,
It sweet me so till
When de lovely Nyame
Look pon me
wid her sparkling eye,
and she sey to me,
'Yes, dear Sam,
You can come to me,
You can come see me
one night soon.'

Oh, Lawd have mercy, that was sweeter to my ears than all of Moses Baker's hymns put together.

The following day, Strap kindly offered to be my messenger, to deliver a letter to my newly found sweatheart at Content Estate.

Tuesday, February 2ⁿᵈ, 1819
My Dearest Sweet Nyame,

I trust that this letter finds you in the perfect state of health. I take much liberty in sharing these words with you. An hour does not pass in the day in which I do not think of our brief encounter at Moses Baker's meeting. Your sweet smile remains forever etched in my mind.

I am asking you a favour that you keep the promise that you made to me that we would meet one evening soon. I ask that you meet me at the bottom gate of Content Estate, this Sunday evening just as the sun is setting.

I send this note with a bearer. I hope that it is received into your hands. You do not need to send me word. I shall be faithful to my own promise and reach bottom gate by sundown. I shall wait for you there and know that the strong attraction, which I feel we have for each other, will bring us together that night.

I hope that you do not think that I have been too forward in writing you this letter, but my desires are so strong that they are leading me to meet with you. I tell you these words with all sincerity.

I trust that you will receive this letter in the spirit with which it is intended.

Yours fondly,
Samuel Sharpe

Strap stole away on a Tuesday night into the dark with my letter in hand. I wrapped up for him in a piece of cloth some cut sugar cane and cassava cake for his journey.

Six

I made a solemn promise to our former slave, Samuel Sharpe, that I would do everything possible to arrange that his narratives be published. Minister Bleby, who took a particular interest in his story towards the end of the slave rebellion of 1831, has kindly offered to assist me in this endeavour.

He handed to me a section of Mr Crawford's diary which he had removed from his dwelling at Cooper's Hill after the man was driven mad and forced to leave the property.

In reviewing Sam's writings, I believe that it is fitting that I include here selections from Mr Crawford's journal.

Mrs Samuel Sharpe

1816

Wednesday, March 27ᵗʰ. I sent Bigga out with a small gang to go crabbing today. Black crabs spawn this time of year, come down from the hills and cross the roads near to the sea. They march in a straight line crawling over anything in their path. The Negroes go out with their torches which stun the crustaceans. Delicious meat. I love also the baracoota which the finer ladies do not eat for fear of poison. They are as fierce as the shark in the water, with sharp fanged teeth, and will strike at anything. They lurk in the mangrove channels in the islands of the Bay. Have seen them six feet long and weighing up to 100 pounds.

Friday, April 12ᵗʰ, Good Friday. The slaves get four days off, far too generous an allotment. They should only be allowed one day every fortnight in accordance with the law. Even outside of special holidays like Easter, Mr Sharpe grants them every Saturday and sometimes Sunday for religious instruction. With this leniency, Cooper's Hill will go to ruin one day.

Friday, April 26th. News of slave insurrection in Barbados, April 14th. Easter Sunday. The Negroes are deluded that Britain promises them emancipation. An uprising in Jamaica could be ferocious with machetes and weapons in the hands of 300,000 savages.

Earlier in the year, there was talk of rebellion in the Parish of St Elizabeth involving 200 Africans who were intent on burning down estates and killing all Whites on the island. The overseer at Lyndhurst Penn discovered the plot. Leaders including a Brown man were apprehended and sentenced to death. The need for martial law in this land is blatantly clear. Little or no government action in this regard. The Duke of Manchester is far too lenient and the country is mismanaged. Despite all the taxes collected, the coffers are still empty.

These days in Jamaica the planters are far more indulgent of the slaves. There are times I feel I should place musketry in the foundation walls of my house to fire upon the savages.

I have an ill sense that the slaves will seek revenge upon my head. I am the only person here who treats them according to their lot. Even Bigga has a surly appearance and does not respond willingly to my commands.

Wednesday, May 7th. Lonely for companionship. I do not have my Mimba any more. Mr Sharpe saw it fit to have her sold. She was a fierce Coromantee but never refused my favours. She used to bring me black crabs, fried fish and sweet cassada and then spend the evenings. She agreed to spend most nights I called for her. I provided for her well: men's jackets, cloth, oil, salt beef, furniture. The last few times, she looked provoked and acted sulky. She said her son, Sam, did not like her coming here at night. Cooper's Hill lost its best slave. I used to work her with the Great Gangs among the males. Mr Sharpe was a fool to have sold her.

Saturday, June 8ᵗʰ. The time is hot and dry. They buried the old fool, Tacky. With Negro burials, there are many superstitious practices which the 'guinea-birds' bring from Africa. They sprinkle rum on the grave, make animal sacrifices, and perform lewd dances. Mr Sharpe requested that I provide them with a hog which they barbecued for the celebrations after the burial.

I used to see Tacky coming across the guinea-grass patch with a bunch of cane tied up in a bundle. He was a damn thief. So are they all. No one is to be trusted. Other times, he would try his favourite pastime of running away. Always unsuccessful, the fool. He would get caught. I would have him duly punished each time with thirty-nine lashes of the cat-o'-nine-tails. Tacky was a stubborn old brute.

Wednesday, June 12ᵗʰ. Port Royal is still not fully rebuilt from the conflagration last July. All buildings were burned to the ground except for the naval establishments and the church. Montego Bay suffered a similar calamity some years ago. Too many risks with wood construction. I should join the construction business. The tradesmen who are employed to build houses are more prosperous than a bookkeeper or small-time overseer like myself.

Friday June 21ˢᵗ. Summer Solstice. Hot as Hades in Jamaica. Mr Sharpe is too generous with provisions for the slaves. Food should be given to strengthen the labourer like the foddering of a horse. You feed it only the right quantities so that it becomes healthy and robust, not fat and lazy.

The government is appointing island curates to each of the parishes. They are to visit the estates to educate the slaves in the ways of Christianity. The Africans do not even read or write. It is nonsense to believe they will be able to understand the Bible. Wretches in England are treated with less attention.

I had a slave boy beaten today with the cart whip for stealing chickens. He assists runaways by providing them with food from Cooper's Hill. I ordered him in the stocks for the night without clothes. The insects will have a feast. Warned him that if he thieves again, I will capture galliwasps to torment him.

Wednesday, June 26th. Suffering terribly today from infection in genitals. Burns when I piss. Sometimes I wonder what fate brought me to be born in this God-forsaken land. My father was captured by man-traders in London, shipped to this island and sold for five years service. He met an English lass and never returned to his homeland. Fie on that!

Friday, June 28th. Tonight is like an inferno. Send for a young female, Sally. She spends the night. Required her to prepare my favourite dish, dokunu: plantain, green banana, cassava flour, sweetened and wrapped in plantain leaf. With some sea turtle soup, port and rum, I settled in for the night.

Wednesday, July 10th. The time is dry and hot. Less output from the jobbers in this heat. The Negro will use any excuse not to work. 'Too hot today, Sar, me head a hurt me.'

The young house slave, Sam, is not to be trusted. He is too favoured and pampered by his master. He tells the master lies about how ill-treated the slaves are. He should be hired out with the jobbers instead of being spoiled as a house slave. He is soft yet thinks himself superior to his mother and other African Negroes. The more removed Creoles think they are from the African blood, the better they feel they are. If you try to punish the Creole, he gets angry and sulky, and with a lenient master, ends up being fully indulged, getting anything he desires.

Friday, August 2ⁿᵈ. Had an older slave, Cudjoe, transported off the property. He's afflicted with cocobay, a disease which causes large blotches and swellings. Toes and fingers rot and eventually drop off. It is highly contagious.

Wednesday, September 4ᵗʰ. The rains break the dreadful heat. Hurricane season. We are spared so far this year. Last year October, the winds were fierce with most of the damage reported in St David and St George. Our livestock pens were completely destroyed. Hurricanes bankrupt us every time.

Monday, September 9ᵗʰ. Purchase five old oxen from Mr James Galloway, Unity Hall Estate. I will have these fattened for sale to butchers in the Bay. Can fetch good prices for old beef.

Thankful for the rain. Has rained steadily for two weeks.

Friday, September 20ᵗʰ. Dreadfully short of money for my personal entertainment. Mr Sharpe hires me for only 100 pounds sterling per annum for my labours. When he is absent in England, I perform all the duties of overseer of affairs of Cooper's Hill. Spend long hours supervising operations from early dawn until after the slaves are fed at six o'clock. Deserving of much better status, for I have a reasonably good education and business sense. I have in mind to seek out employment by a large estate.

Wednesday, October 2ⁿᵈ. Feeling morose this morning. Have drunk to excess. Pissing blood. Must have contracted the infernal clap. Ask Nana to boil the bark of the *lignum vitae* tree, reputed among the Negroes to be a remedy.

Notice a pain in my left foot. Surgeon says it is chigoes that have buried themselves in the toes. Not yet advanced so still curable. Doctor cuts out the parasites and uses the Negro remedy of stuffing the holes with burned tobacco.

Thursday, October 31ˢᵗ. Hallow'd Eve. Strap, the stable boy, comes screaming up from the river that a galliwasp has bitten him. Arranged for him to be taken to the sick-house. The slaves are terrified of them — brownish yellow with green scales and are said to have teeth and a venomous bite. I am most sure the damn thing is harmless. The slaves are cunning. They will do anything to make distractions so they are not worked as hard.

Friday, November 8ᵗʰ. Sally is not available, so I ask Bigga to fetch a young wench from the Bay. She entertains me all night.

Monday November 11ᵗʰ. Sally cooks my favourite meal and spends the night.

Wednesday, December 4ᵗʰ. Thankful for the change in climate with the advent of a cool Christmas breeze.

I often wonder how different life would be in England. Wife, children, home of my own. Instead, I am trapped here with an infernal disease. White women are scarce in this country and, in any case, aspire to be wives of wealthy owners.

Saturday, December 21ˢᵗ. Winter Solstice. Not much change in seasons but Christmas breeze continues to make the nights cooler.

Mr Sharpe has given the slaves four days off for Christmas. They are free to visit the Bay for celebrations. It is quiet at Cooper's Hill this Christmas.

1817

Friday, January 13ᵗʰ. Make report to Mr Sharpe that our supply of mules to the estates is diminishing. I usually fetch thirty pounds sterling per head. I am in need of more investment and a larger number of slaves in order to increase the breeding of livestock. I need a hardier breed of slave to work like the oxen do. Much bigger yield needed to meet expenses. The poll tax is over six shillings per head per slave. Cooper's Hill seems to be more of a hobby than a business.

Monday, January 17th. Yesterday spent whole day in the Bay. On Sundays I often go into town to meet with other bookkeepers and overseers, drinking, gambling and keeping the company of mongrel women. Men dress in their best finery, neckcloths, waistcoats, silk stockings and Florentine breeches. It is a dandy sight to behold the gentry parading around Montego Bay on Sundays. The proprietors do not associate with us and many overseers even distance themselves from the lowly bookkeepers. The wenches give us entertainment by dancing while we look on, and afterwards we find chambers at the tavern to enjoy the evening. They wear tight-fitting bodices and gaudy jewellery, and smell of cheap perfume. They rub their cheeks with Scotch-bonnet pepper to make their brown skin blush.

> Come, carry me in a room;
> Come, carry me in a room
> And give them five-pound piece.
>
> Come, carry me in a room;
> Come, carry me in a room
> And lay me on the bed.*

The wenches are troublesome indeed. Their lustful ways are tempting to any man's heart — virtually impossible to resist their advances. Important not to be seen in public with them after the evenings spent in the tavern.

Saturday, February 15th. Feasted last night at the Great House. Partook of all six courses and drank to excess. Mawby, my favourite drink: a nectar made of rum, sugar, water, ginger and *lignum vitae*. Awoke the following morning in my house with no further recollection of the night's proceedings.

Monday, February 17th. Show Bigga how to salt a hog using a bucket with holes in it. You rub the whole pig with salt two to three hours after it is slaughtered and place it in the bucket over several gallons of water. Repeat process the following day. The water underneath serves to extract the juices from the meat. Negroes love the salted pork.

Saturday, March 1st. Order Bigga to give the slave boy, Strap, thirty-nine lashes. He was out late with the horses without permission. He deserves harsher treatment. Maybe if I fed him his shit, he would change his ways.

Monday, March 10th. I detect a certain unease among the slaves. This morning at mealtime, they all appeared sullen. Bigga will not say what is the matter. I order him to thrash anyone who refuses to work.

Friday, March 14th. Arrange for Bigga to bring a young slave girl from the Bay. She spends the night. I do not perform as well as I used to. My desires for the wenches are not as strong, my moods depressed.

Friday, March 21st. Slaves continue to be restless. I instruct Bigga to keep a watchful eye and give due warning to Mrs Sharpe of any danger.

Monday, April 14th. Escort Mr Sharpe to the Bay for his journey to England on board one of the schooners sailing with the April convoy.

Mrs Sharpe is not hospitable to me when her husband is absent. She appears aloof and suspicious. Melancholic. White women whose husbands are absent live a lonely life in Jamaica.

Friday, May 9th. Mr John Baillie, proprietor of Roehampton Estate, requests a jobbing gang to work the cane fields. I can send only a few slaves suited to that kind of work. Bigga leads five who go on foot. A well-conditioned slave can walk up to forty miles a day, almost as far as a well-groomed Spanish horse.

I feel unwell and stay shut in to sleep most of the weekend.

Wednesday, May 21st. Young slave, Half-Pint, offered me a cool drink of lime juice after the workday is done. Tasted putrid. I suspect that he may have wanted to poison me. I order Bigga to have him lashed the legal limit. Maybe the traitor will learn his numbers better that way. Some Africans learned to count in English from the beatings they received from the driver or Master who would say aloud as he lashed the brute: one, two, three...

Monday, June 2nd. Roach informs me that he has seen Mimba visiting Cooper's Hill at night. She goes down by the graveyard with an old man, a runaway slave who lives in the hills.

Monday, June 30th. I awake with a frightfully high fever. Know not what ails me. Bigga calls for the doctor, who provides me with insipid herbal medicines. I remain confined in my house for several days.

Wednesday, July 2nd. Strange noises in the night, loud bangings on the roof. Delirious from the fever.

Monday, July 14th. Violent cough and loathsome ulcers on my arms. Inform Mr Sharpe that I am unable to continue my duties. Nauseated and vomiting.

Friday, July 18th. Quite beside myself. Roach says the Negroes have set obeah on me. Damn their superstitions.

Wednesday, July 23rd. Fevers persist. Call for Bigga to fetch me some rum.

Friday, July 25ᵗʰ. Roach tells me my door is painted in blood. Damned be this wretched place. Sick to the death.

Fever lifts temporarily. I regain strength to venture out for the first time in weeks. The sunlight is blinding and am able to smell myself, putrid.

Fowl eggs and bird feathers are scattered on the piazza of the house. I kick them off and curse those who look on.

Friday, August 1ˢᵗ. Bigga says that I must see a healer if I want to be cured. He fetches me two buckets of sea water. I spend all night scrubbing the house clean with the salt water. I throw all the beddings and furniture out of the door.

Friday, August 8ᵗʰ. Sweat all night, hot and cold from the fever. My head is not right. Damn this wretched place. Penmanship too poor and my mind too troubled to continue. . .

SEVEN

March 20th, 1832

Father,
I ask you to forgive them all
    For they know not what they do.
Forgive me mine own trespasses
As I forgive all those who sin
Against me and my brothers too.
'Judge not and ye shall not be judged,
Condemn not and ye shall not be
Condemned,' so saith the Lord Jesus.

My fellow slaves are rounded up
Tried, bound in chains, executed.
My friend, George Spence, died for a cause.
My brothers shot down like pigeons.
We thought the King to set us free,
Not spill our blood upon the land.
Buckra left him God in England.
In Jamaica, pure evil reign.
The Parson come to tell me news,
I pain for all those who perish.
Jesus came to save us sinners
No matter how great our sins be.
Father, Massa Jesus tell us
You will answer us our prayers.
Be merciful to us sinners,
Black sinner and White sinner too.

February 1819

I felt nervous about my meeting with Nyame. I had never met a girl in this way before. I made sure to dress up pretty in a white shirt, black trousers and a pair of shiny buckle shoes. I was a dandy young man going to see his sweetheart.

Mr Sharpe would not have given me permission to ride Pebbles to go up into an area of the bush to visit with a woman. I needed the horse, though. So I told Massa a lie about Mama being sick and how she needed my company. I felt bad lying to Mr Sharpe because he trusted me so much and was so kind to me.

As I took the route to Content Estate, I thought about how Tacky must have walked the same paths on those nights he stole away to meet with his queen, Quasheba. I felt an excitement in the pit of my stomach. I arrived early, before six o'clock, tied Pebbles to a fence post and rested under a large guinep tree. I reached for a long stick with a fork on the end of it and twisted off bunches of ripe guineps. The pulp was sweet. I remember when I was a child, Mama used to tell me not to run with the guinep stone in my mouth. It would kill me.

I heard Nyame come down the path to the gate. She was dressed more simply than the first time I saw her. She was wearing a plain frock made of coarse cotton, and a plain, loose-fitting white blouse. Maybe she had not wanted to draw any attention to herself by putting on fancy clothes. I felt I had dressed up too much. She was barefoot and stepped skillfully over the stones along the track. She moved quickly in a spirited and playful way. As she approached the gate, she stopped suddenly by the tree, a couple of feet in front of me, out of breath. She flashed that special smile, and then, unexpectedly, reached forward, opened her arms and gave me a hug. For an instant, I felt her warmth and energy. And then it was over. She pulled back suddenly, as if ashamed.

'Bwai. What a way you dress up.' She said in a joking way. She was looking me up and down.

'It's a special occasion, you know.' I smiled back at her.

'As you can see, I got your letter.'

'I am so glad you agreed to come. I felt that I was maybe too forward in writing it.' I reached both my hands to hold hers, but she turned to one side.

'The young man was so polite. You should reward him. He found me directly and placed the letter in my hands. Said it was from a friend at Cooper's Hill.'

'Strap is a good friend. He had no problem being my messenger. That is the first time I ever asked him a favour like that and it is certainly the first love letter I ever wrote.'

'I should hope so.' She walked across to the other side of the gate. 'This is the path down to the Great River. You want us to pass down there? Some people might come up this big road here by the gate, and I am sure you have no ticket to come up in these parts.'

'You're right. My owner thinks I'm gone only for a little while.' I untied Pebbles and led her by the reins. 'I can't leave Pebbles here. She must come with us.'

'She's beautiful.'

'Yes. The young man you met taught me to ride her. I will teach you someday.'

'I would love that.'

'It's the greatest feeling. The most free a slave can be, I think.'

'I don't think a slave can be free.' She walked ahead, taking the lead through the bush. 'Is your owner mean to you?'

'No. He reads to me and he lets me ride horses.'

'You lucky. Mine is mean to me. Says bad words and orders me around.'

'I will kill him for doing that.'

We came close to the river bank. I tied Pebbles higher up where it was not so sandy. No moon, but the stars lit up every part of the sky, making it look like streaks of milk painted on black.

She broke the silence. 'The night pretty, eh?'

'Beautiful. I wonder sometimes where it all come from.'

'How you mean?'

'How all that light is shining up there and who make it so pretty.'

'Don't the parson teach you in school? "*Who made the heavens and the earth?*" You should know the answer, "*God made the heavens and the earth.*"' She gave me that sweet look from out the corner of her eye.

Lawd have mercy. She look like an angel.

'I know. The Anglican man teach us that, but him don't know nutten. Him just say, "*Say after me. . .*" and you have to repeat every word just like how he say it.'

'You want to rest over there?' She pointed to the roots of the large African tulip. In the month of February, it was in full bloom with red and yellow flowers. Some of the large boat-shaped pods had already fallen to the ground.

She sat with her back against the tree trunk and I moved close to her side, leaning on a nearby log. The night creatures were making noise, especially the crickets that were chirping louder than ever. I could hear the patu making thrilling noises in the trees and flapping its large wings.

'You hear the patu? You ever notice how the white patu is more handsome than the Jamaica owl?'

'It's true, but its eyes are more scary.'

'Yes, and when the male gets excited, it flaps its wide wings to show the full beauty of its white feathers.'

'And why would that be, Sam?' I could hear the laughter in her voice.

'I'm not sure, Nyame. Maybe to attract the female.'

'Maybe.'

I picked up from the ground one of the blossoms of the African tulip. It was a cluster of red and yellow flowers and buds. I took off one of the thin small buds which was about the length of my thumb.

'Watch this.' I picked off the end and squeezed the water on her hand.

'What's that?'

'The bud from the African tulip.'

'It's full of water.'

'Yes. They have a rude name for it.'

'As if I don't know.'

I changed the topic. 'And what about your master and mistress?'

'They miserable.'

'They all miserable.'

'I told you already I want to leave that place. They not good to me, Sam.'

'Where would you go?'

'Run away. Run so far they can't catch me.'

'I wish it was that easy. You ever think about what it would be like to be free?'

'Yes, all the time. What about you?'

When she looked at me, I felt I could look into her soul, her eyes were so clear.

'Yes, ever since I was a little boy. More than that too.'

'How you mean?'

She asked me so sincerely, I felt no strangeness about telling her my secrets.

'Ever since I was a little boy, I felt that there was a spirit greater than all of us and that I shared that greatness in a special way.'

'So what that mean now?'

'I don't know yet. All I know is that the slavery we are in is evil.'

'I could a tell you that, Sam.' She didn't say it in a mean way.

'I know but I have a strong feeling to do something to free myself and help others to be free too.'

'And how you going to do that?

'I don't know yet. Many people tell me that I will do great things one day. So I guess I must wait for the spirit to move me.'

'One thing, Sam. If you find your way, make sure you come fi me, you hear?'

Lawd have mercy. She a mek me head spin round wid love.

'I would never leave you behind.'

'Behind where?' She was trying not to let me get too serious.

'I would come for you and the two of we would be free.'

'And whe you would tek me, Sam?'

'Right up to the highest hilltop in Jamaica and there we would build a house and farm some land, and if you want, we can even have some pickaninny.'

'An if I don't want dem?'

'Then all woe to me.'

We both laughed.

'You want to go down by the river?' She stretched and raised herself up.

'I race you down there.'

I chased her, caught her and held her at the water's edge. We stayed together like that for a while, she looking out at the river, and me holding her from behind with my arms around her waist. I did not want this moment in time ever to end.

She turned to me, and in the beauty of the night, she removed her blouse and pressed close to me. Her breasts were warm and so perfectly formed. I lifted her high about my loins and felt her softness against the strength and weight of my manhood. I carried her back up the embankment. *I don't think all the milk and honey of heaven could have bring more sweetness.*

She gave me her love that night under the African tulip tree. I adorned her with the red and yellow petals and declared my love for her. After, we washed in the cool river, and late into the hot night, found our way back through the bush to the bottom gate at Content Estate.

Before she went back to her house, I lifted her up unto Pebbles with me, and the three of us rode the meadows in the starlight. With Nyame holding my waist and Pebbles moving beneath me, I knew there must be a God, a goodness to life beyond the cruelty of slavery.

When I finally said good night, I showed her my lucky charm, the fierce golden lion, which I told her would give us the strength of spirit to guard us from all evil.

EIGHT

I have taken the liberty to insert here excerpts from my own journals which Sam Sharpe, or, for that matter, anyone else, would not have had the opportunity to read. These I publish in unabridged form with the hope that they will provide another perspective on the events prior to 1831. I trust that they will in no way offend the sensibilities of any persons mentioned herein.

Mrs Samuel Sharpe

1819

Monday, February 1st

I feel unwell this morning. Nana brings me some ginger tea to settle my stomach. I fear she is not well herself. She sweats profusely in this forbidding heat. She is a faithful soul and has served me well. She cares for the children as if they were her own. Some wealthy proprietors believe that the locals are not good enough to care for their children and, instead, import White attendants from England. I can't imagine these imports would be any better than our Nana.

Many times I am morose and do not understand why. The early mornings cheer me up somewhat. They are beautiful to behold, serene and quiet, save for the early crowing of the roosters in the coops. I go about my daily business as usual, exerting myself so that I do not feel the nagging pains of discontent. I am grateful that I have not fallen seriously ill. The English call Jamaica the grave of the West Indies. So many of our countrymen, unaccustomed to this climate, meet untimely deaths soon after their arrival on the island. I worry about Katherine, our second born, who so often looks pale. She cries much of the time. The poor little darling, only four years of age. The doctor says she suffers from colic. Each morning, Nana sits with her in a rocking chair on the piazza to sun her. She says she is too 'whitey-whitey' and that the early sun will give her strength.

Wednesday, February 3rd

It rained thunderously today. It is normally drier this time of year. We are still suffering from the ravages of storms that we experienced last November when public and private buildings were destroyed throughout the island. Militia, who were stationed in barracks on flatlands close to the ocean, were mobilized into the interior. The rain is different here than in England. Large black clouds move rapidly across the sky and the rain pours in torrents, making pelting noises on the rooftops and on the earth. The lightning and thunder frighten the animals in a way unknown in the Northern countries. In the rainy season, in the warmer months, the thunderclouds normally develop towards mid-afternoon and the rains stop as suddenly as they begin. The Negroes are not fond of the rain and are particularly afraid of the dew that covers the ground at night. They believe that anyone exposed to the damp will develop ailments and fevers.

Friday, February 5th

Mr Sharpe has left earlier than usual today to go to his work in the Bay. I spend the morning reading letters which I have received in the post from my dear cousin, John Thorpe, who lives in England. About once a week a Negro boy delivers letters arriving by mule from Kingston. The post has been much delayed of late because of the swelling rivers and muddy roads. Mail conveyed from England takes close to a month to travel each way. Several months may pass before I hear from dear friends and family there. I breakfast today at about ten o'clock.

Thursday, February 18th

I have not written in my diary this last fortnight. I called for the doctor because I was experiencing more serious bouts of illness. After conducting tests, he informs me that I am now pregnant with my fifth child. I pray for the strength to bring it healthily into the world.

Despite this news, my melancholy persists. It sometimes lasts days, even weeks, and then clears as do clouds after a tempest. I wonder if my dear husband notices my shifting moods. Perhaps this is the cause for his unusual reserve, and distance from me.

I turn often to the Good Book for consolation:

A merry heart maketh a cheerful countenance:
but by sorrow of the heart the spirit is broken.

Friday, February 19th

We are without the services of an overseer. Our former employee, Mr C_____, left Cooper's Hill some eighteen months hence. Years of self-indulgence, excessive drinking and cruelty towards the slaves eventually took their toll on the man. He left our employ with great disgrace to himself and to our family.

He possessed some beastly ways. I did not wish Anna to consort with him as I had seen his deportment with the young female slaves. He had received little opportunity for refinement of character or for exposure to English customs. I believe he travelled only once or twice to England in his lifetime. I expect he associates with slaves because no English woman of any standing would deign to be familiar with him.

I began to fear for his safety as I heard rumours the field slaves wished vengeance upon his head. He treated them very cruelly. I have no doubt that some of his actions were justified, yet one must be prudent not to arouse the savagery of the slave. He would drink himself to excess which impaired his better judgement. This overindulgence in alcohol is the ruin of many well-meaning men in the West Indies. Rum is abundant here and few constraints exist by any civil or religious authorities on one's moral behaviour.

Monday, March 8*th*

Again I have been negligent about writing in my diary. I feel unwell during the pregnancy, confining myself to the bedroom for days at a time. Nana brings me a glass of warm milk. The night has been cool, dropping to sixty degrees Fahrenheit, typical of this time of year.

My husband continues to bestow favours on his house servant, Sam Sharpe. It upsets me that he reads articles to the slave from the newspapers and discourses with him on current affairs. Granting him permission to learn to ride a horse shows far too much lenience. These accommodations endow the slave with privileges and freedom, which if abused, will set a dangerous precedent and bad example for the less advantaged ones.

Last week, the slaves were allowed to hold a dance at the Great House. They drank and caroused until early hours of the morning. Many planters on the island believe that one must exercise a degree of discipline and ruthlessness towards slaves if the suitable rewards are to be reaped from their labours.

Thursday, March 18ᵗʰ

My husband has received news from Kingston of an epidemic of malignant fever which has decimated the militia there. This terrible disease mainly punishes those whose immune systems are unaccustomed to the climate. The victim suffers terribly from fevers, nausea and inflammation of the entire body. Fortunately, some of the young soldiers were spared the onslaught of this plague by removing themselves to ships anchored in the harbours and to higher elevations in the mountains where the balmy breezes act as an antidote.

I fear for my dear Katherine who seems susceptible to illness. Thanks be to God that my other little ones, Elizabeth and Jane Gray, have not yet suffered from any serious ailments.

Friday, March 19ᵗʰ

I am anxious about the dear boy, Henry who is now approaching manhood. He becomes more surly and indolent as the days go by. He escapes for long hours from the confines of the house, telling no one of his whereabouts. I have warned him several times about familiarizing himself with the slaves. He needs to learn how to manage them, not in a punitive way, but with an authority becoming of a master. I wish for him to be educated in England like Anna, but he has persuaded my husband that he should remain in Jamaica. His behaviours are very disquieting indeed.

Monday, March 29ᵗʰ

Mr Sharpe reviews our financial affairs. I fear things are not as prosperous as they were. Despite Mr C_____'s darker nature, the man possessed good economic sense and always offered sound advice concerning these matters. I worry that we may go into receivership if the storekeepers and suppliers in the Bay continue to give us unlimited credit. Taxes need also to be paid. There is a poll tax now on each slave that is registered, far in excess of the amount due even for horses or mules, upwards of six shillings per slave. Mr Sharpe has his own business enterprise in the Bay but this too seems to be suffering. Costs are rising and estates are generally not as profitable as they were.

Thursday, April 1ˢᵗ

I peruse the *Royal Gazette* in search of the French novelette that appears in serial form. The series is entitled 'Edward', an English translation of a love story in which the protagonist has lost his senses because of an infatuation with a young virgin.

> I forgot everything; my mind was entirely absorbed in the enchanting idea that I was loved; that our two hearts had been yielded at the same moment; that, notwithstanding all her efforts, she had not been able to detach herself from me; that she loved me; that she had accepted my love; that my life would be passed near her; that the certainty of being loved would stand in the place of happiness for me. I believed this sincerely; and it seemed to me impossible that human felicity could exceed that which Madame de Nevers had just made me experience, when she told me, that, even when she was absent from me, her soul was wandering around me.*

I marvel at this young man's capacity to be consumed by love, yet wonder whether he is delusional. He is about to face the impending tragedy that must ensue if he ever discovers her love for him to be a lie, yet, in believing in her unconditional love for him, he must feel a total abandon of all temporal woes, a transcendence of these in embracing a higher state of eternal bliss.

Tuesday, April 13th

The buzzing of the mosquitoes all but drives me mad. There is an onslaught of them both at dusk and at dawn, especially at this rainy time of year. They are relentless in biting every part of the body, disfiguring the skin by leaving large swollen welts. They are especially partial to the new blood of our compatriots recently arrived from England. Our unsuspecting visitors are eaten alive.

Tonight the cockroaches are also plentiful. After the rain, they fly about in the late evening, finding their way through the jalousies and into every crevice of the house, hiding in the curtains and bedcoverings. They are not harmful but have an unpleasant odour and appearance, some with hard shell-like wings and long antennae. The Negroes do not seem to mind them. I squirm at the sight of them crushing these insects with their bare feet.

Wednesday, April 21st

The stable boy, Strap, showed up this morning by the front steps of the Great House with a big smile across his face. He shouted up to me, 'Look, Mistress Sharpe me catch one big yellow snake. Look how him long, Missus.' He held the reptile dangling from one hand and a bloodied machete standing erect in the other.

'When yellow snake dead, Mistress, you can measure him.'

I was not sure whether his words had a more subtle meaning.

This fair island is beset with creatures of all dreadful sorts. We have heard stories of a gentleman who awoke one morning to find a brown snake wrapped about his legs. Dumbfounded for fear of the reptile, he was unable to call out to his boy servant. When it had become quite late in the morning, the young slave visited his master's bedroom only to find the ghastly sight of his master enveloped by a serpent. He hastily fetched a machete, and his master was petrified at the sight of the hideous weapon descending upon him. In an instant, the boy slave hacked the snake, decapitating it with one blow, leaving his master quite unharmed. I expect this anecdote would sound like a macabre fairy tale to my friends and family in England.

Mr Sharpe is on one of his frequent trips to England. He has not shared with me the full purpose of this voyage. He says that he has matters to attend to. I fear the unpredictable nature of the slaves, and of Bigga who is left in charge of the affairs of the property. I trust Nana, though. She comforts me by telling me she would ring the alarm if she thought anything was out of sorts. If there were a threat of revolt or of actions of cruelty planned against my person, I would be utterly helpless.

Sunday, April 25th

Horrid dreams last night. I miss Anna and am worried that I have not received letters from her in recent months. She is usually a very good correspondent.

Nana brings me a cup of tea just as the first light of morn is showing.

I spend the morning stitching embroidery. I am in want of adult company.

Friday, April 23rd

I read in the papers today that a horde of runaways has been rounded up with the assistance of the Maroons. The Maroons help the militia by capturing and killing troublesome Negroes in and about the areas surrounding Accompong. A handsome reward of fifty pounds is granted per head. The Maroons appear to be fickle, however, in the way that they cooperate with the local officials, taking bribes from slaves looking for a safe haven. Thousands of runaways, it is reported, live in the woods and towns of Jamaica.

Monday, May 3rd

I was awakened in the night by the shock of an earthquake. It made a horrid rumbling noise, rattling my bedposts. It was not violent, yet most unnerving. I called out to Nana but my cries were not heard. I am now five months pregnant, still feeling discomfort, suffering from colic like my dear child, Katherine. She must have inherited this weakness from her mother.

I wonder how my life would have turned out differently had I lived in England. I would perhaps have married into landed gentry, enjoyed the civility of a large country home where it would be safe to take long strolls in the evening. I would have travelled frequently to Europe shopping for the most modern fashions in the finest stores. Alas! The life of a Creole in Jamaica is much different from this, supervising a household of slaves, spending many waking hours indoors because of the dreadful heat, and for entertainment, attending the odd ball, only to watch the men become intoxicated, drinking rum and lusting after the native girls.

I feel as though my youth is passing me by at an alarming rate. I am pregnant again and destined to remain here to breed until I can no more.

I wonder what the English ladies think of us. I am just as savvy and cultured as they, but they think we are bred differently, grown in a foreign soil, darkened by the blackness of slavery.

Tuesday, June 8th

I have not written for more than a month. Katherine is not eating well and cries most of the day and night. I called for the doctor to attend to her but the medicines he provided do not seem to offer any relief. My dearest Katherine, I pray for your recovery! A part of me I know will die should anything happen to her. If she shows no recovery within the coming weeks, I shall take her to England where the doctors may be able to better diagnose her ailment.

I am heartened that Anna and Mr Sharpe will soon be arriving from England.

The heat is intense today. I do not venture far from the house but, to catch the ocean breezes, sit on the piazza. This gives some temporary relief.

The lack of morality among the privileged classes never ceases to amuse me. I wonder what disgrace would befall a White woman were she to exhibit behaviours typical of Englishmen who reside in Jamaica. Adultery among the White gentry is widely accepted here. Men of planter class keep their Black or Brown mistresses in the very homes where their wives reside. I have not known of a White woman to have a Brown baby, yet I expect these things do happen in secret. Women, after all, are in possession of similar passions and instincts, as base as these may be.

Wednesday, June 9th

Sam serves me my morning tea on the piazza. The morning fog still hovers close to the land, the silk-cotton tree towering up through it not far from the side of the Great House. It looks eerie in the misty light.

The Africans have superstitions about the silk-cotton tree. They believe it to be sacred, The God Tree, the dwelling place of ancestral spirits. The Creoles, however, are more fearful of it than reverential. One night, Strap was returning to the slave houses with a glass of red rum and a bowl of roasted yams. He said that as he passed in front of the cotton tree, the spirits, or 'duppies' as they call them, grabbed the drink and food from his hand. Ever since that day, he takes another route from the stables to his hut. Other Creoles do not like the tree for they say it is the favourite place for wicked planters to hang their slaves.

Sam Sharpe has been groomed by my husband to take care of many of the affairs of the household. He has a gentle manner for a slave. His eyes reveal a certain brilliance and he has shown an exceptional gift for reading and writing. Henry's tutor has commented on occasion about the rapidity with which the slave learns. He has a deep black complexion and generously fat lips, characteristic of many of the Africans. His look is almost contemplative, as if he possesses the capacity to think profoundly. We have treated him well. How he will use this privilege is anyone's guess.

I know that his mother debased herself by earning favours from the overseer. This did not sit well with my husband.

Saturday, June 12*th*

Katherine's condition worsens. I make arrangements for a passage to England.

Monday, June 28*th*

I buried my dear sweet Katherine today on the hillock behind the Great House. Nana brought her to me Saturday morning, dead in her arms. She had breathed her last during the night. I did not hear her cry.

I can only pray to God that she passed peacefully and without pain. It seems cruel that a life be taken away so young.

She was a darling child. My very own, my very first girl. May your soul, dear little child, forever rest in peace and may God give us the strength to understand His will.

Thursday, July 1ˢᵗ

Anna has arrived. She shows such maturity, her speech refined like that of an English lady and her manners genteel. She comforts me in my loss.

My husband does not share many details of his stay in England. He is deeply saddened by the loss of our second child. He knew she had been ill but was not aware that her condition was critical.

Everyone is glad to see the master home. It is the most peculiar sight to behold the servants gathering around to greet my husband. They smile, clap and curtsy along the road in front of the Great House.

Saturday, July 3ʳᵈ

I asked Nana to arrange for a feast to welcome home Mr Sharpe and Anna. In true Jamaica style, there was more food served than one could possibly consume: pepper-pot soup, turtle steaks, the most succulent of the snappers, the deep water silk, barbecued hog decorating the middle of the table, pigeon, bald-pate, land crabs, vegetables, fruits and sweets. My husband insists on these indulgences.

Sunday, August 8ᵗʰ

I am large with child and feeling the intensity of the summer heat. It has been wretchedly hot.

I read often of slave revolts. They are alarming and unsettling. In the Parish of St Elizabeth, a few years ago, a slave from Saint Domingue led a bloody revolt. The character of the African, especially the Coromantee, can be fierce and warlike. I remember my father speaking of the general massacre of Whites by General Toussant L'Ouverture at the turn of the century. Black regiments mutinied, forcing a complete evacuation of all Europeans. The ninety-two Whites remaining in Port-au-Prince were hanged. In Jamaica, we continue to be haunted by these stories.

And now, I hear rumours of Wilberforce's intentions to set the Negroes free throughout the British Empire. This is a complex issue. The planter class in the colonies will not easily surrender their way of life, and if there is resistance on their part to change, then surely the slaves will revolt.

It is uncertain what kind of life awaits the slave should he be freed. I expect that he would be happier and freer under the care of a benevolent master than to be left to his own demise, roaming the woodlands without food or shelter. Mere savagery would result, surely.

Wednesday, September 8th

I have asked Nana to make the necessary preparations for the birth. I am due to deliver any day soon. My health has improved and I feel more cheerful, expectant of the new arrival. The Lord hath taken a little darling from us but in kindness giveth us another.

Henry tells me today of some shocking news of Samuel Sharpe's behaviour. He has betrayed the trust that my husband and I placed in him. It has become known that for several months now, he has been stealing books and other personal articles belonging to Mr Sharpe and also various items of foodstuffs from the kitchen. In addition, his dealings with other female slaves are of a questionable nature. I assume that Mr Sharpe will deal with him in a fitting manner.

Friday, September 17th

Mary Gray was born into our family on this day. She is a beautiful child with a rosy complexion like her sister, Elizabeth. We welcome her into this world with a gaiety of heart.

Friday, September 30th

Nana screamed, wailing like a woman who had lost her senses. She entered my chambers, 'Missus, de Lawd tek weh another one from you.' She carried my baby dead in her arms.

The doctor is not sure of the cause. 'Cot death,' he says. She stopped breathing during the night and lay dead in the same position in which she was lain down to sleep.

My little, little darling. I cannot explain why you have been taken from me, your very life plucked away. It is a heinous crime.

Time is cruel, I know. It carves lines in our fair brows and makes beauty to fade, but my sweet Mary Gray, she was devoured before Time had his chance to be unkind.

Next to her sister, Katherine, I buried her tiny body in a box no bigger than a shoe.

Part II
THE BAY

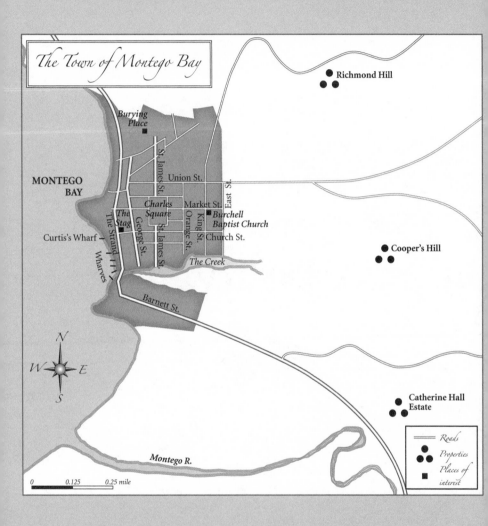

The Town of Montego Bay

Richmond Hill

Burying Place

MONTEGO BAY

St. James St.
Union St.
East St.

Charles Square
Market St.
Burchell Baptist Church

The Stag
George St.
St. James St.
King St.
Orange St.
Church St.

Cooper's Hill

Curtis's Wharf — The Strand

Wharves

The Creek

Barnett St.

Catherine Hall Estate

N
W E
S

Montego R.

Roads
Properties
Places of interest

0   0.125   0.25 mile

NINE

March 25th, 1832

I *have not written for several days. My spirits have been*
low.
James approaches the cell door. His large lips and broad
nose soften his otherwise stern look. Strong he looks, the kind
of man who could break your neck with one snap.

'One letter come fi you from Minister Burchell but de gaoler
sey dat Mr Coates, de justice man, shoulda read it fus.'

'So why dem gwine on like dat?'

'Cause de authority nah trust de parson dem.'

I tease him, 'So why you wouldn't show it to me?'

'You mussi mad, prisoner, dem would a heng me before you
if dem did ever find out.' His expression is kind and soft, not
vexed.

I am surprised that Mr Burchell has replied with such haste.
'Thank you, Mr James, you know me jus a joke round wid
you. You look after me good still.' I like when James is on
duty. He is kind to me, bringing me extra portions of food
and providing candles so that I may write by night.

The screams and moans from other prisoners keep me
awake.

There is no escape, no mastery of my own destiny. There
has never been. I thought at one time there would be but I
was wrong. A slave is no different from a prisoner, his life
owned and his fate controlled by the master.

Latter Part of the Year, 1819

'I have decided that it is best for all of us that, Sam, I hire you out elsewhere so that you may take leave from Cooper's Hill. I have made arrangements with a lady by the name of Miss Garcia of Montego Bay. She is desirous of having you as her slave to assist with the operation of a lodging house which she holds in town. She is a woman of a generous heart and will treat you kindly.'

Mr Sharpe sat on his favourite chair facing the upstairs veranda. I stood to one side, facing him, remaining there at his command the whole time he spoke. No one else was in the great room.

'I had considered making some provisions for your manumission, but in light of the circumstances, I will postpone this plan. I should like to inform you, however, that I have made allowances for your mother and her sister in my will.'

'Maas Sam, I want to say that —'

'I do not wish for you to speak at this time, Sam. Bigga has been instructed to transport you to the Bay tomorrow before sunrise. I shall insist also that you return to this house all items in your possession which you have unlawfully removed from here. The punishment for your actions normally would be quite severe. If I were to listen to the advice of Mrs Sharpe and Master Henry, I would have you receive fifty lashings and be sold to auction. You will speak nothing of our conversation today.'

'No, Massa, not a word, Massa.'

He drew on his pipe and blew rings of smoke which drifted out to the piazza.

In the auctions, I have heard they bid a price for you, no different than they would for cattle. You are naked and they all stare at you to make sure that you are not sick, no sores, no bleeding gums, no swollen feet. Then you feel them poking at you with a stick to test if everything is as it should be. They talk about you, thinking you do not understand what they are saying. The bidding starts at a few pounds, the healthiest male slaves going for 100 pounds sterling.

'Miss Garcia is prepared to pay handsomely for you. She knows that you are healthy and of a willing nature. She has offered me the generous sum of 200 pounds, but I will choose to keep ownership of you for the time being.'

I wanted to explain to my master that I was grateful for what he had done for me, for the graces he had bestowed on me, for sparing me hard labour with the jobbers, and for giving me the opportunities to read and write and to learn how to ride a horse. He would not understand if I told him that I did not really mean to steal the Bible, I only borrowed it for a while. I did not know what other lies Master Henry may have told him but I had no choice in the matter. I had to accept my fate.

'You have proven to be an intelligent slave, Sam, but you have made some mistakes and for this you must pay your dues by leaving us for a while.' With that, he raised his right hand and motioned to me to leave as if he were shooing a fly or running a dog out of the room. My heart felt heavy and tears came to my eyes to know that I was humiliated by the man who had shown me such kindnesses. He seemed not to care now, his face turned away from me, his eyes fixed on the rings of pipe smoke.

My departure from Cooper's Hill was sudden. Bigga escorted me in the early hours of daylight. I did not know then if I would ever see my childhood friends, my master and mistress again.

And so it was that the Bay became my place of residence. My new owner was Miss Maria Garcia, affectionately known as Miss Mary. She was a Brown woman but different looking from the mulatto ladies in Jamaica. She had straightish black hair which she tied back with a fancy silver pin. Her eyes were black too, black like coal, her skin, smooth, the colour of coconut oil. She referred to herself as a *criolla* from the island of Cuba, where her master, a Spanish count, lived in a big palace. A few years earlier, he arranged to buy her freedom and a passage to Jamaica.

Miss Mary owned and operated a lodging house and tavern called *The Stag*, located on the Strand by the water's edge, very close to Curtis's Wharfe. Travellers from Kingston and Falmouth would stop there, some for lodging, others to have their horses refreshed. In May and June, when there were many tall ships in the harbour, sailors would also frequent the tavern for a drink of rum and to smoke hand-rolled cigars.

The house was similar to but smaller than Mr Sharpe's. The second floor had a piazza with shutters and four bedrooms which gave to a drawing room in the middle. The kitchen, dining room and tavern were downstairs. The walls of the saloon were decorated with swords and pistols. I stayed in the slave quarters round the back next to the horse stables.

My chores included the busy routines of operating the lodging house, including errands which Miss Mary needed me to run. She treated me fairly well but would show a hot temper if I complained about the long hours she made me work. I was up before cockcrow to draw fresh water for the guests and to ready the horses. I was coachman, footman, butler, storekeeper, waiting servant and house cleaner. Anything that needed to be done she called me to do. She made me scrub the floors with oranges and dried coconut husks. She would also assign me to kitchen duties, peeling and slicing fruits and vegetables, and washing pots. Miss Mary hired a separate washerwoman and a young boy to help out a few times a week, so that gave me some relief from the workload. There was a full-time cook whose name was Strumpet. The sailors knew her as Miss S. After the mariners had drunk too much of the sweet cane juice, Miss S would offer them other services which they paid for handsomely.

I enjoyed the errands Miss Mary sent me on because I was able to leave the house to go into the Bay. That is how I got to meet Miss Nelly at Sunday market.

The Bay fascinated me. I visited stores where the dry-goods merchants sold cheese, ham, tea, port, and other wares like boots and saddles. I loved watching people of all colours, black, brown and white, all walking the streets together. I was not used to seeing free persons of colour mingling like this. Very few lived on the plantations. As soon as they gained their freedom, they moved to the towns and villages to make a living — the mulattos, quadroons, mustees, anyone with a mix of White and Negro blood. Many became craftsmen, working for themselves, some hiring their own slaves and others apprenticed to White men. They always had employment, the millwrights, coopers, blacksmiths, carpenters, wheelsmiths and masons.

I was told that I should not go to the upper part, to the top roads on the hills behind Charles Square. There the big massa villas stood overseeing the whole town. I spent time instead walking down by the wharves to see the tall ships up close. When they were anchored, their white sails were down, and I could see long ropes tied to massive masts and beams stretching way up to the sky. Below were two decks where I would count the cannons all lined up in rows, sticking out of huge portholes. There were usually thirty on each side. I wondered what it would be like to sail on a big frigate far off into the deep blue sea. I wished that Miss Mary would help to buy me my freedom.

Early Sunday morning in the Bay, Barnett Street was lined up with slave women coming down from the mountain, balancing on their heads big baskets full of fruits, vegetables, rum, sugar, salt, anything they could grow in their provision grounds or tief from buckra on the estate. To cushion the burden of the heavy loads, they wrapped their heads in cotta, the plantain leaf, dried and plaited for the purpose. The mamas carried their pickaninnies strapped to their backs. The older children walked in front, pulling on the ropes of the jackasses which did not want to carry the baskets strapped to each side of their fat bellies. Sometimes, the asses would stand up in the road, coming to a full stop, and no matter how hard the children pulled the rope, they would not budge, not one inch, stubborn as can be. Then the mamas would lick their backside with a stick, not once but many times. And some of those mamas were strong. Only then would the jackasses move, slowly but surely down the hill towards the market.

When the higgler women reached the shoreline they walked across the Strand where the wharves are, and then up to Charles Square at the centre of town to begin market day in the Bay.

Miss Mary would give me a few shillings each time to buy foodstuffs for the guests at her lodging house. I always went to Miss Nelly's stall first. She had the loudest voice of all the vendors, the best prices and the most produce. She generally had a round, happy face, but that could quickly change to a nasty scowl. Her right cheek was marked with a scar large enough to have been the brand of a bill, a cutlass with a sharp hook used for chopping cane. Miss Nelly was a hefty market woman with bosoms round like melons. She flashed her smile when she sold her wares, but you did not mess with her. She had a machete, hidden under a crocus bag close to her side, ready for use if anyone stole from her or gave her any boderation.

'Ripe plantain, sweet potato. Nice White pickaninny, tell yuh mumma fi come here and buy some ripe plantain.' She directed her words one day to a little White girl who was walking by, hand in hand with her mama.

Then ignoring the child, she shouted so all could hear, holding up a middling-sized bunch of plantains. 'Four bits for dis bunch of plantain.' She sat on a box, her legs spread wide, carefully guarding what money she had tucked away in the deep pockets of her frock.

The little buckra girl began to cry, pulling at her mama's skirt. Her mother picked her up and moved quickly away from Miss Nelly.

'Don't fraidy, fraidy, lickle girl. Come here, let me give you one sweetie.' Miss Nelly called after her, but neither the girl nor her mother seemed to hear her amidst all the confusion of the market. They became lost in the crowd.

'Five pence for de sweet potato. Yam, cocoa, yampy, sweet cassada, cassada cake. All fi sale from Miss Nelly,' a young boy hollered above the crowd, making sure to hold up each fruit or vegetable as he called out the price. He was about ten years of age, a slave boy whom Miss Nelly hired to help carry her baskets and sell her produce.

'Ten pence fi one quart of peas, nice fresh pigeon peas.

'One sugar-loaf pine, sweet as sugar cane. One pineapple, ten pence.

'Two coconut fi five pence. Buy yuh coconut here.

'Ripe mango here fi sale. One dozen mango fi five pence.

'Pindar fi buy here. Sweet roast peanut. Buy yuh pindar here. Miss Nelly have de best price.'

Miss Nelly sold more than any of the other higglers in the market. She also carried foodstuffs from foreign like strawberries, grapes and apples. The buckra especially liked the fruits from overseas. All kinds of people came to buy from her, White, Brown, Black, some even speaking strange languages. The Spanish ladies always wore black veils on their heads, carrying fans and parasols to match. The Brown people, Miss Nelly did not like too much. She said dem did go on too fancy with dem long frock, buckle shoes and big ring pon dem finger.

'Dem follow fashion de backra too much,' Miss Nelly would say. 'Dem try fi talk big-people talk. Me tell you, Sam, one day when de heat de was killing we all, one of dem fancy Brown lady wid de parasol come up side me and sey, "Well, Miss Nelly, I don't know how you stand it these days, this heatment is very greatment. Don't you think?" Well, Sam, me couldn't help meself, me jus a bus out wid laugh same time, one raucous laugh.'

This did not stop her, though, from selling the Brown people her wares. Miss Nelly would even give some braata to those women she knew would come back, week after week.

I used to stay back late on Sundays to help load up her baskets with the produce she did not sell. Miss Nelly had not been a higgler for that long. She told me that when she was younger, she was so pretty that men flocked to her like bees to the jasmine flower. She received pieces of jewellery and Spanish coins from sailors who came off the ships in Montego Bay. But she stopped that after a while and turned to the higglering instead. It wasn't long before she became big and fat. All higglers are supposed to be big and fat, she said. She still loved to dress up, and at Christmastime, her mistress bought her fine linens for her to parade in the streets. But she didn't business with men any more.

Long ago, she had a daughter from a White planter, but she was forced to leave the child when a new young couple occupied the house.

'Dem was de days when dem did treat me good. De buckra man did love me so-till.' She sat and counted her money while I stuffed the crocus bags and baskets with the leftover fruits and vegetables. 'Dem sell me fus to one massa who live in de Parish of St John. Me did go on so bad dem did send me back to St James.' She burst out with a belly laugh. 'Lawd have mercy pon my soul, Sam. What a life of tribulation and boderation. Me nah know how we tek it sometime. All me know sey is now me a go bout me business and sell me provision dem. And if anybody try fi mess wid me, me a cut up dem raas.'

'Do you know what happened to your baby?'

'Me think dem did keep her in de house with de new mistress. Dem did christian her Bessy. Me nah know whe dem get de name from, Sam. But you know, me would a love fi set me yeye pon her one day and stroke her 'traight hair and tell her dat her mama love her. She mussi big child by now.'

'She is a pretty brown skin gal.'

'What you saying to me?' She looked up at me, her eyes bulging out of her head like a mad woman.

'The Bessy I know live in Mr Sharpe house at Cooper's Hill. And she is a sweet gal.'

'Don't go on wid yuh foolishness, Sam. What you saying to me? You know me Bessy?'

'Yes, Miss Nelly. Me mama did grow me de same place as she.'

'Who is yuh mama, Sam?'

'She name Mimba, Miss Nelly.'

'Lawd have mercy, Sam. What you saying to me now?

Maybe de Lawd forgive me, maybe him forgive all me transgression dem — but me nah know how dat possible, me have nough of dem still. But today is a blessed day, today the Lawd bless me. Today on de Sabbath Him send me an angel fi give me good news.'

'Dem did tell me bout you, Miss Nelly.'

'You is fi me own flesh and blood, Sam.'

She stood up, using the machete as a crutch. I thought that she was going to be sick, she was sighing so heavily. She reached over to grab two water coconuts, and shaved the tops off with the cutlass, leaving two small drink holes with the white flesh of the jelly showing on the rim.

'You must be thirsty, bwai. Drink it up, Sam, it will mek you strong.' We gave thanks and drank the coconuts dry.

She said nothing more. She reminded me of Mama in that way, talking up to a certain point and then turning dead silent.

Before long, I followed her up to the hill to the foot of Barnett Street by the creek and bade my auntie farewell until the next Sunday.

~

Miss Mary used to complain that I spent too long on the errands.

'The customers are waiting for you and you are walking about the *pueblo* as if you own the place. *Díos mío.* I need a man so that he can beat you.' When she scolded me, she became flushed and her bosoms swelled big.

'I always come back as soon as I can, Miss Mary.' Whatever I said in my defence would be wrong. A slave could never properly defend himself to his master or mistress.

'*Mal criado.* Don't be rude to me, Sam. I have a house to run and mouths to feed. You do as I tell you. ¡*Mala criatura eres!*'

She frightened me when she spoke Spanish. I felt she was obeahing me. I had heard of some White women from foreign who did cruel things to their slaves. They reached Jamaica from an island called Santo Domingo.

When she was in her kinder moods, I learned many facts from Miss Mary. She told me how she missed her country. There were more free people in Cuba than in Jamaica, more Coloureds, Whites, and more priests and nuns walking the streets. Ladies, elegantly dressed with veils and expensive jewellery, strolled the promenades of la Habana, and rich men, who courted them, lived in big palaces. Music filled the air, from Spanish guitars, and there were *fiestas* every night in the town squares. '*Todo el mundo es músico en la Habana,*' she would say.

She was born in a place named *San Marco,* which the Cubans called the garden of paradise. The earth was bright red there, the flowers sweet and the fruit so abundant that the mangoes and guavas ripened and fell to the ground with no one to pick them. Tall palm trees grew around the houses to keep them cool, and the mountain breeze they called *el doctor* because no one ever became ill there because of it. The district of *San Marco* was always green, always fertile.

'Why you would ever want to leave such a paradise, Miss Mary?' I inquired of her innocently one day.

'You ask me too many questions, Sam.'

'That is what my mother always tell me.'

'Well then, Sam, you should know that it is true. *Es la verdad.*'

She showed me books written in her language and I learned to say a few words in Spanish, but I soon gave that up. It was too different from what I knew. I became discouraged because

131

I could not understand her when she spoke her language. She rolled her tongue, trilled her R's and became so excited that I thought she was going mad.

'The language too foreign for me, Miss Mary.' I finally told her.

'It is the language of romance, Sam.'

'Tell me then about the Count of Habana, the man who bought your freedom.'

Her mood suddenly changed. 'You shut up, Sam. I tell you that you ask too many questions. What are you doing listening to stories of Cuba, you lazy boy. Get up out of your seat and go do your chores. *Pendejo eres.*'

I missed Cooper's Hill, especially my friends, Dove and Gardner. I wondered when I would see them again.

TEN

April 1832

I write the following in the hope that Mistress Sharpe or Parson Bleby will publish this plea and show it to those persons for whom it is intended.

To the Gentlemen and Lords of the British Parliament and to all free citizens of the great United Kingdom of Great Britain in the second year of the reign of our sovereign King William IV, I, a wretched slave who is very shortly to be condemned to death, exhort you to listen to my pleas, not for my sake but for the sake of all the slaves of the West Indies who are still bound in chains. I make an appeal to you to do whatever is in your power individually and collectively to fight for the cause of freedom and to expedite the passing of bills in Parliament for the abolition of slavery.

I was born a slave and will die a slave. My mother was sold to traders off the coast of Guinea and brought here to Jamaica in chains across the ocean, separated from her kin and her ancestors. She was abused and ill-treated, sold to different owners, and finally became a fugitive, a runaway, no family, no master, no place to rest her head. I ask you, for a moment, to reflect on how it must feel to be the chattel of someone else, to be bought and sold in the marketplace, to be driven like oxen to the field to labour all day, to be beaten by the master so that you will work harder, and to be fed along with the other animals, not when you are hungry but when it is decided that it is feed time. You are fed not for the enjoyment of food or the satisfaction of hunger but so that the master may keep you strong and fit for his own economic gain.

The beasts of the earth, the asses, the cows, the pigs do not receive the harshness of treatment that we do. Even though we are all the property of the landowner, the animals in the pens are treated with more respect. Their heads are not cut from their bodies and hung upon poles. They are not flogged until they bleed. Buckets of salt are not thrown on their open wounds. They are not bound in chains and placed in stocks.

For those who tell you that we do not want to be free, do not listen to them. They are liars and false as hell. They say that we will not be happy if we gain our freedom. How do they really know? They have never been slaves. How can we be happy now, bound in chains, denied our very birthright, our freedom before man and God?

Do you not think that we have feelings just as you do? Am I not a man like any other who resides in any other region of this earth? If this is so, tell me how one person can be the property of another? This I do not understand. I am sure that, if you appeal to your own reason, you will find it is not logical.

I urge you to act out of mercy, to listen to the teachings of your Christian faith, to the voice of compassion in your souls, to do everything in your power to rid this great Kingdom of the evils of slavery. And the Bible tells us that you shall be blessed for being merciful.

I know that the Lord will change our condition because He is a just God. I have told my fellow slaves to be of good courage for He will strengthen their hearts, all those who hope in the Lord. I teach them Psalm 34 which tells us that blessed is the man who trusteth in the Lord. None shall be desolate who trust in Him.

I urge you to turn to your own Christian belief as a counsel to help end this evil. Does not Christianity, the faith you profess, teach you to love one another and treat others with dignity? What honour can you have in your hearts, what salvation can be yours if you torment another human being? Christ calls us all to act with justice, not to judge according to appearance.

Our Christian faith teaches us, 'Do unto others as you would have them do unto you.' Would any one of you want your children to be taken from you, or your husband or wife to be stripped naked and sold at an auction in the marketplace? Would you want to be put in chains in the hold of a ship and sent to Africa to serve as a slave to another King? This should not be. And why should it not? Is it the complexion of a man's skin that explains why he should be in slavery?

On this earth, surely there are many persons who are of many different complexions, different from yours, and they are not made to be slaves.

I implore you to open your hearts to what I am saying and not to renounce these pleas just because they come from a paltry slave who is to be tried for committing acts of insurrection and rebellion.

I know not whether I shall be given a chance to speak in my own defence but I do solemnly swear that it was no intention of mine to incite others to murder or to the use of force against any man, Black or White. I appealed to my fellow slaves, and will continue to do so if the occasion should ever present itself, to use their capacity of reason, to show our masters the injustice of forced labour by peaceably withdrawing our services. This force of non-resistance I still believe we should use to strike terror into the hearts of our oppressors, to compel them to understand the strength and power of free will.

I do not propose these measures because I belong to any political party or because I am a disciple of Thomas Spence whom you no doubt hold in scorn. I believe that we need, however, to bring our message to the planters, that freedom is a right that no one, not even God, can take from us.

Is he not a liar who saith that he loves God and hates his brother?

You have reaped the fruits of our labour, but no good will come of this reward. Jesus tells us in the Gospel According to Matthew:

> Even so every good tree bringeth forth good fruit;
> but a corrupt tree bringeth forth evil fruit.
> A good tree cannot bring forth evil fruit,
> neither can a corrupt tree bring forth good fruit.

We shall not despair because I know your hearts to be true. Where is the man who does not have the heart to rejoice to see our brothers freed? May the good Lord inspire within you the benevolence, the wisdom and the will to set us free.

Slavery is living in a hellhole. Hell is where there is no light, only darkness, no love, only hatred, no freedom, only bondage, a place where goodness is always out of our reach, never within our grasp. The more we try to have it, the further it slips away.

But we shall be free, free from this hell because 'God hath not appointed us to wrath, but to obtain salvation by our Lord Jesus Christ, Who died for us, that, whether we wake or sleep, we should live together with him.'

Just as Moses chose able men out of Israel, so too I believe God will choose us to rule over our own land and to control our own destiny.

I wish that I had the chance to address you personally but I know this is not possible. I do not pretend to be a man of letters who is trained in the ways of rhetoric but I write from the heart to make this plea to you to lift the yoke of slavery from around our necks. To hold another in chains is against the laws of God.

Our Lord is a God of forgiveness and redemption.

Signed this _____ day of April 1832
Samuel Sharpe
A West Indian Slave

ELEVEN

April 1832

I lose sense of time, the days and nights seeming all the same in here, long and dark. I need to try to keep track of them by marking my own calendar on the cell walls.

James tells me it is still the month of April.

My fellow inmates, Plato and Thorpe, were taken from the cell this morning. There was no telling whether they would go directly to the gallows or if they would appear before justices at the Slave Court. Plato did not go willingly. His eyes were fiery red and he wore a scowl on his face. James, and another guard whom I do not know, tried to shackle him but he refused to get up off the floor. He sat firmly on his hands and kicked the men when they came near. James fell backwards onto the cell floor when Plato tripped him.

'You stupid raas. You gwine pay for dat.' The other guard removed a baton which was strapped to his side.

Plato showed no fear. 'You black raas. Why you dress up in a de soldier uniform? You fava monkey.'

'Who you a call monkey?' He lifted his club and smashed Plato across the head.

They then dragged him from the cell. Thorpe followed, weak from fright.

I tried to find words to comfort him as he was removed from the cell. 'Tell them that you will depend on salvation from your Redeemer. Believe in the Lord Jesus, Thorpe, and you will not perish.'

He reached for my hand and his eyes welled with tears.

*I heard from one of the sentinels that both were executed
later that day in Charles Square. The rope which they used
to hang Plato proved to be too frail for his robust self, and
for some time, he hung from the gallows, a broken noose
about his neck. They hanged him a second time.*

Christmas 1820

December in Jamaica is a special time of year. The weather
is cool with the Christmas breeze blowing and the sweet-
smelling Jack-in-the-bush in full white bloom. It is the season
also for the alligator pear and the Christmas mango which
bear in plenty. It is the time when the buckra open their doors
wide for us slaves to come in to dance, sing, drink and be
merry. It is the time of year when the sweet rum flows freely
and the masters let us barbecue our own hogs. They give us
provisions of oil, mackerel and salt beef. They give us days off
work to wile the hours away, Christmas Day and Boxing Day.
All is merriment, all bout, street dances with John Canoe and
their drunken followers, and travelling troupes of players
performing shows of song and parody.

Many visitors passed through Miss Mary's lodging house
during the Christmastime of 1820. I enjoyed talking with the
gentlemen from Kingston, two Brown men, in particular, Mr
Watkis, a barrister from town, and his friend, Mr Lewin. They
were sympathetic towards our cause, maybe because they
themselves had been born into slavery and received
manumission from their masters. They also spoke
knowledgeably about what was happening in England at the
time. I learned about William Wilberforce and the abolitionist
movement, and about mulatto men like Robert Wedderburn,
who were fighting for the freedom of slaves. He was born in
Jamaica of a female slave and a White planter from the Parish
of Westmoreland and later became a freed man in England.

The gentlemen showed me a pamphlet by Mr Wedderburn entitled 'The Axe Laid to the Root or a Fatal Blow to Oppressors, Being an Address to the Planters and Negroes of the Island of Jamaica. (1817).' They had smuggled it in from England where it sold for sixpence per copy, but here in Jamaica it was considered seditious material. I first learned from his writings about a plan of slave resistance. His exact words were:

> My advice to you, to appoint a day wherein you will all pretend to sleep one hour beyond the appointed time of your rising to labour; let the appointed time be twelve months before it takes place; let it be talked of in your market place, and on the roads. The universality of your sleeping and nonresistance, will strike terror to your oppressors.*

Mr Wedderburn's political views first implanted in me the seed for my own struggle for organized rebellion.

The local newspapers also gave me information about what was happening in Jamaica. I remember reading at the time that the magistrates in Jamaica were demanding from the Governor a closer look at the items of public expenditure. Monies were being managed badly. At the end of 1820, I remember reading about the Governor, the Duke of Manchester, having an accident. While travelling Jamaican roads, he fell from his carriage and was trampled by his horses. His skull was smashed open, but with proper medical care, he survived. He rewarded his doctors with large sums of money.

Visitors came not only to talk politics but also to take part in the Christmas festivities. One of the favourites of these was the Sett girls. They were especially fine that Boxing Day of 1820. The White mistresses would help the slave girls by buying them jewellery and finery of all sorts, shoes, silks and hats. In each Sett, all the women dressed alike, with matching frocks, bodices, shoes and hats, some groups in red, others in blue. They began marching after breakfast, before the sun got really hot. They made their way through the streets, singing and dancing, starting from the top of Barnett Street, along the Strand and ending the parade in Charles Square. People of all kinds lined the streets to watch and join in the celebration.

Each Sett had a queen and a king. That Christmas, I noticed none other than Miss Nelly, dressed to kill as queen of the Blues, a band of about twenty Black females, grown women, young girls and pickaninnies. The Black women were always separate from the Brown. They never mixed, they were always in different Setts.

Miss Nelly proudly led her group of Blacks with a little girl walking behind her holding her train of white and blue. She wore a lavish dress cut low in the bodice with puffy sleeves and a frock that spread out wide, stiff and round. Her stockings were white and her pointed shoes were a bright blue which matched the colour of her silk dress. She wore huge pieces of jewellery, long earrings and gold bracelets, and a necklace with a large pendant looking like a donkey's eye. Feathers several feet in length stuck out of her hat, matching the rest of her attire, all blue and white. She was the queen, the 'Ma'am' of the Sett girls, the prettiest and most fashionable there was that day. She carried a cow-skin whip which she used with great pomp and authority, swishing it to make sure everyone kept in step.

Her king was dressed in full British admiral uniform with a white satin sash, huge cocked hat and magnificent sword. He wore tight-fitting white stockings, and a long blue coat with shiny brass buttons, left open to show off his frilly vest underneath. He was handsome with his hat upon his head, golden lapels and medals and pictures on his breast. His face looked familiar but I was not able to say who he was.

Master Henry used to tell me stories of the Battle of Trafalgar and the tragic fate of Admiral Nelson. The Sett King's dress reminded me of the descriptions of the Admiral's fancy uniform, which, it was told, was so decorative that he was spotted by the enemy and shot through the spine while commanding the British fleet against the French and Spanish. That was in the year 1805. He died minutes after his shipmates told him of Britannia's great victory.

The words *Long Live Britannia* decorated the banners carried by the Sett girls that day.

The Reds were not to be outdone by the Blues. They came dressed in elaborate regalia resembling the Redcoats, the militia which the government brought out when there was a threat of a slave uprising. They even carried the same long rifles with which the officers used to hunt us down. The ones the Setts carried, I am sure, were not loaded with ammunition.

The crowds grew bigger and more excited as the day went on. As evening approached, the freed men of the town copied the styles of their former masters by putting on lavish balls with an abundance of victuals and drinks for all. The ladies of the house opened their doors to their friends and slaves alike, who ate and drank and danced all night, eating and drinking, and having a very merry time.

Another attraction of the day was the John Canoe. Bands of men went from house to house calling out, 'John Canoe, John Canoe', entertaining each household by dancing and singing. If their audiences appreciated their performances, then the troupes would be lucky enough to earn some shillings.

My friend Gardner appeared as one of the John Canoes that night. He wore a white mask and a long wig of curly brown hair. He had a close-fitting bodice of red and white with thick brown gloves covering his big hands. He danced in a pair of pointed shoes, his doublet, striped in blue and white, tied about with a red satin sash. On his head was a board on which was pasted a model of a great house with feathered palm trees crowning the top.

I followed along with Gardner and his party. He was true to form that night, a bold and talented leader of his group. Each place we stopped, we were given rum and port to drink, received praise for our antics and were rewarded with British and Spanish coins of great value.

At the home of one gentleman, Mr John Manderson, we were invited to enter into the great hall. There he extended to us the warmest greetings. I discovered in later years that he was a leading merchant in Montego Bay and that he became a magistrate and member of the Assembly, one of the select brown-skin men who helped our cause for freedom.

Gardner was one of several John Canoes invited inside to perform for the guests. The party was a bustle of activity. To one side, little Black children hovered about, not dressed for the occasion but looking on in awe of the proceedings. Beside them were groups of fiddlers who provided the music for the evening. On an upper balcony, a crowd of revellers chatted and laughed out loud, loud enough for their voices to be heard above the din. A mix of Blacks and Whites were decked out in colourful costumes. On the main floor, male servants in the most formal attire were serving cake and port to the guests. In the middle of the floor, the host and hostess were dancing, each at the head of a set of dancers arranged in pairs. Very few of the dancers were Black people. I saw one couple, a Black man with a White woman — that I had never seen before. A few militiamen decorated the hall too, dressed in their Redcoat uniforms.

Eventually the host and hostess excused themselves from

the dance floor and began mingling with other guests. Our group caught Mr Manderson's attention.

'You have provided us with much gaiety this evening and I am proud to have you in my home.' He was handsome, with striking features, a round face, muscular jaw and robust body.

His words of kindness and hospitality took me by surprise. 'Thank you, Sir.' I answered for Gardner who was too drunk to talk coherently.

'Where do you young men reside?'

His question seemed genuine. 'I live here in the Bay, Sir. I am slave to the proprietress of a lodging house on the Strand. Miss Mary is the owner. Gardner here is my friend from Cooper's Hill.'

'Me belong to Greenwich Estate,' said Gardner.

I had not known this, and was surprised that he was even listening to the conversation.

'Hello, John.' Two gentlemen approached Mr Manderson in the most cordial fashion. They introduced themselves as Mr William Dyer, editor of the Falmouth newspaper, the *Cornwall Courier,* and Mr Samuel Vaughan, proprietor of Flamstead Estate in St James.

'What brings you gentlemen to the Bay?' Mr Manderson's attention was now turned away from us.

'Dem too f___in rude.' Our drunken John Canoe was not the most polite guest.

The gentlemen turned in astonishment, but then chose to ignore the situation, and resumed chatting.

I signalled to one of Gardner's friends to move him outside.

'You are from Flamstead, Sir. Are you the gentleman who is providing shelter for a Black Baptist preacher? The name escapes me.' Mr Dyer directed his question to Mr Vaughan.

'Moses Baker. Yes, he has brought many under the fear of

God. Many he has converted have left their wanton ways.'

'No doubt, Mr Vaughan, but surely you must have your challenges in trying to limit their religious practices.'

'They act well within the law, Sir. What brings you to St James on such a lovely Boxing Day evening?' Mr Vaughan seemed to want to change the topic of conversation.

Mr Dyer did not answer his question but continued instead on the same subject. 'My knowledge of these matters tells me that, in order to practise, missionaries need to apply for a licence from the magistrate who then decides whether their credentials qualify them as ordained ministers. If I am not mistaken, I believe this man's churches in Kingston were shut down.'

Mr Manderson interjected, 'I understand, William, that some planters have been granted permission to be the patrons of these Black preachers. Enough of this, gentlemen. Let us enjoy the levity of the evening. What does bring you here tonight, William? Not that you would not always be welcome as my guest.'

'As a journalist, John, as a newspaper man, I am always curious about social events in the Bay.' He chuckled as if this was somehow humorous.

I was disappointed that I did not have the opportunity to talk more with Mr Manderson. He acted sympathetic towards us slaves and curious about our condition. This was unusual. No one of Mr Manderson's social status had ever shown so much interest in me.

Later in the evening, the music stopped and the guests assembled to one side of the main floor to sit on the benches and chairs set out for them. Mr Manderson had invited to the party a troupe of actors to perform scenes from Shakespeare's plays. The cast grouped themselves opposite to the guests on the dance floor area. They consisted totally of Black boys, dressed fantastically to present themselves as kings and warriors.

One of the young actors opened the night's performance:

'This play is about the history of England. Buckra people like this play because it tell the story of how War of the Roses finally came to an end after many years of fighting. From then on, a line of kings started in the House of Tudor, to which our present King belong, King George IV, Sovereign of the United Kingdom of Great Britain and Ireland and Jamaica and so forth and so forth.

'It is the story of King Richard III. He was a wicked man, uglier than sin. He had a big hunchback and he love to play with the devil:

> *Now is the winter of our discontent*
> *Made glorious summer by this sun of York;*
> *And all the clouds that lour'd upon our house*
> *In the deep bosom on the ocean buried.*
>
> *And therefore, since I cannot prove a lover,*
> *To entertain these fair well-spoken days,*
> *I am determined to prove a villain,*
> *and hate the idle pleasures of these days.* *

Everybody clapped at how well the boy recited the lines.

'Richard was a murderer. He murder his brother, his wife and his brother's sons. In the part which you are about to see, he is haunted by the duppies of those him kill. He face his enemy, Richmond, on the battlefield. Two great generals dem meet pon Bosworth field.'

Much commotion and fighting followed as actors entered with cardboard horses and long metal swords.

King Richard: A horse! a horse! my kingdom for
a horse!

Cate (his servant): Withdraw, my lord; I'll help you to
a horse.

King Richard: Slave! I have set my life upon a cast,
And I will stand the hazard of the
die.

The audience gave a loud round of applause.

Richmond entered, and he and King Richard engaged in a prolonged duel. The King killed Richmond in the fight.

King Richard: God and your arms be prais'd,
victorious friends: Their day is ours,
the bloody Richmond is dead.

Cate: Courageous King, well hast thou
acquit thee.

King Richard: Let them not live to taste this land's
increase,
That would with treason wound
this fair land's peace!
Now evil wounds are stopp'd, peace
lives again: That she may long live
here, God say amen!*

The End

No one clapped, not a puss said a word. There was total silence. Then, one young man stood up out of the crowd and yelled, 'Bravo, Bravo,' and clapped really loud. Then gradually others joined in, laughing nervously.

The slaves had changed the ending, turning it all around by rewarding the evil King with victory. In his play, Shakespeare shows how the evil King Richard is slain in battle by the good

Richmond, who is then crowned the new King of England. The message the slaves wanted to give the audience was immediately clear: badness lived on in the House of Tudor, in the line of the kings of England. How could one praise Britannia when so many of its subjects are slaves to His Majesty?

The party broke up soon after that.

After leaving Mr Manderson's house, I found Gardner slumped down on the street, his mask and wig removed and trampled in the dirt. I propped him up by holding him under his arms. He could not stand straight on his own. He was black-up fi true, his breath stinking of rum.

'Sam, my friend, you ever did hear of de song, my friend?' His speech was slurred.

'Which song, my friend?'

'De one where de jackass tief me gal from me.'

'No, Gardner, sing it fi me.'

Gardner bellowed out the verses to his song as we wandered through the streets of the Bay:

> *Jackass with the long tail,*
> *Bag of cocoa coming down!*
> *Jackass with the long tail,*
> *Bag of cocoa coming down.*
> *Him worry me, him teasie me,*
> *Him make me dandy leave me!*
> *Jackass with the long tail,*
> *Bag of cocoa coming down.**

That night we drank even more of the coarse white rum we call john-crow batty. We met up with Dove and looked for entertainment in the Bay until sun-break. The rest I cannot tell here.

TWELVE

March 15th, 1832

My Dear Sam:

I have received into my hands from Mr Bleby your letter dated yesterday, March 14th. I write this hastily as I have made arrangements to set sail tomorrow for America from the port of Montego Bay. Even though I have been set free by the Chief Justice, my person is in grave danger from those gentlemen who, having no regard for the law, still wish to lynch me. Besides my personal safety and that of Mrs Burchell, I have concern also for the public good of my faithful and for the just treatment of my brethren, Messrs Knibb and Gardner. For these reasons, I have taken the advice of friends to depart from the island.

Upon receiving your letter written from the Montego Bay gaol, it occurred to me that you must have been one of the prisoners for whom I was praying whilst I myself was confined within the same prison. A separate room to the common gaol was offered to us by the kindness of the gaoler. Through the grating of my window, I recognized some of the prisoners to be members of our church but I was not aware that you were among them. Unfortunately, due to the position of my room, I was not able to converse with them even though I was anxious to hear of their tribulations. I have heard that, for no other reason than that they professed to be Baptists, some were severely flogged and sent ignominiously to the workhouse.

These are troubled times indeed, Sam. Mrs Burchell and I are attempting to recover from the barbaric treatment we

149

received from the magistrates and militia. Madness has consumed the hearts of these individuals who want nothing but bloody revenge for me and other missionaries whom they hold responsible for the rebellion. I fear that I have not always been courageous in the face of all this danger. I have needed to place more faith in the Lord and to understand more why we have been subjected to such hardships.

The Custos exercised authority under martial law to apprehend me and confine me to prison. When I first arrived on the Garland Grove in the early part of January, Captain Pengelley was immediately surprised by the boarding of officials who arrested me and transported me to another vessel, a man-of-war of the British navy; this scarcely gave me any chance to say words of farewell to Mrs Burchell or to pack my personal belongings. I was confined to a cabin, no larger than a gaol cell, for eleven days. I was permitted to go on deck twice only during this time, and on these occasions, was heavily guarded by two militia men with rifles which they were ready to use at any moment should I make an effort to escape. Whither they thought I would go, I have no idea. Nevertheless, the authorities saw it fit that I should be so heavily guarded.

I had no knowledge of why they had imprisoned me or why they were treating me with disdain. Such an insult to my person I had never before experienced. When I asked for an explanation, the guards told me martial law was the rule of the land and orders had been given for my apprehension.

I requested an interview with my wife whom they had detained on board the Garland Grove. With much reluctance, they afforded me this meeting but insisted that a sentinel be present to supervise us during our discourse. I pleaded with them that this was preposterous, and they kindly granted my request to be alone with my wife. I was fearful for Mrs

Burchell's health as she was disconsolate and weak, not understanding why we should be subjected to such harsh and cruel treatment. Before she departed, we both prayed and recited Psalm 91. I had not even been given the privilege of retaining my Bible, which they had confiscated along with my other papers and possessions.

Except for this one visit, I remained for the eleven days on board the Blanche in total isolation from all human contact. My only recourse was prayer, which gave me some consolation during this dark period.

Custos Richard Barrett instructed that all my papers be handed over to the authorities for examination. They seized both my personal letters and those papers belonging to the Mission. Having found no evidence of my complicity with inciting rebellion, they released me to reunite with my family on board the Garland Grove, but they still held me under arrest. The Governor, as you may know, arrived in Montego Bay on February 1st, and shortly thereafter proclaimed an end to martial law. I then demanded my immediate release, as I explained that they no longer had any authority to hold me prisoner. A few days later, the head constable, Mr Lewin, along with a few of his subordinates, boarded Mr Pengelley's ship with an official warrant for my arrest with instructions that I must report before the magistrates in the Montego Bay courthouse. They had an affidavit from a Coloured man, Mr Stennett, claiming "That Mr Burchell had said to him [Stennett] and other leaders of the Baptist society, to go among the Negroes and tell them that freedom was theirs; and that they, the Negroes, must fight and pray for it, and they will get it." I became even more bewildered by this news as I had no knowledge of Mr Stennett or of any reason why he would utter these falsehoods.*

By this time, Mrs Burchell was suffering from extreme mental anguish. It debilitated both her body and spirit. We knelt and prayed the whole night, reciting psalms, asking the Lord to deliver us from all evil and harm. We gained strength from Psalm 46:

> *God is our refuge and strength,*
> *a very present help in trouble.*
> *Therefore will not we fear,*
> *though the earth be removed,*
> *and though the mountains be carried*
> *into the midst of the sea.*

The good Lord, I believe, heard our prayers, for the next morning, even though we had not slept the whole night, we felt stronger in spirit and more confident that we would come to no harm.

Arriving on shore, we met with an angry throng that was awaiting us. The militia could scarcely protect us from the pushing and jarring. One gentleman burst through the crowd and thrust his dagger at my breast. Fortunately, it did not pierce me for I had moved quickly to avert it. Such danger to my person and to my family I would never have imagined possible. The crowd was jeering, 'Have his blood!' 'Shoot him!' 'Hang him.' Some coloured gentlemen intervened on our behalf, protected us from the crowd and hurried us to safe shelter.

Sam, I do not know how hearts can be so hardened or the passions of hatred so aroused as to make men insane. They blame me for inciting you and others to rebellion. How do they think I may have done this when I was in another place thousands of miles across the ocean? 'I can and do most solemnly assure you, that I am as innocent of any connection *with, or any knowledge of, this unhappy insurrection, as an infant child.'* There is no doubt that I abhor all the vestiges of slavery, and you know how strong these sentiments of mine are. I also believe that you and I and all men are equal before God and I admit that I was not shy to preach these truths which the Bible tells us. This message frightened them, and I have become a martyr for the profession of God's truths.*

You find yourself in a similar condition. Unhappily, you are not yet free from danger as I am now but you must trust in God as I have done. Do not stop for one moment to offer prayers for your salvation and for that of your brothers. The authorities may harm our mortal bodies but they will never be able to punish our souls, which, if we remain faithful to Christ, will live for all eternity, praising God and His heavenly host of angels.

Mr Joseph Bowen signed the warrant for my arrest and I was committed, along with Reverend Gardner to the common gaol to await trial by the magistrates of the town. Mr Bowen was the gentleman who had said to Mr Manderson the day the chapel was demolished that 'the house of any person should come down that protected the missionaries.'* The demolition of the houses of God can only be the work of the devil. Almost all the missions we built at Salter's Hill, Falmouth, Montego Bay and Lucea were destroyed and fired upon by the militia. The furniture and contents of the buildings were used for bonfires. They have gone mad, Sam, driven by a frenzied desire to consume all that is sacred. My personal belongings from my retreat house, Hillington, in Hanover and the small chapel we built at Gurney's Mount suffered the same fate.

When they bring you to trial, Sam, you must be strong and steadfast in your faith.

I heard a story of a magistrate from Lucea who took a Negro man to trial and interrogated him thus:

Did not Mr Burchell tell you to rebel?
No, Sir.
Tell me the truth; confess that he told you so, or I'll
blow your brains out.

While uttering these words, the interrogator pressed a pistol to the man's head. The poor slave, fearful for his life, was compelled to say what the magistrate wished to hear. He exclaimed that I had preached words of sedition to that effect the night before I departed for England. The slave was never brought forward as evidence in my trial and I can only imagine what a dreadful end he suffered.

My trial came to naught. The coloured man, Mr Stennett, who had signed an affidavit against me, volunteered information to one of the magistrates that he had indeed lied and that he had been bribed to tell his falsehood. He testified that three gentlemen, Mr Delisser, Mr Morris and Mr Bowen, had offered him money to make the accusations against me. The Attorney General could not proceed with the trial with the knowledge that the only witness for the prosecution had perjured. God works in mysterious ways, Sam. He has answered my prayers.

I have received a recommendation from the Chief Justice and the Attorney General to leave the island, not only for my own well-being but for the sake of my brother ministers and for the restoration of the mission. After I sought refuge with Mrs Burchell in the home of Mr Brown, it was not long before a large crowd of White gentlemen congregated outside, shouting threats on my life and demanding that I exit from the house. The Chief Justice, Mr Tuckett, and a large group of coloured militia came to my rescue and conducted me to safety on board ship.

The Lord has spared my life, Sam, and I pray that he will do the same for you. You have fought valiantly for His sake, and have been a good Christian and loyal member of the Church. I was always able to depend upon your judgement when you presented cases to me of inquirers who wished to be converted to our faith. You led your own people as a class leader and Daddy with more Christian zeal than I have seen in anyone. You spoke brilliantly on matters of the faith and were always orthodox in your views. For all of this, the Lord will reward you, here and in eternal life. He is our only salvation and in Him we must always put our trust.

I came to Jamaica as a very young man, educated in the ways of the Christian ministry, and have laboured for my flock here, perhaps too zealously, at the price of my health and the welfare of those whom I tried so earnestly to convert. Our mission, as you know, grew a thousandfold, from a handful of worshippers at Crooked Spring, to thousands, across several parishes, from one mission chapel to fourteen, spreading a distance of many miles across this fair island.

I will miss this place deeply. I loved my people more than myself. I do believe it is God's will, though, that I depart to spread His word in a new land. I know that the seeds I have sown here in His name will continue to grow. If it is God's plan, I will return one day to finish my work.

My heart is with you, my brother. I know the suffering that you must be undergoing at the hands of those who are blind with rage and unforgiving in their actions of revenge. I pray for your soul, and you will forever be in my thoughts, my brother in Christ.

I hope that you do not consider me a traitor for leaving the mission. The Chief Justice told me that people perceive that I am the cause, albeit the innocent cause, of many of the events that transpired and that the best way to clear myself of this reputation is to depart from the island. I did nothing, as you know, to incite rebellion. I go of my own free will, and having pondered much the situation in which I have put my wife and child, I think it best that I take the advice of the Chief Justice.

I leave you with the words of Jesus from the Sermon on the Mount:

> Blessed are ye, when men shall revile you, and persecute you, and shall say all manner of evil against you falsely, for my sake.
> Rejoice, and be exceedingly glad: for great is your reward in heaven: for so persecuted they the prophets which were before you.

Yours very truly in Christ,
Thomas Burchell

THIRTEEN

1822

J amaica suffered a terrible drought. The land became scorched once again and my soul felt that it needed nourishment. I had been spending too much time carousing with Gardner and had no one to speak with about matters of the spirit. I missed Mama and wanted to arrange to meet with her. I did not know where she was residing as I had heard she was now a runaway.

I spent what free time I could find reading the Holy Book. Miss Mary had several copies in her lodging house. I consumed every part of the scriptures, the Books starting with Genesis and the stories of Abraham, Isaac, Jacob and Joseph, the Books of Moses who led his people out of Egypt, the adventures of the Kings of Israel, Saul, David and Solomon, the sayings of the great prophets, Isaiah, Jeremiah, Daniel and Ezekiel. I read the psalms of David and the story of Christ in the gospels. I studied sections over and over again until they stuck in my mind. After that, I was able to recite verses, psalms, and whole sections of chapters.

My mind became so preoccupied with reading and learning the scriptures that I was scarcely able to think of anything else but God's covenant with His people and His wrath for those who did evil. These thoughts possessed my mind and my sleep was full of fits. I became disconsolate, moods of darkness taking over my spirit. Miss Mary scolded me every day for not attending properly to my chores. When I was younger, slaves at Cooper's Hill warned me that something would go wrong with my brain if I read too much. Maybe they were right.

Wild thoughts came into my head. I had dreams which frightened me. The sun no longer shone in the heavens and everywhere was covered with a dark cloud. Huge battles were being fought, with men and women taking up arms and the rivers turning to blood. On the earth and on the seas, in all the countries, everyone wore a shield and carried a sword. The fighting was fierce. There seemed to be no end nor victory.

I was losing myself. Evil spirits spoke in my head, drawing me down to the edge of a huge pit. There below I heard men, women and children screeching and crying for help. I wanted to rescue them but I could not. My soul was being pulled and I feared that I might fall, that I might join all those who lost favour with God. I smelled the burning of flesh and felt the scorching fires of hell.

The words of Zophar to Job came to me in a dream:

> Knowest thou not this of old, since man was placed
> upon earth,
> That the triumphing of the wicked is short,
> and the joy of the hypocrite but for a moment?
> He shall suck the poison of asps:
> the viper's tongue shall slay him.
> He shall not see the rivers, the floods,
> the brooks of honey and butter.

I lay in bed, night after night, the cold sweat drenching my body.

The old man at Flamstead will help me. I remembered Moses Baker's sermon at the chapel. I remembered his stern voice telling me that the unrighteous shall not inherit the kingdom of God.

~

Moses lived alone in his own house and yard on Flamstead Estate. Four poles stuck out of the ground in front of his dwelling, a bright red flag tied to each stick. One of the rooms of his house was a kitchen where he prepared medicines and oils, and in another was a bath which he used for healing waters. The estate owner, Mr Finn, was very kind to him. He had brought him from Kingston to preach to the Negroes and had even bought slaves from Mr George Lisle, who, like Mr Baker, was an American preacher who had set up the Windward Road Chapel in Kingston. Mr Baker was sad these times because he had to hold service in secret. The magistrates would not approve a licence for him to preach. So, he invited Baptist ministers from England to come to help him out. The most recent arrival was Minister Tripp who preached at Crooked Spring.

This did not stop Moses Baker, though, from having his own prayer meetings. He would hold service most often in a class house in the Negro village. He appointed sect leaders who came from all over St James and neighbouring parishes. They learned about the Good News from their teacher and eventually began to hold their own prayer meetings, reporting back from time to time to Parson Baker about the state of his flock. Many of these leaders were drivers who were given great privileges and authority by their masters. So it was not too difficult for them to arrange for meetings at night-time when all else was quiet on the estates.

This time when I met Mr Baker up close, I noticed ugly scars around his eyes. His hair, and there was lots of it, was white like the wool of a sheep. He spoke with vitality, but I detected a drawl in his speech, and he pronounced words with a twang. Now and again, he would use different words like *whooping* instead of whipping, *Missus* instead of Mistress,

Marse instead of Master, *chillun* instead of children, and so on.

'You must see it as a sign from the Almighty.' He leaned over to me as if he was telling me a secret.

'The dreams are not good dreams, Parson.'

'They good dreams, boy, if you only listen, listen to what the Spirit is telling you.'

I tried to make light of what he was saying. 'I so frightened, Minister, I can't hear nothing.'

'This no joking matter, Sam. The angels will come visit you, but they must find you in the light. If they find you in the darkness, they will leave you. You understand what I mean?' When he stared at me, his eyes bulged out of his head.

'I don't see no angels, Parson.'

'An angel will appear to you when you ready. He will tell you to go spread the Word of God to all His people. Then once you start to preach, there's no stopping you. You will go to the ends of the earth to praise His holy name.' When he said these words, he raised his head and stared at the heavens.

'Then how will this angel come to me, Parson?'

'He will come in a dream, but you must prepare yourself. You need to be ready to receive the Spirit into your heart. You must go into the wilderness, you must fast yourself for many days and nights, and then, only then, will the Angel of the Lord come to you.' There was conviction in his voice.

'How I know I supposed to do this?'

'I know you supposed to, you listen to me. I am telling you that you are chosen and your chillun will be blessed too. You listen to old man Moses.'

'Yuh words comfort me, Parson.'

'After the Spirit possess you, you must make yourself holy. Then you will come to me one day and say, "Marse Baker, Praise the Lord, I have seen His light, I am ready to receive the holy oils of baptism." And we will go down to the river, and there you will be cleansed in the waters.'

'Then I be a Christian?' I thought I should soon leave, as his voice was beginning to tire, his words to slur.

'Yes, Sam, but you don't listen to me. You will be more than that, you will be a preacher.'

'I not ready for that, Parson.'

'I believe you are hard-headed, Sam. I'm in the right mind to give you a good whooping, boy. Listen to me, you will be ready when the Lord wishes you to be. And once you are chosen, you need then to make yourself pure. You will not fornicate or keep anyone except that you be married to her. We put away from us anyone who is a fornicator, an adulterer, an idolater, a drunkard or whore monger.'

He rose from his stool. 'Before you go, I want you to wash in the herbal bath. One of the healers will attend to you. It will be a balm to your body and soul.'

'You have been very kind to me, Minister, and you have lightened my grief.'

'I am old now, Sam, and maybe I will not be here much longer. Mr Winn and the Missus, they be kind to me and all. It's the other folk, they won't let me preach no more. But you will continue the Lord's work, you will learn how to walk on fire, to send curses to your enemies, and defend yourself against all harm. All this you will receive through the Spirit, Sam. Go now in peace.'

And so it was that I received Moses Baker's blessing.

~

After that encounter, I took every opportunity to attend service at Flamstead and there it was that I met Mama one Sabbath. I had sent word with someone who knew where she was residing that I should like to meet with her after service at the Crooked Spring Chapel.

'Dem send word sey you did waan fi see me.' She still looked strong, but more tired than I had ever seen her.

'It's good to see you, Mama. I been thinking of you plenty. Where you staying now?'

'Me live up in a place dem call Accompong, some good way up de road from here.'

'Dat far enough from here, Mama. How you did manage to go up there?'

'Massa get vex wid me all de while and him call me all kind of bad name. Me did know from de first, de first time me did set me yeye pon him, dat him was gwine miserable. Me nebba did much work fi him, so him start fi flog me like me is some pickaninny. "You are some useless nigger,"' she said, trying to imitate his angry, high-pitched voice.

'So he get rid of you just like that?' It pained me to hear her story.

'Not as easy as dat. Him decide fi hire me out, rent me out to a big chief in Accompong. Him tell de chief sey me is a great worker and dat is why me fetch such a good price. If me should give him any trouble, de chief should just use de cart whip pon me and then him will get me fi work.' She spoke in a very matter-of-fact way, without emotion.

'Yuh massa treat you bad fi true, Mama.'

'Him is a facety raas.' There was hatred in her eyes and anger in her voice.

'But, Mama, being a slave to the Maroons is not good either.'

'Dem treat me better than where me was, Sam. Dem train me fi fight like a warrior, to hide in de bush and surprise de enemy. And dem let me join in wid dem singing and dancing.' Her eyes were now smiling.

'What kind of work they make you do, Mama?'

'Me help round de village and me a wuk pon one road dem cutting through de bush.'

'That is hard labour, Mama.'

'You know a strong and can handle de work. De Chief nice to me, not like Massa.'

'The Maroons, they can be bad to us, Mama. Some of dem friends with the militia.'

'How much time a tell you, Sam, you must keep yuh mouth shut bout things you don't know. You chat things you not supposed to.' She raised her voice at me, squinting her eyes and giving me that scornful look I knew all too well. 'I do what I must do and you look after yuh own business.'

I changed the subject because she was not going to listen to me about the Maroons. 'I need to tell you about someone I met. I run errands in the market for Miss Mary, my new owner, and every week I do business with the same higgler woman. She is a lovely lady, Mama. You would never guess who she is.'

'Who you a talk bout, Sam?'

'You would never believe it, Mama.'

'What you trying fi tell me, Sam?'

'I trying to tell you, Mama, that I came to know your sister, Miss Nelly.'

'What you saying to me?'

'She was asking bout you and her pickaninny who she never see all these years.'

'What Nelly doing selling in de market? You sure is she?'

'Sure thing, Mama.'

'I don't think she ask fi me, though.' She sounded indignant.

'She ask for you, Mama. She ask for you all the while.'

'Miss Nelly and me used fi fuss all de while. She like man

too much and she get herself in a whole heap of trouble. She mussi have bout twenty pickney from de buckra man dem.'

'She change now, Mama. She is a respectable higgler woman and she done with all that other business.'

'You tell her fi me, Sam, when you see her next, dat her sister is strong still, dat me know sey we is both blood and have de same spirit, de same faada and de same mada.' She looked me straight in the eyes.

'I will tell her that, Mama. Do you ever think about Tacky, Mama?'

'Don't worry bout Tacky, him spirit travel long time now to de land of de elders.' Both of us remained silent a few moments. She had that faraway look on her face. 'Dat raas man Crawford, is him mek Tacky get ol' and sick before him time. People dem sey Missa Crawford still de bout, sey him join de militia.'

'Is better we don't talk about Mr Crawford, Mama.'

'Is plenty o ting you don't understand, Sam.'

I did not want to continue speaking to her about Mr Crawford. It was bringing back too many gloomy thoughts. 'Tacky never told us the end of the 'Nancy story, Mama.' I wondered whether she knew it.

'He used to tell us all kind of stories from Africa.'

'The one when Bro Tiger make believe that he is dead and he tell his wife to shout it out to the whole village so that 'Nancy can hear.'

'You remember good, Sam.'

'I always did want to know what happened between 'Nancy and Brother Tiger.'

'I can't tell it good like Tacky.'

'Well, just tell me like you know it.'

'Well, me don't think Bro Tiger could fool 'Nancy dat easy.

'Nancy didn't believe him was dead cause Bro Tiger was so strong and powerful. Bro Tiger could nebba just lie dung and dead like dat.

'Anancy hear all de commotion, and you know how 'Nancy like fas in people business anyway, so 'Nancy find himself in Bro Tiger yard and him start fi gwaan bad. In de loudest voice him could a muster, him start fi ask all de people whether dem ever hear bout Bro Tiger and him sickness.

'"Me nebba hear a ting, 'Nancy."

'Bro Dog don't hear nutten, Monkey don't hear nutten, Puss don't hear nutten, Jackass not a ting, not even Patu, and you know how Patu see and hear everyting dat a go on.

''Nancy ask everybody whether Bro Tiger even call out to de Lord before him dead. Everybody sey, "No, Bro 'Nancy, not even one word come out of him mouth."

'Then, Bro 'Nancy shout out as loud as him can so everybody can hear. Him talk in him most cunning way. "Well, me nebba see s'madi not even call out to him Lawd before him dead. No good man would a ever do dat."

'And then all of a sudden, everybody hear a big hollering coming out of Bro Tiger house. Bro Tiger feel shame dat everybody think him bad, sey him don't sey him prayers before him dead.

'Then everbody realize wah a gwaan. Oh my God, Bro Tiger try fi fool Bro 'Nancy, but Bro 'Nancy more trickify than him. What a shame come dung pon Bro Tiger. Then everybody leave Bro Tiger de so. Not a soul talk to him, not even him wife.

'Then Bro 'Nancy leave de yard feeling happy dat everybody tink him smarter than Bro Tiger.

'And dat is the story of 'Nancy and Bro Tiger.'

'So, Brother Tiger can be tricked after all. I never knew you could tell those stories so good, Mama.'

'Dem go way back, Sam. 'Nancy is de spider-god of the Ashanti.' She sounded proud when she said that. 'We have a whole heap of lesson fi learn from 'Nancy.'

'Yes, it look that way, Mama.'

'Mek sure, Sam, mek sure Bro Tiger don't trick you in dis life.'

'I wish I knew more.'

'You will do jus fine, Sam. You will do great things in dis ya life.'

'I don't know what.'

'When de time is right, it will come to you. You still have de lion me give you?'

'I guard it with my life.'

'Then, you must be patient and you will attract good things to you.' She got up from the tree stump. 'Me must reach back before dark. De ticket no good after sundown.'

'I will try to get word to you again.'

'Don't het up yourself so much, Sam. You look after what you haffi do and don't bother bout me.'

'Mama, tell me something.'

'Wah you waan fi know?'

'You ever have any other pickaninny beside me?'

'How much time me must tell you not fi ask so much question.' She didn't seem as angry this time.

I waited for her to calm herself.

'Me have one boy pickaninny when me did come from Africa.'

'Where is he now?'

'How a mus know, Sam? Dem tek him from me when we fus come off de boat.'

'What was his name?'

'Maybe jus like you find Miss Nelly, you may lucky fi find him one day. De name don't matter, Sam, for dem would a change it long time. De boy name was Cuffie cause him was born on a Friday.' She turned to go. 'You get me all bothered, Sam, talking bout dem ting deh.'

'They are good things to know, Mama.'

'De chief gwine lick me dung if me don't reach back soon.'

'You take care, Mama, and I'll send word when I can.'

'You must make me proud, you hear?' She looked into my eyes, and then disappeared up the rocky hillside paths which took her miles back into the interior to Accompong.

I felt an emptiness which I did not know how to fill. I wondered whether I would ever see her again. We made no plans for that. Plans are stupid to make when you are a slave. They make no sense because other people control your future.

I felt comforted to know that she was strong of spirit. I hoped that if she became a warrior, she would fight for us, not against us.

FOURTEEN

I did as Parson Baker suggested and fasted for three days and three nights. I left Miss Mary's lodging house, knowing that after my sojourn into the bush, I would be punished and, more than likely, sold off to a new owner.

At all times, I carried with me a ticket from Miss Mary so that if I ever got apprehended by the authorities, I could try to convince them that I had permission to be away from my owner's place of residence.

I set out one evening and chose to follow the banks of the Slippery River rather than any of the more travelled roads. I had no special destination in mind but wanted to go far enough into the interior that I would not be easily discovered. I must have walked about four hours before I turned off from the river to climb farther up into the bush along a rivulet close to Hampden Estate. The ground was rugged and the underwood too thick for most people to venture there. Only wild hogs made runs through the thicket.

I cotched myself near to the riverbank up against the trunk of a few bamboo trees which creaked and moaned with the coming of the land breeze. I remember Bigga telling me that the whoopingbwai lived in the bamboo, the duppy of the slave driver cracking his whip in the wind. *'If you get too close, he will tek you up and grab you and lick you wid him whip. You musn't go near those trees when dem meking de crackin noise.'* As I sat beneath the branches, the long stalks rubbed against one another making the lashing noises of the cart whip, the branches bending down low so they touched the other side of the river. It was deep with dark pools of water close to where I was, but up farther into the bush it was shallower, running quickly over the stones. All the sounds of the night came into my head, the crackling noise of the crickets, the mating calls of the lizards, the croaking of the frogs, the swishing of the bats, the scurrying of the rats and the occasional hooting of the patu. For most of the night, I remained alert, unable to sleep and feeling unwelcome in this place.

As morning broke, I removed myself from the bamboos and travelled up the river a bit to cross where it was shallow. A tall cotton tree gripped the bank, with big open roots twisting and knotting themselves high up out of the water. The massive roots formed a deep, dark cave. I crawled inside to lay my head down but soon sensed duppies swarming around me. Mama used to tell me about how spirits of the ancestors lived inside the silk cotton tree.

A great depression of spirits overcame me. I felt gloomy as I had before, but this time more fearful, my body weak and cold, shivering from the early morning dew. My thoughts were confused, so mixed up that I lost a sense of where I was. I felt that my spirit was going to travel to another place, dark and foul. My body was going to be dead and my soul was going to cry out for mercy so that I would not be damned to hell.

My God and Saviour, help me, this poor and hated Samuel. I am worthless before You, the Almighty who gives breath and life to all things. Save me from the pit of hell, do not let my spirit leave me, my body to rot. Do not forsake me. I will be Your servant to do Your will and to be at Your command. Save me from the bad spirit who calls to me so that he may push me down into his darkness beneath the earth. Show me Your light and send Your angels to surround me. Do not let me perish. I will praise Your name for always.

No matter what I said in prayer, I could not ward off the hosts of devils circling my head. They said bad words to my brain, calling me down into the wretched pit to be lost forever in the darkness. I sweated cold all through my body, which then became numb and senseless. For what seemed to be a long time, I lay lifeless like a piece of rock with no movement, no feeling. The spirit in me could not move any part of my body, not talk any thoughts, not hear any sounds of the forest or of the river. All was quiet.

Two nights passed with neither food nor sleep. The bats swarmed through the hollows of the tree and the insects tortured me by night. At last I began to feel the stirrings of a spirit within me and the desire to go farther up the river. I managed to loosen my limbs, to feel sensation enough to raise myself onto all fours, crawling like an animal into the bush to follow the crooked path of the river. The ground was high at this point and I could look far down the mountainside where the water coiled its way over the rocks, round and round through the bush.

By the third evening, I felt totally exhausted and fell off as if into a dream. My body began to burn all over, around my neck and belly, right down to my feet. I removed my shirt for the heat was so great. And then I saw bright lights shining in my mind's eye.

I felt the presence of good spirits speaking in my mind. I saw, as did John in Revelations, seven golden candlesticks, and in the middle of these, a man clothed in a long white garment down to the foot. His eyes were like flames of fire and his feet like fine brass and his voice the sound of many waters.

I managed to raise myself up to a kneeling position. A power came up inside of me. I felt the blood flow in my veins. I felt the skin tighten on my muscles all over my body.

I heard then in my head the words of Jesus as He spoke them to John, 'Fear not; I am the first and the last: I am He that liveth and was dead.'

I feared it was the devil who was tricking me with his words. Then I wondered if duppies were getting me. I started to tremble again from fright and wanted to run from my place by the river, but I could not move. My feet were fixed to the ground.

Mercy on me. Help me to find the faith to understand this madness.

More voices came into my head:

> You must know, Samuel, that you will become a faithful servant. He has chosen you to do good work for Him. God has loved you more than any human can love you because His love is eternal.

I did not know who was speaking to me, or where the voices were coming from, but I started to speak back, to say my thoughts out loud, so loud I could hear them echo back to me.

'So tell me. Who am I to do the work of the Lord? I am no master. I am a mere slave. You spirits must be fooling with my head.'

I heard again voices of many spirits and saw in my mind's eye a throne that was set in the heavens, and all about the throne were the beasts of the earth and the elders of time, and they all knelt down and praised God.

> And every creature which is in heaven, and on the earth, and under the earth, and such as are in the sea and all that are in them, heard I saying, blessings and honour and glory and power unto him that sitteth upon the throne.

My spirit became calm and my body warmer. It felt good, like the time Mama hugged me close when I was a pickaninny. My heart opened up with a love I wanted to share, to tell Nyame, Mama, Gardner, Dove, Miss Mary, Maas Sam, everybody I knew, that the Lord is good, that He liveth in our heart, that He cometh to save us wretched people.

And the words of Christ came unto me as they did to John:

> Fear none of these things which thou shalt suffer: behold, the devil shall cast some of you into prison, that ye may be tried; and ye shall have tribulation ten days: be thou faithful unto death, and I will give thee a crown of life.

I knew the voices were of the Good Spirits, because I felt no fear again. My soul was lifted and the burden of sin removed from me.

The Lord was in my heart. The words of Revelations kept coming into my brain 'To him that overcometh will I grant to sit with me in my throne, even as I also overcame, and am set down with my Father in his throne.'

I raised myself up, strength returning to every part of my body. The tears welled up in me and I dropped back down on my knees, bowing my head to the ground. I wept silently, wept heavy, joyful tears. I wanted to offer my body and soul to God, for Him to bless me, to protect me from all evil and to grant me the faith to tell others the good news of salvation.

The river water was cold, smooth and clear as glass. I dropped down into a small pool, bending low so that my whole body became wet. It was as soothing as a healing bath.

Words of blessing and offering floated up into my head:

> Soul of Christ, sanctify me
> Body of Christ, save me

Blood of Christ, inebriate me
Water from the side of Christ, wash me
Passion of Christ, strengthen me.

I prayed in my heart for Him to look after me as a mother would her own child. And He came to dwell in my soul. He removed from me temptations and distractions so that I might be quiet enough to listen to what He had to say.

He told me that if I had faith, and did not doubt, that someday I would be able to move mountains and cast them into the sea.

I saw myself in my mind's eye as a grain of sand on the beach, as a drop of salt water in the big ocean, as a speck in the vast creation of the skies, the sun, the moon and stars. I was so small and He was so great, I so wicked and He so pure, and I so weak and He so mighty. I was to dash away my pride so that I might praise His greatness forever.

My tongue was loosed and I sang praises to His holy name. I saw a great light and heard the words of the covenant which God spoke to Moses:

> I am the God of thy father, the God of Abraham, the God of Isaac, and the God of Jacob.
> I have surely seen the affliction of my people which are in Egypt, and have heard their cry by reason of their taskmasters; for I know their sorrows.
> And I am come down to deliver them out of the land of the Egyptians, and to bring them up out of that land unto a good and large land, unto a land flowing with milk and honey; unto the place of the Canaanites .
> Now therefore, behold, the cry of the children of Israel is come unto me: and I have also seen the oppression wherewith the Egyptians oppress them.

Come now therefore, and I will send thee unto Pharaoh, that thou mayest bring forth my people, the children of Israel out of Egypt.

I burned with passion to bring the message to everybody who was in slavery, to tell them that I had gained a vision and sign from the Lord that He would lead us out of bondage. I will say unto them that the God of Abraham has visited them and knows of their tribulations, that He will bring them out of their affliction and smite their oppressors.

The people would think me mad, but in my dreams and in my vision those three nights, I knew I was stricken with the grace of God. I knew that He had anointed me as His servant to lift up my soul, to rejoice and to do His holy will.

I prayed in my heart to Jesus, who is the Prince of all the kings of the earth, to love me and wash me from all sin, to wash me clean in His own blood.

To you be glory and dominion forever.

Before I left that holy place in the woods, I knelt down one last time to praise the Lord for saving me from damnation and for calling me to be His servant.

I made my way back out of the bush singing praises to the Lord, knowing well that the direction of my life as a slave had changed forever.

FIFTEEN

April 8th, 1832

A couple days ago when the guard brought in my breakfast of boiled green banana and a cup of warm water, he also handed me a copy of <u>The Holy War</u> which he asked me to keep hidden under my clothes. Minister Bleby kept his promise but the guard does not like that I have it or want anyone to know that he delivered it to me.

I first started to read this book while I was at Cooper's Hill. I enjoyed the story of the battles between good and evil. It frightened me to know that both spirits could dwell in the soul at the same time. It is a tale of a war within the individual souls of the people of the world.

There was a time when a mighty giant by the name of Diabolus attacked the famous town of Mansoul. He was the terrible Prince of Darkness. He wanted total dominion over Mansoul which the great King Shaddai had reserved for his own son.

Mansoul was a beautiful, magnificent city in the country of the universe. King Shaddai had made it in his image. It was fortified with strong walls so that it would be difficult for any enemy to destroy.

Diabolus spoke to the people of Mansoul with words that were so sly that he was able to persuade many of them to the ways of evil. The people of Mansoul were so innocent and trusting that they believed everything they heard. He told them that the King was holding them in bondage and that if they would only believe in Diabolus, he would grant them all their wishes.

The townsfolk began to disobey the laws of their King. They started to hear of the forbidden fruit of the tree of paradise. They forgot about King Shaddai and let Diabolus and all his army into their houses.

The tyrant Diabolus and all of his evil captains invaded every house of Mansoul and drove the good King from the town.

That did not mean, though, that Shaddai gave up on his people. Without warning, he tried to invade Mansoul, but Diabolus's forces were too strong for him.

That is as far as I read the first time. I wanted to know how Shaddai, with all his might and power, could be beaten by the dark prince. It did not make sense to me that the King could not defeat Diabolus.

When I read on, I discovered that there were many more battles and that in the end the people of Mansoul were the ones who had to decide which King they wanted, Shaddai or Diabolus.

The people found out that Diabolus did not really keep his promises. He locked up in jail the good captains like Lord Understanding and Mr Conscience so that they could not persuade the people to start a riot.

The King became so vexed that he sent his strongest army to rescue the people of Mansoul. He sent his own son, Emmanuel, who rode a chariot with his army of captains, to come for the deliverance of his people. Emmanuel came into the hearts of the people to deliver them from bondage. And many listened to his word.

When Diabolus realized that he could not win the battle, he instructed his men that they should destroy the palace. The people came to realize that it was the Prince of Peace, not Diabolous, who wanted them to be happy. All Diabolus did was tell them lies. He wanted to ruin them by keeping them prisoners.

Emmanuel was victorious and his people begged for mercy: 'Prince Emmanuel, the great Lord of all worlds and master of mercy, we, your poor, miserable town of Mansoul, confess that we have sinned against your father. We are no longer worthy to be called your Mansoul, but we should be cast into the pit.'*

And the good Prince had mercy upon the people of Mansoul. He did not drive them into the pit but delivered them from evil. He blessed and pardoned them for the wrong they had done. He took possession of their castle, and in preparation for the coming of their Prince, the people of the town went out into the country to lay tree branches and flowers on the street.

The chiefs of Diabolus, who were left in the town, were put on trial. Mr Lustings, Mr Unbelief, Mr Forget-Good and Mr False-Peace. All those responsible for the wickedness were brought to justice. All the traitors them. Many received a sentence of death according to the law.

The story teaches me about the salvation that the good Lord will deliver unto us if we drive out the evil that dwells within our hearts.

I have about half of the book left to read.

December 1823

By the end of 1823, rumours of freedom were all bout the land. We found out that some of the White people in England were actually our friends. They wanted to bring an end to slavery. One of the men who took over from Saint Wilberforce was a Thomas Fowell Buxton, who told the lords in England and all His Majesty people everywhere that they must pass laws to improve the condition of us slaves here in Jamaica. That meant we would come to enjoy the privileges and rights as free subjects of the King.

Everybody was talking bout how slavery mus come to an end and the chat was causing unrest inna Jamaica.

The planters were livid, saying all kind of bad word to the slaves, telling them that there was no way their life was going to improve. They would be crazy to think that the flogging was going to stop or that they were going to get an extra day off work. The people in England were going mad, they said, to say that the laws should change here in Jamaica where everything was just fine.

The magistrates held public meetings in the town hall in Montego Bay and the freed Blacks and Coloureds reported back to us that the buckra passed resolutions to make petitions to the Crown. The planters did not want to take any instructions from England because they knew what was best for Jamaica. They were the ones who knew how to improve the character of the slave population.

The newspapers carried all the news. The walking buckras shared stories with the slaves and the parsons read articles aloud to the congregations at church service. It was said that the Governor had received a dispatch way back in the month of May and that he got further instructions which he was supposed to send out to the people in July month. But up to then, December time, no one had heard of any change in the slave law.

The slaves became anxious. Word was about that freedom might soon come and that the White man in Jamaica was hiding the truth. The slaves were saying that we were tired of being slaves and that we should work no more for massa. What a tribulation! It seemed then that everything was going to turn about.

Part II: The Bay

Many conversations about the state of affairs in the country took place right in Miss Mary's lodging house. Her establishment attracted magistrates and other important persons, some travellers, and others, local residents who gathered to talk about business and to relax with their friends over a glass of port and a Jamaican cigar.

On one such occasion, the Customs Collector, Mr Roby, was at the tavern. He had come to talk with one of the sea captains concerning goods he had brought to the island. Three other influential gentlemen joined them, Mr Richard Barrett, Custos of St James, and two magistrates from the parish, Mr John Coates and Mr William Grignon. I had heard about Mr Grignon whom we slaves called Little Breeches because of his clothes, which always fit too small. He was a short, White gentleman with deep furrowed lines in his face. In his left hand he carried a cane which he seemed to use not for walking but instead for pointing at people when he spoke. His face had a stern look, emphasized by a white, broad-rimmed hat which cast a dark shadow when he wore it out in the sunlight. He had a loud mouth and a reputation for being mean to his slaves at Salt Spring where he was the attorney. Little Breeches had a pointed nose like a wudpika, eyes small and close together, and a voice screechy like the patu.

The gentlemen were seated at one of four round tables in the tavern. Miss Mary had instructed the cook to prepare a large bowl of soldier soup, made from crabs caught on the honeycomb rocks by the sea. She placed one at each setting. Miss Mary was cross with me again for being absent so much but that was not the appropriate time for her to give me a scolding. I would get that from her later. She instructed me to fetch a decanter of madeira and glasses for the gentlemen and to stand close by them to attend to their wishes. She made up

179

her face ugly and talked rude when she was giving me the orders. I have noticed that even the nicest owners go on bad and treat us slaves worse when other White people are about.

'We met in October last, and the majority has decided not to make any changes to the existing slave code. I am in full accordance with this position for it would be far too dangerous to modify any clauses at this time.' I was sure Mr Grignon would have continued talking about this and that, if Mr Barrett had not interrupted.

'Maybe so, but perhaps it would be wise to make alliances with the free Coloureds and Blacks. They have already come forward with petitions and grievances for their own rights to be considered. I do believe they are becoming a force to be reckoned with.' Mr Barrett had stern eyes but he spoke with compassion. He was dressed in a formal black suit of clothes with a high ruffled white shirt about his neck.

'That seems to be beside the point, Richard.' Mr Coates sided with the opinions of Little Breeches. 'To be honest, I cannot tell you how delighted I am by the resolutions of the Jamaican Assembly. William, I believe you have been instrumental in putting these forward and should be congratulated highly for your efforts. We have called for a condemnation of the measures adopted by the House of Commons.'

'"A decree has gone forth whereby the inhabitants of this once valuable colony (hitherto esteemed the brightest jewel in the British Crown). . ."' Mr Grignon let out the strangest laugh which sounded like a cackling fowl. '". . .are destined to be offered as a propitiatory sacrifice at the altar of fanaticism."* These are the exact words, I might have you know, gentlemen.'

'Bravo!' replied Mr Coates. 'Fanaticism indeed! I do believe the lords have gone mad! They know not the interests of their colonies. How would they? Most have never set foot in this part of the world. There is yet some hope, gentlemen. We have spoken with such eloquence and boldness that I cannot imagine how they would ever refuse to admit to the good reason of our arguments.'

'We need to be cautious, gentlemen,' Mr Roby interrupted. He did not seem as involved as the others in the discussion and spoke with less passion than Mr Coates or Mr Grignon. 'I understand that the House has called for the abolition of slavery. We need to be careful not to exaggerate the situation. The measures are for the improvement of conditions of the slaves, and they do not seem to be too radical or, for that matter, out of keeping with our own practices.'

Mr Grignon and Mr Coates both started to speak at once. 'Mr Roby!'

I was not sure whether it was the effect of the port or the excitement of the moment but both men suddenly became flush and red in the face.

'What is the matter, Sirs? Have I said something offensive?' Mr Roby seemed surprised.

'Do not be deceived, my dear Roby,' Mr Coates replied. 'These measures are a step towards total abolition of slavery, and, I may add, our own ruination here in the colonies. The tone with which we received the edicts is inexcusable. I honestly believe that the home government forgets that its colonial legislature in Jamaica is chosen by the people! If we do not let our voice be heard, our friends in England will leave us in total mayhem. I dare say, Roby, you sound much like those nigger lovers in England.'

'I beg your pardon, Sir.' Mr Roby got up out of his chair and approached Mr Coates.

'I wish for you not to stand over me in this fashion, Sir.' Mr

Roby was standing close, his legs up against Mr Coates's chair.

'Then you shall apologize for your remarks.'

'I say only what appears to be the truth, Roby.'

'Then, I shall ask you to step out of the tavern with me and do what is the only right thing for a gentleman to do in the circumstances: to challenge you, man to man, to a duel.' He moved away from the chair.

Mr Barrett had been talking to other people in the tavern, but when he heard the commotion, stepped in between the two men. 'Gentlemen, I think the port to be too potent. I am sure we can find a way to conduct ourselves in a manner more becoming of English gentlemen.'

'It is best I leave, gentlemen,' said Mr Roby. 'I have finished with my business here. Mr Coates, I think we should all be wary of divine retribution for our actions and thoughts. None of us is above God's law. Good evening, gentlemen. God's speed.'

Mr Barrett waited for Mr Roby to leave the tavern. 'With all due respect, John, you may very well be exaggerating the case.' Mr Coates did not seem to be listening. His face was as red as beetroot and his head was bopping around like a nervous chicken.

'I must say John may have a point, Richard.' Mr Grignon's voice sounded squeaky again, this time like the wheel of an ox cart. 'The Act is despicable. It aims to prepare the wretches for freedom. There is no question about it. What is more, all the talk has put crazy ideas in their heads. I have heard at Salt Spring some say to the driver that freedom time *soon come.*' He let out his gaggle-cluck-cluck laugh again, but this time, more nervous.

'Have not the sectarians been preaching this for some time now?' I was not sure whether Mr Barrett was beginning to agree with the two red-faced gentlemen.

Mr Grignon seemed to love that question. 'Indeed! And this new talk of amelioration has given the orangutans the notion that King George wishes them to be free.'

'I am sure, gentlemen, that you would agree with William, that there is general unrest among the population.' Mr Coates poured himself another glass of port. 'We have heard of uprisings in the Parish of St George and the holding of slave meetings in other parishes.'

Mr Grignon interjected, 'It has been recommended to the Governor that those who have been taken prisoner recently in St George's be executed before Christmas.'

'And so they should,' replied Mr Coates.

'We may be overreacting, gentlemen.' Mr Barrett tried to calm them by lowering his own voice. 'There has been no destruction of property or general uprising in any of the parishes of Jamaica. I know that some of the alleged plots in St James are based on hearsay. This may surprise you, gentlemen, that I say this, but I have seen, over the last ten years or so, a general improvement in the character of the Negro.'

'So you are saying that this qualifies the slave for equal status, for admissible evidence in the courts, for easier access to manumission? My dear Mr Barrett.' Mr Coates was becoming increasingly impatient and stood up as if he was ready to leave the party.

'You know, John, that we have seen atrocities in slave courts on account of their evidence being inadmissible.' Mr Barrett paused and looked about the tavern. 'It is probably time that we go home to join our families. I am pleased this argument has ended civilly without challenges to a bloody duel.' He chuckled.

'Do remember, John, that we are the civilized ones,' Mr Grignon cackled.

'The truth is, gentlemen, that Jamaica is in dire straits.'
Mr Coates seemed to get the attention of the others with his
serious tone. 'The value of our property is in decline, the Duke
is not responding swiftly enough to oppose the antislavery
bills, and the sectarians are being allowed free rein to preach
what they bloody well want. We are putting ourselves in
grave danger.'

'We are prized no longer as the jewel of the crown. The
hypocrisy of it all! I wonder what amelioration is being
afforded to the factory slaves of Lancashire? Damn it all. This
cursed country!' Mr Grignon started to pound his stick, digging
into the floor with the pointed end of the cane.

'I think it time we leave. Otherwise, I do reckon the landlady
will call the constable for a disturbance of the peace. Having
the Custos and his magistrates arrested would not be too civil.
Would it, gentlemen?' Mr Barrett laughed. 'A pleasure as
always, gentlemen. Adieu.'

Mr Barrett left at that time, but Mr Grignon and Mr Coates
remained at the tavern for a few more hours of loud chatter,
heavy drinking and smoking.

One thing I knew for sure was that I would never want
either Mr Grignon or Mr Coates to be my massa.

~

It was in January month of the following year, 1824, when
I first met Mr Thomas Burchell. He had dropped anchor in
Montego Bay on the 15th day of the new year and wasted no
time in starting his ministry by preaching on every alternate
Sunday at Moses Baker's chapel in Flamstead. He was
supposed to reside there but the house which the proprietor
had intended for him was converted into a hospital for the
Negroes.

He arrived by mule at Crooked Spring on the Lord's Day, the 25ᵗʰ day of January. Crooked Spring is at Flamstead, just off the Orange River about ten miles up into the hills from Montego Bay. He was accompanied by a young slave assigned to be his guide. Mr Vaughan, who was the attorney at the estate, showed him the way into the chapel. A small crowd, mostly slaves from the area, gathered that morning for service.

When I first set eyes on Mr Burchell, I was struck by his youthful ways, the energy he showed in his walk and expression. He was no more than five and twenty, a medium-height White man with light hair that stuck up high on his head. His eyes were kind and sincere.

The elders of the community stayed around after service to meet their new parson, and shortly after that I had an opportunity to speak with him as he was leaving to go back down the hill to the Bay.

'I like your sermon, Preacher. It is from Luke, chapter 2, verse 10: "Fear not: for, behold, I bring you tidings of great joy, which shall be to all people." I glad you come to bring us good tidings, Preacher.'

'I am very impressed that you know your scriptures so well. Thank you very much.' His voice became softer and weaker. 'I was not sure what would appeal. I am glad that you have said this to me for I did not think I was very well received.'

'Why you say this, Sir?'

'At the start, few would enter the chapel, and those who did seemed not to welcome the message of the gospel. I expected a larger crowd. I think the number did not exceed 300.'

'They not sure bout you, Massa. The parson they had here before, Mr Tripp, him wife did get sick and pass on, and then he left everybody to go back to England with his children. Now, the new parson come with no notice. They never see you before and they wonder what happen to Parson Tripp.'

'He needed to return to England because of personal illness and I have been asked to take his place.' He started to wipe the sweat from his brow with his long sleeve. 'I am unaccustomed to this heat, I am afraid.' His face filled red from the sun-hot.

'No mind, Parson. As long as you preach the gospel of salvation and the people know that you bring them the Good News, they will love you.'

'That is my mission and the reason I have come to this place.'

'I thought you to be a Baptist minister.'

'Why, I certainly am. Why would you not think so?'

'You preach just like the minister from the Anglican Church, Reverend Smith.'

'Well, how do Baptists preach?'

'They sing more, Preacher, and they talk bout John the Baptist and they baptize the faithful in the river.'

'I see. I do all these things. You seem to be very knowledgeable about religious matters. What is your name?'

'My name is Sam Sharpe. Yes, Preacher, I am a devout Christian and I have been saved. Moses Baker has taught me well.' I felt proud to say my name, to profess my faith and to know that a White man was showing respect for what I was saying.

'What sorts of things has he taught you?'

'That Jesus is the Son of God, that the Baptist come to prepare His way, and that Jesus shed His blood to be our Saviour.'

'Do you truly want Him to be your Saviour, Sam?'

'I would die for His name sake, Sir.'

'Then I should like you to attend one of our services in Montego Bay. I procured there for my use a small house on the corner of Church and King streets. I also intend to hold meetings.'

'What kind of meeting, Sir?'

'I shall invite worshippers who have been baptized or who follow in the ways of Christ.' His voice became more alive. 'We shall pray and I shall tell them of the nature of the Christian faith and of the obligations and duties of becoming members of the Church.'

'I would like that very much, Mr Burchell.'

'This is good, Sam. I am pleased to hear. I believe that you have an ardent faith which will make you an excellent follower of Christ. Soon enough, there will be many hundreds like you, God willing, under my special care and protection.'

'That is good, Preacher.'

'I am concerned about the doctrine of the elders whom I have met here today. Their interpretations of the Bible leave much to be desired. They seem not to follow those of the established church of England. They tell me they are leaders in Mr Moses Baker's church. I shall need help to train those who are eager to do God's work.'

'I will help you, Massa.'

'Why do you call me that?'

'Massa?'

'Yes.'

'It is a sign of respect, Sir. We call White boss, who have authority, the Massa. You have authority, you are a minister, you ride a horse and you have a servant.'

'Some of the massas whom I have met in the last ten days have not been what I might call respectful or civil.'

'Some of them do not like the Baptist. That is why.'

187

'And why would that be?'

'It is because the Baptist tell the slaves too much things. You will soon find out for yourself, Mr Burchell.'

'I expect I shall. Where do you live, Sam?'

It felt good again to hear him call my name. When buckra talk, they don't always call my name in a polite way. 'I live in the Bay at a lodging house in the service of Miss Mary.'

'Well then, it will be convenient for you to attend the service next Sunday.'

'I will try my best to be there, Massa. Miss Mary is vex with me and she might send me off to a new owner, but I will try my best.'

'Have you been a bad slave?'

'She think of me as bad because I spend too much time away from the house and she don't like that.'

'I see how that would upset her.' There was a slight pause in the conversation and I did not know what to say to him. He continued, 'Well, Sam, I do hope I can see you on the Sabbath. Perhaps you might persuade others to accompany you. There is no limit to the size of Christ's flock.'

'Thank you for staying to talk with me so long, Preacher. I will bring a friend of mine. She go to church here sometimes.'

~

'You bad boy. *Maldita su madre.* I give to you so many chances, Sam, and still, you do not listen. *Necio eres.*'

I should have known that Miss Mary would be in the worst of moods. I had been staying out long hours at Sunday market, and at Content visiting with Nyame. I had also disappeared for three days when I was fasting in the bush. She made a report to the authorities that her slave had run away.

'Sam, you know that I am a good owner to you, just like no

other one here in Jamaica.' Her face was red and her bosom moving up and down. '*Mala criatura.*' As she talked, she was fussing with her hands behind her head. She pulled at the pin in her hair which made it fall out long like a horse's mane right down the length of her back.

'You put me in a nervous state, Sam. *Tú eres pendejo.*'

I knew that she was swearing at me but there was nothing I could say or do to stop her.

'What are you thinking, Sam? I have a lodging house to run. I need to give attention to my guests.' She pinned her hair back up on her head. 'You need to give care to the horses. I have errands for you to do. They say in Jamaica, you need a good licking, *a lo menos, cincuenta.* I need for a man to beat you. *Pendejo, su madre.* You not good, Sam. You not listen to what I say to you.'

'Miss Mary.' I wanted the conversation to end.

'Do not say nothing to me. You people are all the same. I try to give you kindnesses and you treat me as if I am a fool. *¡Carajo!*'

'I will tell you something, Ma'am, if you give me one chance.'

'I do not want to hear nothing from you. I will give you over to the authorities. You know what they will do to you, Sam? They will lock you up and they will beat you and give you hard labour for ten years or more. I think much on it, Sam. What am I going to do with you? One thing I know, Sam, is that you are a bad slave.'

'I know I did not keep my word, Miss Mary.'

'*Pendejo.* You not feel sorry, Sam. Do not give me a look like that. You look down. Put your eyes down when I am speaking to you.'

She was carrying on very bad. I knew I had no more chances with Miss Mary. 'You can give me stricter hours, Miss Mary.'

'I try that, Sam, over and over.'

'I am sorry, Ma'am.'

'I have arranged with Señor Sharpe that you go to one of the big estates to do hard work.'

'What did you say, Ma'am?'

'I tell you that you are going to do hard labour on a sugar plantation.'

'You would not give me one more chance, Miss Mary?'

'I give you chance and chance again, Sam. If you stay here, you are disobedient to me again and again. ¡*Ay, díos mío!*'

'I sorry, Ma'am.' I tried to look away from her as she had instructed.

'I have made a report to the authorities that you came back to me and that I punish you myself. You leave this house as soon as Señor Sharpe make the arrangements. Where is the fiddle that I gave to you?'

Miss Mary had shown me how to play notes on the violin. 'It break, Miss Mary.'

'I do not believe you. Where is the violin I give to you, Sam?'

'It break, Ma'am.'

'Then bring it here to me and I will fix it.'

'It mash up, Ma'am, into little pieces.'

'Ay, you make me like a lunatic. ¡*Carajo!*'

'It is all right, Ma'am, I bring you the pieces.'

The truth was Moses Baker had told me that I should give up all those entertainment — music, dance and gambling. I loved to play the violin so much that the only way to get rid of the temptation was to break it.

'Come here, Sam. You do not leave until I say to you to go.'

Then she struck me hard against the face with the back of her hand. I stood silent before as her obedient slave. This time I looked at her.

'*Vete, vete*, go, go.' And it seemed that she was going to cry.

Miss Mary would not say, but deep down I think she felt sorry to part with me. She had no choice. Leaving the lodging house was to be my punishment for disobeying her. Even though Miss Mary had a bad temper and she cuss and go on bad, she had a good heart. She missed her country terribly and did not adjust to life that well in Jamaica. Maybe she had left some children behind in Cuba, or maybe the Count, who had bought her freedom, had been cruel to her. Something was bothering her, but she never said what it was.

I never saw Miss Mary again.

Part III
CROYDON ESTATE

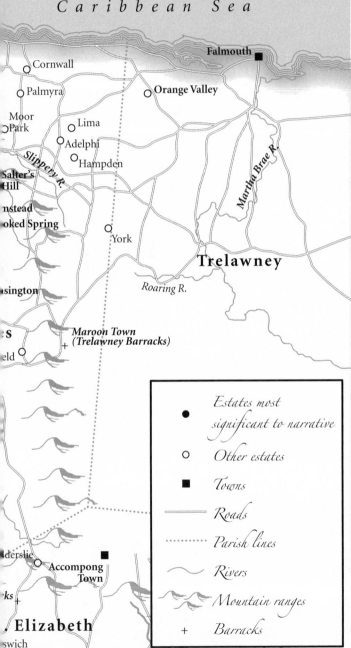

...ions of Estate Properties in the ...ey, St. Elizabeth and Westmoreland

C a r i b b e a n   S e a

Falmouth ■

Cornwall ○

○ Palmyra

Orange Valley ○

Moor
○Park

○ Lima

○Adelphi

○Hampden

Slippery R.

Martha Brae R.

Salter's
Hill

nstead

oked Spring

○ York

Trelawney

Roaring R.

sington

s

Maroon Town
(Trelawney Barracks) ✝

eld ○

derslie

○ **Accompong
Town** ■

ks ✝

Elizabeth

swich

●	*Estates most significant to narrative*
○	*Other estates*
■	*Towns*
—	*Roads*
········	*Parish lines*
～	*Rivers*
～～	*Mountain ranges*
✝	*Barracks*

0   5   10 miles

Rose Hall
Tryall
Easthams
Salt Spring
Blue Hole
Bogue Islands
Area of sectional map
Cooper's Hill
Bay and Town of Montego
Round Hill
Reading
Orchard
Unity Hall
Bellfield
Montego R.
Orange R.
Wiltshire
Prospect
John's Hall
Fla...
Anchovy Bottom
Cre...
Springmount
Roehampton
Anchovy R.
Hanover
Lethe
Ke...
Content
Copse
Great R.
Old Works
Golden Grove
Montpelier
New Works
St. Jam...
Shettlewood Barracks +
Vaughansf...
Belvidere
Seven Rivers
Silver Grove
Ramble
Chester Castle
Hazelymph
Alexandria
Argyle
Roaring R.
Greenwich
Cambridge
Hermitage
Ducketts Spring
Springfield
Richmond Hill
Mocho
Retrieve
Catadupa
Struie
Croydon
Lapland
Cow Park
Belmont
Westmoreland
Woodstock
Chesterfield
F...
Barra...
Leamington
Ginger Hill
S...
Bluefields
Ip...
Flint R.

SIXTEEN

April 12th, 1832

The gaol guard lets Mr William Knibb into my cell.

'My dear Sam, God's blessings be with you.'

'It is good to see you, Minister.'

He looks haggard, *maaga* and drawn down. His eyes are dark and he is slightly stooped over.

'Given the circumstances, you look in reasonably good health.'

I cannot understand why he is saying this because I smell bad and have not cleaned myself for weeks. 'I don't feel that good, though, Sir, but I trying to keep the faith.'

'Prayer is sometimes all we have.'

'The last time I saw you, you was at Salter's Hill just before the fires started. You were trying to tell us that the rumours were false, that no freedom was coming.'

'There was reason for my concern, Sam. I had received word that slaves from Cornwall were refusing to work. The estates all around were in trouble.'

'It was too late by then, Mr Knibb.'

'Perhaps, but I had an obligation. I feared for my wife and two daughters, for my flock of 5,000.'

'What was there to fear?'

'Bloody massacre.'

'The people panicked. It was time, Sir. I don't think anybody, not you or any other preacher, could have stop it. Our time had come. We would be slaves no more.'

'What a terrible mistake.'

'What kind of mistake, Minister?'

'The bloodshed, the terrible loss of life. "As Christians, we can never condone unlawful acts to obtain freedom."*

'But don't Jesus teach freedom?'

'Yes, Sam, of course, but Christianity must not only enlighten us, it must sanctify us.'

It feels like he is insulting me so I change the topic. 'How is the Missus and the children, Mr Knibb?'

'We are all safe, thank God, but have been subjected to utter humiliation by the authorities.'

I feel suddenly bored by his self-pity. 'What day is it today, Sir?'

'I believe it to be the 12th day of April.'

'What day is that?'

'Thursday.'

'How they keep me in here so long, Minister? One month now.'

'I understand your trial date is set for next week.'

'Nobody tell me nothing. You were saying that the authorities giving you trouble.'

'More than trouble, Sam. They have locked me in goal, put me on trial, driven me and my family from our home, burned my church in Falmouth. You know of this.'

'I know they burn the churches.'

'The magistrates are holding us missionaries responsible for the rebellion. They say you slaves call it "The Baptist War". They tell me that shooting would be too merciful a death for those of us who have caused so much bloodshed and loss of property. What an outrage!'

'It is because you and Mr Burchell preach the gospel of freedom.'

'But to be tried by court martial for inciting slaves to

rebellion? Preposterous!' He furrows his brow and looks as if he is going to cry. 'The indecency of it all, treating licensed ministers of religion in such fashion.'

'They set you free, Minister?'

'Yes, there are some to whom we owe the deepest gratitude. Mr Roby rescued us from the mobs on more than one occasion and Mr Manderson posted bail and offered us refuge in his home. On returning to Falmouth, I needed to depend on the kindness of some Coloured ladies to provide safety for me and my family. <u>The Cornwall Courier</u> was advising people to tar and feather any missionary they met.'

'They put you on trial?'

'Yes, but nothing came of it. The indictment stated that I was a person of depraved, impious and unquiet mind and that on one particular occasion, on December 4th, I endeavoured to stir a group of slaves to rebellion. <u>Nolle prosequi</u> was entered in the case, which means that there was no evidence for the charges they brought against us. As you know, slave evidence must be corroborated by the independent testimony of a second person, but they could find no one.'

'And the people testify for you, Sir?'

'Three hundred or more were there, Sam. I was able to collect many of the witnesses myself. They were willing to swear that the missionaries had nothing to do with inciting them to rebellion, but before they were given a chance to testify, the case was thrown out.'

'That is good, Minister.'

'It is not the end of it, I am afraid. It will take many years to restore sanity to this island. And what of you, Sam? Is there anything that you can divulge that may help in your case?'

'You already know about me, Sir.'

'*I know you to have been a faithful member of Thomas Burchell's congregation.*'

'*Yes, I was one of his church leaders and I preach the gospel as it was taught to me and as I see it.*'

'*You are saying that you meant no harm to any man?*'

'*You know I am not a murderer, Mr Knibb. Did someone send you here to talk to me?*'

'*A very good friend of mine is the major general of the militia, Mr William Miller, the Custos of Trelawney. He has asked me and Mr Bleby to gather evidence that will assist in your case.*'

'*So why he want to help me?*'

'*You are up before serious charges, Sam. They are charging you with being director of the whole rebellion.*'

'*And what I can tell you that will help free me, Mr Knibb?*'

'*The truth, Sam.*'

'*I tell Parson Bleby I writing it all down and I will give him my story, just as I see it.*'

'*I shall ask to give evidence at your trial.*'

'*That is good, Sir.*'

'*Just as you say that you yourself are not a murderer, then you must believe the same for me and Mr Burchell. The Baptists did not incite you to rebellion.*'

'*You know I don't believe you is a murderer, Minister. We all wanted the same thing, dignity for Christ's people. Just that we slaves could wait no longer.*'

'*I will be very interested in reading your narrative.*'

'*God's blessing be with you, Sir.*'

'*And to you, my brother. I may not see you often again because Mr Miller has recommended that I reside in Kingston. He cannot guarantee my safety if I remain in these parts.*'

'*Blessings to you and the Missus and to the children.*'

He comes over, stares at me at length in silence, and then

reaches for my hand. He pulls me from the floor and embraces me with much affection, pressing his bosom to mine.
I feel deeply sad.

February 1ˢᵗ, 1824

Anxious to meet the new minister, the people came in big numbers, packing the little house on the corner of Church and King streets. It was the Lord's Day, the first of the month, the first time Parson Burchell preached to the people of the Bay. The crowds were especially large because the Methodist minister was away, so many of his congregation joined the Baptists to worship that Sunday.

He stood before a crowd of about 200 people, mostly slaves, but also a few Whites, sailors, a sea captain, and several Coloureds who sat in the chairs at the very front. The Black people sat to the back in what spaces were available, others having to stand, spilling out through the doors at the side of the church.

The minister wore a long black gown, far too hot even for the ten o'clock morning service. Bible in hand, he looked out over his congregation, his eyes youthful and excited, but his voice a little shaky.

'I bring you good tidings of joy and peace.' A hush came over the crowd. 'I am a soldier of Jesus and you are my brothers. Welcome to the house of the Lord. I carry His banner and speak to you here today so that you will come to know your Saviour and join me as part of His great army.

'From the time I was a little boy, I always yearned to bring the Good News to those who lived in conditions such as yours. I spent many years in prayer asking for God's guidance to lead me to the right choice. He has brought me to this place, to ask you to repent of your wrongdoings so that you may be saved and live in the peace and joy of Christ. His Word will bring you out of your darkness and bondage so that you may see the true light of freedom.

'We are saved, dear brethren, through repentance and through grace. We must recognize that we have done wrong in the eyes of God and confess it to be so:

> *I acknowledged my sin unto thee, and mine iniquity have I not hid. I said, I will confess my transgressions unto the Lord; and thou forgavest the iniquity of my sin.*

'I want to welcome you to the house of the Lord. In the words of David, I say unto you from Psalm 122, verse 1: "*I was glad when they said unto me, Let us go into the house of the Lord.*"

'I ask you today to leave your wicked ways and lift up your hearts to God. This Bible reading is from Psalm 84, verse 11:

> *For the Lord God is a sun and shield:*
> *the Lord will give grace and glory:*
> *no good thing will he withhold from them*
> *that walk uprightly.*

'Let us pray.' Everybody in the church bowed their head. 'Heavenly Father, look down on your people today, open their hearts so that they may confess to you their transgressions. Send them your grace, let the Holy Ghost dwell in their hearts and give them the knowledge of your Son, Jesus Christ, who died for us on the cross and shed His blood so that we may be forgiven and one day enter into eternal life with You, the Father, the Son and the Holy Ghost. Amen.'

More prayers and hymns followed. One slave asked if she could lead the congregation in a song that Moses Baker had taught us. The parson obliged and stepped to one side, allowing the woman to come to the front.

'Let us all begin, all together as one,' the woman bawled out and the whole crowd immediately hushed. Her name was Mamas, and she was one of those Jamaican ladies with the big bosoms and large girth. Sturdy, strong and tough. She was dressed in a long white frock with a tie on her head to match.

The Black people sang out with one voice as if they all belonged to a single choir. Some knew the song so well that they began to harmonize:

> *Go down, Moses,*
> *Way down in Egypt land,*
> *Tell ol' Pharaoh,*
> *Let my people go.*

The people were swinging their bodies and clapping their hands, and all the while Mamas was leading them:

> *Thus saith the Lord, old Moses said.*

Everybody sang out the refrain:

> *'Let my people go.'*

Mamas clenched up her fist and drove her hand up and down through the air:

> *If not, I will smite your first-born dead.*
> *Let my people go.*
> *Go down, Moses,*
> *Go down, Moses,*
> *Way down in Egypt land,*
> *Tell ol' Pharaoh,*
> *Let my people go.*

'Amen. Let we give praise to the Lord for He has chosen this to be a blessed day. He has brought us the Good News. He has answer our prayer and bring a preacher to us this day.'

After church Mr Burchell mingled with the congregation, the White people mostly demanding his attention.

I spotted Nyame in the crowd. I had tried to catch her eye during service but she looked as if she was avoiding me. I was not sure what was wrong.

'I don't see you this long time.' I went over to her.

'It only been a few days.' Her black skin looked soft as silk, made even more beautiful by the lacy white dress she wore.

'I know and I miss you even still. I have a whole heap to tell you. You look pretty today, girl.'

'You and your sweet talk.' She turned away.

'No, I serious, I not joking. You look like an angel.'

'Thank you, Sam.' She broke out in her usual big smile.

'I been talking to the new Minister, and he invite us to join a meeting he having at the end of the month.'

'What kind of meeting?'

'He want to find people to join his church.'

'I not so religious as you, Sam.'

'No matter. You can come anyway and hear what he want to tell us.'

'And why me would waan do dat?' Her question had a serious tone.

'I want us to get baptize in his church.'

'But, tell me something, Sam, you don't baptize aredi?' She sounded a little annoyed.

'They say Mr Sharpe father and mother did Christen me when I was born, but now that we are grown and become big people — '

She interrupted me. 'Then what we goin' baptize for?'

'He will tell us, Nyame. It will give us the strength to follow the Christian way.'

'What kind of Christian way?'

'We would have the Church blessing so you could marry me if you want.' I flashed her a tender smile and reached out to hold her hand.

'And who say me would want do dat?' She asked me sort of half joking and turned her back to me.

'Come here, Nyame.'

She turned back to me, looking serious. 'You shouldn't say dem ting if you don't mean dem.'

'I mean them, Nyame.'

'You sure?'

'Sure as my name is Sam. I know I would want that very much.'

'And why so?' Her voice began to soften.

''Cause you are sweet and lovely and I would want no other man to have you. Then the Lord will bless us if we marry, and then you will be fruitful and bear children.'

'You can really do the sweet talk, Sam.'

'So how the meeting sound to you?'

'When you say it is?'

'He say it is at the end of the month.'

'So me gwine haffi use me Christian name when me baptize?'

I found myself falling naturally into the patois. 'Him will baptize you with yuh Christian name, but plenty people have more than one name.'

'You send word to me and me will try fi come but me nah mek no promise bout no baptism yet.' She started to go.

I wanted to talk more with her. 'Otherwise, how is things with you?'

'Same like always. Dem work me too hard.'

'That's because you is strong and healthy.'

'No kind of life, Sam, where s'madi can own me like dat and tell me what fi do all de while.'

I tried to console her. 'A lot of people talking now bout how de free paper soon come.'

'Me nah know bout that.'

'Me think de best way is for we to join de church.'

'And what dat gwine do fi we?'

'It will help, Nyame, it will help we find freedom. De Lawd promise we deliverance.'

'Me better galang, Sam, otherwise, de driver gwine flog me fi staying out too late. Me have something fi tell you.' She had a glint in her eye.

'What is it?'

'Later.' She was teasing me.

'You kyaan do dat to me, Nyame.'

Her tone changed, more serious. 'Me tell you later.'

'Me will send word to you bout the meeting. Me stay far now, you know, up in de Great River Valley. Miss Mary get rid of me and Maas Sam have me doing field work up by Croydon Estate.'

'So why dem move you?'

'She say me stay out too late a night-time.'

'And what you doing out a night-time?'

'Visiting with you.'

'You galang, you hear, Sam. Me hear bout you still.'

'What you hear bout me?'

She seemed not to pay attention to my question and sprinted off towards the distant mountain track. Before she disappeared, she turned her head back to flash me her special smile.

~

Croydon Estate became my new home. It was located way into the interior of the Great River Valley, which resembled one giant yabba, a flat, fertile stretch of land forming a basin with misty blue mountains in a smooth rim all around. On many properties within the area, natural springs came up out of the rocks. The owners drew this water through high wooden bridges and stone aqueducts into dams which harnessed energy for the mills. The aqueducts stood tall through the land with their huge arches.

The estates were much larger than those closer to the Bay, with 200, sometimes 400 slaves on one plantation. Along the river, there were many including, Lethe, Copse, Montpelier, Shettlewood, Belvidere, Seven Rivers, Hazelymph, Greenwich, Cambridge and Croydon. Croydon was between Catadupa and the big river, close to the main road which came up from the Bay past Ginger Hill, clear through to YS Falls into the Parish of St Elizabeth.

The Great House at Croydon was much bigger than Mr Sharpe's. It stood on several acres of land away from the cane piece, the slave houses and the works. The works yard had several buildings, the mill, the boiling and curing houses, the distillery and trash houses. The overseer's house was near to the yard so that he could keep a close eye on everything. Many roads passed through the yard and into the estate, all of them big enough for the ox-drawn carts to carry the cane in crop time. The distances between the estates were great, but when we travelled from one to the other, we used the footpaths instead, which wound and curved through the bush, hidden from busha's sight. Over the years, I came to know these parts very well, the footpaths, the river and the slave villages.

Mr Gray was my new boss. He treated me quite well, maybe because he was the father of my former mistress, Mistress Sharpe. Gray was her name before she was married. She would have put a good word in for me. He took a liking to me also because he saw that I was strong and was able to work the fields from first light until dark.

Mr Gray put me with the Great Gang which did the hardest labour of any group of slaves. We spent the first part of the year harvesting the cane, and in August time, we were digging the cane holes and planting the shoots. Rain or shine we were in the fields. If the driver was in a good mood, he would let us sing a digging song:

> The one shirt I have ratta cut ahm
> Same place him patch, ratta cut ahm
> Rain, rain, Oh! Rain, rain, oh!
> Rain, rain oh fall down and wet me up.*

Another gang of slaves brought the cow dung from the barns in ox-driven carts and shovelled it into the trenches along with other waste. In the rainy time when the cow droppings got wet, they became very heavy. And they smelled stink too. Towards Christmas, we still worked the fields, nursing the ratoons, weeding, trashing and removing dead leaves from the cane stalks. From January month on, the harvest started. We chopped the cane, carrying and loading it on to the wagons for other slaves to feed into the mill. We started at shell-blow, at about six in the morning, stopped for an hour to eat, and then worked until the sun went down.

I also came to earn the respect of the overseer. I became stronger with the hard labour and was free of disease, my teeth white and clean, no fevers, no swellings, no leprosy, as healthy as his best workhorse. He told me I possessed a commanding way, and in the opinion of all, a good character, patient, civil and, most important of all, polite to Massa. Before long, he gave me a house in the slave village, all to myself, with furniture, a bed, table and chair. I came to earn the status of slave-driver.

My particular gang worked the fields, and the estate had

slaves doing other kinds of jobs. The majority were cane cutters but Massa had gardeners who cut the grass and tended to the grounds, and craftsmen like carpenters, masons, coopers and blacksmiths who worked in the shops. White men, who were desperate for jobs, also worked at these trades. Other slaves looked after the grazing of cattle, the pens, the hogs and sheep. In the main house, Massa had about ten or twelve slaves who did the cooking, washing and other chores too laborious for buckra and his family to do themselves. Mr Gray owned 200 slaves in all, 100 oxen and 50 mules. He was rich because each slave was worth, on average, 100 pounds. As long as we were healthy, it made sense for him to work us and not to sell us off. He was reaping good value for his money. But if we became sick, old or tired, then we would have no use any more.

My immediate boss man was the bookkeeper who lived in the barracks with other White workers, separate from the Great House and from the overseer's house. We called him Bulldog. He had eyes which bulged out from his head and a big fat nose and mouth which curved upwards to meet his nostrils. He even growled like a dog when he spoke, 'Grrrrr, you wrrrretch, come here, you filthy wrrretch, grrrrrr.' His voice would go harsh and then he would cough and choke on his words.

He asked me one day to fetch him the slave logbook from his room. There I saw entries which kept track of the names of slaves he had.

Cudjoe, forty-three, Negro, African, right leg amputated for vagrancy. 10th November, 1823.
Sidney, twenty-one, Negro, Creole, placed in dungeon for two weeks for refusal to work. 12th January, 1824.

Hamlet, eighteen, Negro, Creole, left hand amputated for stealing chickens. 20th March, 1824.

Cockcrow was his favourite time for punishing the slaves. Hector, a young man of about twenty, was always getting a thrashing for running away from the estate. Bulldog would instruct the slave to remove his trousers. And if he did not obey, Bulldog would lick him with a stick until he did. He then would command four of the strongest slaves to hold Hector down with his face in the dirt. Two men at his head would stretch his arms out wide and the other two at his feet would pull his legs far apart. Then the buckra would start snorting and turning red in the face, cart whip in hand. The strap would come down on the man's bare back and buttocks, 39 lashes. As a routine, he would order one of the slaves to bring a calabash full of salt water to throw on the wounds.

If the bookkeeper was in a sour mood, he would carry the punishment one step further.

'Will it be the ears or the feet this time, boy?' the bookkeeper asked Hector one day.

The young slave could barely talk. 'Do, Massa, have mercy pon me.'

The bookkeeper gave the signal to a head slave called Caesar.

'Please, Massa. Look pon me, me young and strong like bull.' He tried to raise himself up but fell back down on his face.

'You of no use, boy.' The buckra seemed to enjoy teasing Hector.

The young slave managed to raise his head to speak one last time. 'Do, Massa, do. Me do anything you ask me fi do. Do, Sar, a beg you.'

The bookkeeper went over to Hector and pushed his right boot under his belly to roll him over on his back. For a moment, I thought the White man was going to show mercy for I saw a smile come over his twisted face.

'Do what needs to be done,' the bookkeeper instructed the head slave, and then he walked away.

Four men rolled Hector back over on his belly, pushing his face down so it rubbed in the earth.

'Hold his head firm,' Caesar commanded.

One man sat on Hector, holding on to his neck-back with both hands and driving his face deeper into the dirt. Another sat on his legs facing the other way, pinning both his feet to the ground. The other two men held his arms out straight.

Hector was strong. He squirmed and slithered like a snake in the dirt.

'I sey fi hol' him.' The driver raised his machete.

Other men joined in, this time grinding his head farther down into the ground so it would not move.

Caesar came closer. He reached down to grab hold of Hector's left ear which he stretched out as far as he could. Not a sound we could hear coming from Hector because his face was buried in the earth. I thought he was going to be dead for he had no way to breathe.

With one quick chop, his ear was ripped from his head.

Blood spouted out of the hole just like when you cut off the neck of a chicken.

The slaves standing nearby started wailing.

The men let go and Hector pushed himself up and away from them. He stood there naked, looking like a madman. He held on to the side of his head to stop the blood and then he went wild, kicking and screaming.

Caesar could not catch him to carry out Bulldog's orders to cut off his other ear. Hector fled into the bush, never to be seen again.

~

As planned, Nyame and I attended the religious meetings which Parson Burchell arranged. She was not too keen about the instruction but she joined us anyway. One Sabbath, while we were sitting together after service, I noticed something different about her. Her rounded belly was showing big through her frock. *My God, was it really true that Sam was going to be a Daddy?* I did not know how to ask her. She had not mentioned it to me. My tongue was all tied up. My thoughts were swirling around in my head, nervous and excited both at the same time. The worst of it was that she was acting normal as if she had nothing to tell me.

'Nyame. Me nebba did know.'

'Nebba know what, Sam?'

I became speechless.

'Come, Sam. Tell me what you nebba know.' She spoke in a teasing way. 'So you going to be a Daddy, Sam.' She moved her hand over the curve of her belly, patting it slightly.

'Me sing praises to God for dat, Nyame.'

'And what about me?' she asked, still in a jokified way.

'Me happy for all three of we, Nyame. You happy, girl?'

'Me feel me gwine get fat and so-so but, yes, Sam, me happy fi bear yuh pickaninny.' She looked at me loving-like.

'All me hope sey is him favour you when him born.'

'Why you sey dat?'

'Cause you so pretty, gal.' I came closer to her to hold her hand.

'You know what dem sey in Jamaica?'

'What is dat?'

'*Man nebba ugly.*' She laughed out loud and stroked my face with her hand in a gentle way.

'Me not too sure bout that. Me see some man in Jamaica well ugly. Me just hope de pickaninny favour you.'

'We will see. You must promise me someting, Sam.' Her tone was serious.

'Me honour anything you ask me, Nyame.'

'You must promise fi look after we.' She reached for my hand and placed it on her belly.

'Me will guard you and de baby to de end of time. You know dat still.'

'You musn't mek promises you kyaan keep, Sam.'

'You don't believe me?'

'You galang, Sam. Me tink you tell me all dem fancy word cause you read too much Bible.'

Mr Burchell instructed twelve of us in the ways of his Church, telling us of the commitment to the Christian faith and preaching to us from the scriptures, Acts chapter 2, verse 42. There were many rules. We did not understand why we had to give up buying and selling on Sunday and the men were not too happy either about refraining from drinking rum. Pardoning and salvation were worth more than any material goods or world pleasures, the parson told us. The lesson to be learned was that when you were a true Christian, you were more concerned about obeying the Sabbath than about selling food at the market and getting drunk with your friends.

The numbers of faithful grew so big that Mr Burchell had to find another building that would hold the crowds, a large hall on the second floor of the old courthouse. In the early mornings and evenings, we held secret prayer meetings, which were strictly forbidden under the slave code. Regardless, the minister gave us permission to hold these Negro gatherings in the church. He himself was never present. We prayed and talked about ways in which we could spread the Good News of Jesus Christ to all our fellow slaves.

As time went on, the preacher gathered many followers he thought were ready for baptism. He put questions to them to test their faith, and when he thought they were prepared to receive the Spirit, he would write the names in a big book he had in the church. I rejoiced the day he wrote my name and Nyame's name in his records.

A few chains from the Bay on the west side of town, Minister Burchell met with a large crowd at the mouth of the Montego River at the early hour of four o'clock in the morning on the appointed day, the 6th of June. It was dark, a time even before the first crow, a time of night when the animals are quiet and the air feels soft on the skin. Hundreds of people came to watch. They lined the banks of the river, and when the ceremony was ready to begin, a hush came over the crowd.

The minister started the service with a short prayer. He then told everybody present that we, the faithful, had been specially chosen by Christ to be renewed in the Spirit through baptism. He was fully satisfied with regard to our character and our faith, having received testimonies from people who knew us. 'And John also was baptizing in Aenon near to the Salim, because there was much water there: and they came, and were baptized.'

Like John the Baptist, Mr Burchell walked waist deep into the river water. All dressed in full-length white frocks with white ties on the head, thirty-three of us followed him and walked down into the water that night. As each of us came up to the minister, he held us, one hand on the waist and the other on the neck-back, and he bent our body down so that our head went under the water, baptizing us in the name of the Father, and of the Son, and of the Holy Ghost. We came up out of the water, cleansed from our transgressions.

And Jesus, when he was baptized, went up straightaway out of the water: and lo, the heavens were opened unto him, and he saw the Spirit of God descending like a dove, and lighting upon him.

Later that morning, those of us who were baptized were permitted to partake of the Lord's supper, which Mr Burchell administered at the ten o'clock service. He broke the bread and blessed the wine in memory of Jesus. Many of us, including the minister, wept with joy, rejoicing in the wonderment of God's blessings.

Nyame and I were sanctified that day. My hope then was that she would agree to be married to me sometime soon.

In the same month of June, word was all about that the estates in the Parish of Hanover were going to be set on fire and that the Whites in those parts were to be killed off. On the night that it was planned for, Roach, the same one Mr Crawford used to have as a slave, told all the buckra what the slaves were scheming. So the militia came in fas fas and took care of everything. They hanged ten slaves at Argyle Estate and five more at Golden Grove. It was at Golden Grove where the slaves put out the fires on the estate and recovered the ammunition stolen from the overseer. But there was no recognition for their efforts. They received no reward, only punishment — punishment by death.

We were becoming anxious to obtain freedom. Since the massas were not giving us what we wanted, we started going to church in even larger numbers to hear if the parson would give us the freedom message of Massa Christ.

SEVENTEEN

In the October month of 1824, Nyame gave birth to a beautiful girl pickney. She sent word for me to go visit her at the slave village on Content Estate. The baby looked glorious just like her mother, with the same smooth black skin and happy face. She named the child Juba because she was born on a Monday. The Africans say that a child born on a Monday is clever like the spider Anancy.

'Hold her, Sam.'

What a beautiful moment it was. It felt like the glory of God was coming into my soul. I reached down and cupped the baby with my hands, cuddling and rocking her back and forth.

'She sweet, Nyame.'

'What you expect?'

I joked with her. 'Me know, she is fi me own flesh and blood.'

'Is fi we both, Sam.'

'A know but she favour you still, Nyame.' I snuggled the baby close under my ribs and felt her warmth against my naked skin. 'How come she so warm?' I placed her back on Nyame's belly.

'She spend nine month inside me, dat why she still warm.' She drew Juba close to her left breast, and with two fingers on her nipple, started to suckle the newborn.

'Me don't want dem tek de baby from me, Sam.' She kept looking down at Juba.

'Dem not gwine do it jus now. Dem want you fi feed her till she strong. When the time come, we will have a plan.'

She started to sob. I bent down to hold her and the baby close to me.

'Dem time ya wicked, Sam.'

'A know but look ya, look pon disya gift from God.' I caressed the baby's smooth head with my hand. 'De Lord give us hope in time of trouble.'

'You mus tek care of we, Sam.'

'A did promise, you remember?'

'Yes, you did tell me.'

'Me want you fi come up to Greenwich in a couple week time. We having a prayer meeting up there and me going to be doing the preaching.'

'Me soon goin haffi call you Parson Sam.'

'Me want you fi come hear me talk.'

'Me haffi go see how it go, Sam, wid de new baby and everything.' She paused a while and looked up at me. 'Only if you good, you promise?'

'Me always good, girl. But if me good, you know, Nyame, you haffi get serious wid me.'

'How you mean?' Then she seemed to pick up on what I was saying. 'You galang, you hear, Daddy, 'nough time fi dat still.'

~

The meeting was held in secret at ten o'clock at night behind the slave houses at Greenwich Estate where Gardner was the head slave. People gathered in multitudes because they heard that a Black preacher was going to talk to them that evening. They came from all about the Great River Valley district and from the parishes around, Hanover, Westmoreland, St Elizabeth and Trelawney. Many head slaves got word out to the field labourers and others from the neighbouring estates, and the news spread fast. These men shared the same vision of the fight for freedom. They became my friends: Thomas Dove from Belvidere, Johnson from Retrieve, George Reid from Cambridge, John Tharpe from Catadupa, and George Taylor, a saddler from the Bay. Three of Gardner's friends also joined the prayer meeting to play the goombay drums and shakas.

The night was clear, the stars shining like peeny-wallies in the sky. Gardner and I stood by the trunk of a silk-cotton tree to wait for the crowd to gather. Hundreds were assembling. Those who were approaching from the distant hills resembled duppies floating in the dark in their shimmering white clothes. A hush was over the crowd, an eerie silence, a knowledge full well that slave meetings after dark were strictly forbidden under the law.

Nyame waved to me from the crowd. I blessed her in my heart before I spoke.

'Our parson friend, Mr Moses Baker, cannot be with us tonight.' My voice was nervous. 'He sends his blessings to you all. He is old now, almost blind, but we mus not feel sorry for him for he sees with the Spirit of God. His legs move slowly because he is close to his grave. The masters were bad to him, my friends, when he was young. They put his legs in irons, they flogged his face, his eyes and his ears but they could not break his spirit. Yes, my brethren, they could not break his spirit. He walk straight in the eyes of the Lord and one day soon he will see His glory. Glory be to God! Let us always praise the name of the Lord. Praise be to the name of the Lord Jesus. Parson Baker had been a poor slave once upon a time, poor like you and me, but he was saved. He found the way of the Lord and gave up his old ways of drunkenness and waywardness. We too can do the same. We too can follow the way of Moses. Yes, my brothers and sisters, we can all be saved. Massa Winn took pity on him and brought him to Crooked Spring to convert us slaves. Moses has been our messenger from God. He taught us the redemption song which we can all sing now:

> *Shall we all go on in sin,*
> *Because Thy grace abounds,*
> *Or crucify the Lord again,*
> *And open all His wounds?* *

'The answer, my brothers and sisters, is no. We shall no longer live in sin, we shall no longer crucify the Lord. Why do I say this, my friends? I say this because the Lord's good grace abounds, it abounds eternal, abounds for you and for me because He loves us, my brethren. He is our Saviour, our King, our Massa.'

My voice was excited and more confident. I felt the Spirit, the Spirit of God and of the people before me. They were responding to my words, rocking their bodies back and forth, their white frocks swaying with the rhythm of the night. The chanting began:

> Praise be to Jesus,
> Hallelujah.

'Let us all sing what the Parson teach us:

> *We will be slaves no more,*
> *Since Christ has made us free,*
> *Has nailed our tyrants to the cross,*
> *And bought our liberty.*

'Before Brother Gardner talk to you, I want to tell you bout a vision I had. Yes, my brothers and sisters, I had a vision. I had a calling from the Lord. Praise be to His holy name. I was driven down into the deepest pit of hell where the flames consume the body and spirit. I was swallowed by a lake burning with fire and brimstone. In my darkness, I saw the souls of you, my friends, trapped in burning hell. I saw demons swallowing us and throwing us into the dark hole to be slaves forever. When I awoke, the Lord spoke to me and told me that I should not be afraid, that if I put faith in the Lord Jesus, He will free me. I said to the Lord, "Why me, Lord? I am just a slave, a wretched sinner." But an angel of the Lord appeared to me and I repented for my evil ways, my brothers. Yes, I repented for my evil ways, and the Lord blessed me and take me under his wing and he breathe the Spirit of God into me. I say to you tonight, my friends, that you too must repent of your bad ways and accept the Christ Jesus as your God. Massa tell we dat we is fi him slave but I am telling you tonight that this is false as hell. The Lord God create you and me just like him create buckra massa. No different. All the gold and silver of the world, the cows and the goats, the earth, the skies and the sea, all of this belong to the Supreme God, not to massa, not to busha. Don't look to the sun, the moon or the stars. They can't help you, for the God Almighty mek dem too. Look to God alone. He dwell right in your soul.'

Three women came forward and knelt down on the ground calling out for mercy, calling the name of Jesus.

'Give thanks, sisters. The Lord will never forsake you. Repent ye, confess to God that you are sinners, and be saved unto Him who is all-forgiving. Amen, amen, amen. Praise be to God.'

'Let us sing. Sing out loud for Massa kyaan trouble you. The Lord will protect you:

> *O shout, O shout, O shout away,*
> *And don't you mind,*
> *And glory, glory, glory in my soul!'* *

I stepped forward and sang out the verses:

> *And when 'twas night I thought 'twas day,*
> *I thought I'd pray my soul away,*
> *A glory, glory, glory in my soul!*

'Sing out the chorus:

> *O shout, O shout, O shout away,*
> *And don't you mind,*
> *And glory, glory, glory in my soul!*

'Let us shout glory unto God the whole night through so that we turn night into day. Blessed are those, my brethren, who have not seen yet believe.

> *Come in, Kind Saviour,*
> *No man can stop me.*
> *Walk in, sweet Jesus,*
> *No man can stop me.*
> *See the wonders Jesus done*
> *O no man can stop me.* *

'Jesus is our second Moses. Let us pray.' Some bowed their heads in reverence. Others raised both their arms in the air, swinging their bodies back and forth. 'Oh, Jesus, You will lead us out of Israel to the new Kingdom of God, You will free us from our bondage. Oh, Lord, look down on us poor people and give us the strength to believe in Your name:

> Jesus, you is fi we Massa.
> And the Lord said unto Moses,

I am the God of thy father,
I am the God of Abraham,
The God of Isaac.

'Oh Lord,

And you said unto Moses,
I am come down to deliver,
deliver them out of Egypt.

'And

The Lord said unto Moses,
I shall bring them unto a good land,
a land full of milk and honey.

'Oh Lord,

And you said unto Moses,
I will send thee unto Pharaoh
so thou mayest bring forth my people.

'Oh Lord,

Here are your people,
the children of Israel.
Look down upon them
and bless them.
Oh, yes, Lord,
bless thy people.

'And

The Lord will deliver us
out of the land of Egypt.
Oh, yes!
The Lord will deliver us,

free us from massa chains
and lead us,
lead us to the land
of milk and honey.

'Let us sing praises to the Lord. Praise the Lord.'
And they shouted out in the night:

Praise the Lord.
'Praise the Lord, my brethren.'
Praise the Lord.

'The Israelites passed forty days and forty nights in the wilderness. We must believe in the Lord and He will rescue us from evil, deliver us from slavery. When you are baptized in Christ, then you tek Him, you tek de Lord as you Massa and leave busha fi do him own work. Jesus tell us in the Bible, Matthew, chapter 6, verse 24:

No man can serve two masters:
for either he will hate the one, and love the other;
or else he will hold to the one, and despise the other.
Ye cannot serve God and mammon.

'Praise the Lord, my brethren, for when we are baptized into Christ, we put on Christ, when we are baptized into Christ, there is neither Black man nor White man, slave nor freed man, male nor female, for we are all one in Christ Jesus.'
The drums started and the crowd swayed to the music. The bongo music rang out in the quiet of the night, reaching the hills and valleys of St James and beyond. We sang praises of freedom to the Lord, rocking our bodies and swinging our arms high above our heads. Nobody seemed to worry if buckra was going to hear the noise.

As the drums increased their tempo, the dancing became more frantic. We held on to the motion of the music and did not let it stop for fear the demon would come into our bodies. The rhythm would keep the evil ones at bay. So the joy lasted — it lasted until the drummers were satisfied that the devils were quieted and satisfied. The music could then stop and we could feel the presence of the Lord.

Gardner stepped up. He looked over the crowd in a commanding way, his voice strong and confident. 'Brethren, you have heard Brother Sharpe talk to you tonight of de truths that will set you free. Some of you have heard me preach before and me send you de same message, but me want to say one more thing to you, that you must be strong, that you must not. waver in your belief for there are many who will tempt you, who will tell you that you are a fool fi believe in Jesus. You mussi strong cause de White man is trickified and he will tell you that your lot is to be a slave, that you were born a slave and that you will be most happy dying a slave. But me tell you him is a lying raas, false as hell. You must believe in yuhself, you mussi strong and steadfast. You mus not waver. Him will tell you that if you talk freedom that him will cut out you tongue, that him will tie you up and flog you, but you mus not listen to him. Him want you to feel coward. Him want you to feel fraid. Him want you to be his slave forever. You must tell him sey dat we is all born in de same spirit of Christ and dat you will pray for him soul and the soul of him mistress.'

He raised his voice, 'If him try fi beat you, kneel dung and call on de name of de Lord, ask God to forgive him wickedness and start fi sing, sing praises to de Lord. Yes, sing praises to God, right in him face. Buckra don't like when we sing de Christian hymn dem. Him get vex. But you will see what will happen, you will see dat him will stop flog you for him will catch him own fraid, him know sey dat Christ is fi him God too, and him will get coward and think dat God goin' damn him to hell. So, be brave, my brothers and sisters, be strong. De time will come when we will fight fi we freedom. De time is not right yet, but God will tell us when Him ready. The Lord spoke to the prophet, Joshua, chapter 8, verse 1:

> *And the Lord said unto Joshua,*
> *Fear not, neither be thou dismayed:*
> *take all the people of war with thee,*
> *and arise, go up to Ai:*
> *see, I have given into thy hand the king of Ai,*
> *and his people and his city, and his land.*

'De time will come, brothers and sisters, when we will speak wid one voice, we will tell buckra dat enough is enough and we will be slaves no more, dat we have de birthright just like de buckra dem, to be free, to walk de land, to own de land, to work fi an honest wage, not to toil in de hot sun like de horse and de ox under threat of de cart whip. De time will come, my brethren, when we shall tek no more. We will stop wuk, you will see, we will rise up and tek what is rightfully ours.'

Gardner's words alarmed and confused the people. They became silent, not knowing how to respond. They did not know whether he was preaching the Christian message or if he was telling them to disobey their masters and rise up against them. They were not sure what connection one had to the other.

But the drums played on into the night and soon everybody made merry. Helpers brought food and we feasted on roast goat, rice and green banana. We gathered banana leaves, split them into squares to use as plates and served food for all to have. When bellies were full, some people lay down and fell

223

asleep under the cotton tree. Others walked through the night to the safety of the slave villages.

April 1826

'I have been very ill, Sam. I also fear for the health of Mrs Burchell and of our newborn son.' Mr Burchell had called me aside one Sabbath after service in the Bay. His face was white like chalk, his cheeks so hollow that his jawbones stuck out from his face.

'God will tek care of everything, Minister.'

'I know it is God's will that I serve my people here, but I must return to England now to seek medical help. I shall return for there is much left to be done.'

'Whole heap of people waan to join the church, Mr Burchell.'

'I know this, and your mission in converting souls to Christ has been remarkable. My church must have 800 members now.'

'It's cause you talk bout freedom, Massa.'

'I have promised them nothing, Sam. I talk the gospel of Jesus Christ. I feel a great attachment to the people at the Bay church, and I feel honoured that the Lord has chosen me to be his instrument for gathering them here.'

'They love you too, Minister.'

'I am so much aware of this, Sam. The affection they show me is so strong that I know not how to repay it.' Tears came to his eyes.

'They expect nothing in return, Massa.'

'You understand that it is with mixed emotion that I depart. They will need careful attention when I am gone and this is why I should like to ask you to preach in my church when I am in England.'

'It would be a great honour, Sir.'

'I can continue no longer, Sam. I suffer from an inflammation of the lungs. The doctors have bled me and still I experience the most dreadful convulsions in the night. I have requested that two ministers be sent out from England to continue my work, but I have not yet received an answer.'

'I will do your work, Parson.'

'And I trust that you will do it well. You will be Parson Sam. But you must promise me to be careful. I have been more than once castigated by Mr Coates for baptizing Negroes without the permission of their owners and for allowing you and others to hold night meetings.'

'We can take care of things, Sir. You don't worry yourself.'

'You must be especially careful about the interference of Mr Coates. He is particularly adverse to the practices of the Baptist Church.'

'Cause they don't want us to be free, Parson.'

'They know slavery to be wrong, Sam, but they are protecting their way of life.'

'I don't think they all think it wrong, Mr Burchell.'

'You must be careful. Mr Coates has informed me that he will dispatch constables to apprehend any slaves who are about earlier than five o'clock in the morning or after six o'clock at night.'

'As I tell you, Parson, we will take care of everything, Sir.'

'It is especially dangerous if he learns of your preaching, for he has requested that I expel from the church all Negro elders and teachers. The magistrates have treated me with the utmost scorn, paying little or no attention to what I have to say in defence of our mission.'

'The Lord will be the final judge, Mr Burchell.'

'You offer much comfort with your words of faith, Sam. Yet, I did not expect to find this hatred and persecution from my fellow countrymen. Members of our congregation are being apprehended on their way home from service and are being sentenced to the workhouse on the pretence that they are runaways.'

'Not to worry yourself, Parson. You tell us yourself that the Gospel is "the power of God unto salvation."'

'You are called by God, Sam, to do good works. Your faith is strong.'

'You help us with the faith, Parson. The people call you Massa Missionary. You are their friend. They say they will follow you because the Good Spirit is with you.'

'They will follow you too, Sam. You will have the assistance of Brother Mann who will be in charge of the mission while I am away.'

'I will continue your good work while you are in England. I shall do as you ask, Sir, for I believe it is God's will.'

'My fear is that when the shepherd is gone, the flock will suffer.'

'The Chief Shepherd is always near, Mr Burchell. Massa Minister leave us but Massa Christ stay with us. Poor nega weak, but Christ all strong.'

'And God willing, I shall return strong and healthy from England with Mrs Burchell and my son to continue His work in this heathen land.'

'We will tek care of everything, Parson. You don't worry yourself.'

EIGHTEEN

December 1826

The Good News of the gospel spread throughout the Great River Valley. The head slaves on the estates held secret prayer meetings at night and the people sang freedom songs to the Lord. The time was soon coming for us to see a new day, to come out of the darkness of Egypt into the light of the land of Canaan.

The magistrates and their friends continued to wage war against the Baptists, but this did not stop me from preaching God's Word and from baptizing the faithful. Mr Burchell had asked me to continue his work while he was in England, and no one, not even Mr Coates, was going to prevent that. Under the supervision of Brother Mann, I held service every other week at Flamstead and on alternate Sundays I preached in the Bay. From the surrounding districts and parishes, the slaves came in the hundreds to hear Jesus' message. Talk of the Black preacher, Sam, was all bout:

'Parson Burchell tek sick and him go back a England.'
'Me know, and him put Parson Sam in him place.'
'Iin-hiin, and me yerry say him preach good, you see.'
'Him tell we sey Massa Christ will set we free.'
'Iin-hiin, and me yerry sey him talk wid de spirit.'
'And him have a vision inna de night-time.'
'Iin-hiin, and de white angel a come talk to him.'
'Say him is de chosen one.'
'What a ting. What a jubilation.'

'Lawd, me haffi go dung a de Bay fi hear him.'
'Yes, man. Inna de bush dem a call him Daddy.'
'So me hear. Dem a call him Daddy Sharpe.'
'Iin-hiin, him is de shepherd of de flock.'
'Him will lead we out of slavery.'
'Come, let we tell everybody sey dem should a go dung a de Bay.'
'Yes, man, fi yerry Daddy Sharpe a talk bout Massa Christ.'
'Let we go dung a de Bay and sing de song him teach we:

> *We will be slaves no more*
> *Since Christ has made us free,*
> *Has nailed our tyrants to the cross*
> *and bought our liberty.'*

One Sabbath in December when I was concluding the service, two White constables barged their way right into the Baptist church in Montego Bay. They did not even let me finish the prayer I was saying. They grabbed me, one on each side, and pulled me out into the street. They were tall blond men dressed in uniform and carrying long muskets at their sides.

'Are you not the slave they call Daddy Sharpe?'

'My name is Samuel Sharpe.'

One was holding both my hands behind my back and the other was so close in front that I felt his spit on my face when he spoke.

They led me to a small room in the gaol house where I remained in chains for a long while. The two constables returned with a short White gentleman dressed in formal wear, a waistcoat, neckcloth, pantaloons, fancy stockings and shoes with large brass buckles. His nose was long and pointed and his eyes slit as if he was straining to look. I remembered him to be Mr Coates, a visitor to Miss Mary's tavern.

'I believe you to be Mr Coates, Sir.'

'Don't be an impudent ass. You wait to be summoned to speak before uttering a word. Do you hear me?'

'Yes, Sir.' I held my head down and dared not look at him.

'You are Samuel Sharpe, property of Mr Gray, slave at Croydon Estate.'

'I believe Mr Samuel Sharpe is my rightful owner, Sir.'

'Are you not the head slave at Croydon Estate?'

'I am one of three, Sir.'

'Are you a teacher in the Baptist church of Mr Burchell?'

'I teach the Good News of Jesus Christ.'

'You imbecile. Do not blaspheme in my presence or I shall have you flogged and put in the workhouse. Who appointed you teacher in the Baptist church?'

'I appoint myself teacher of the Gospel, Sir.'

'Did not the minister appoint you as a leader of his church?'

'I take my direction from God alone, Sir.'

'You are mad and I should have you hanged and quartered.'

'Beg you pardon, Sir. What is my offence?'

'You are a wretched slave and you have no authority in this land to preach the Gospel.'

'The Good Shepherd came to let all in through the door, Sir. He knows His sheep, and those who are not of His fold. He will bring them in and they will hear His voice too, and there will be one fold and one Shepherd.'

'Take this lunatic out of my sight. If you are found about the streets in the dark or found to be preaching in the churches, you shall be apprehended, flogged until your back is raw, and sentenced to six months' hard labour in the workhouse.'

Some say that backra is a good name for the White man because he clap us so hard with the whip that our back turn raw.

That was not to be my last encounter with Mr John Coates.

~

Mr Burchell returned to Jamaica on December 16th of that same year. I met him and his wife at the wharves and assisted them by loading and carrying their luggage to the mission. He came back with his health restored, but he and his wife, Miss Lusty, were low in spirits.

'Sam, I lost my little boy while in England. He died of the croup. He was the specimen of health at birth, such a robust infant boy, but I fear that the medicines the doctors so lavishly administered to him in Jamaica weakened his constitution. Mrs Burchell is beside herself. We do not understand the workings of Divine Providence which has chosen for us the loss of our only offspring. He was a darling boy, and with each day, the remembrance of him increases, not fades. The Lord tests us in mysterious ways, Sam.'

The minister brought back news from England about how people there were fighting for the cause of our freedom. He also shared with me letters written to friends in Jamaica by members of the British Parliament. These were printed in the *Jamaica Gazette*:

> You will observe that in the whole course of these debates there is not one person who did not admit the extinction of slavery to be the whole object of parliament and the country — an object which they were determined to accomplish, and that the only difference was as to the means and time of its accomplishment.*

It was comforting to know that in England there were White people who were our friends. Parson Burchell said they argued back and forth among themselves in Parliament. Some did not want to see slavery end, but most agreed that the time was soon coming for everybody to find a way to free us with the least amount of disruption to the planters' way of life. News of this discourse spread fast through the slave population. Domestic slaves stole newspapers from the Great Houses and those of us who attended church received our membership ticket wrapped in a piece of English newspaper.

The buckra massa in Jamaica did not like what was going on in England. They also hated the White missionaries who were preaching the gospel to us. They posted and read proclamations in the public square in Montego Bay so all could know that the slave laws in Jamaica were not going to change:

Let it be known that the slave laws of Jamaica will be reenacted, as passed by the House of Assembly. Slaves found preaching and teaching without permission from their owner shall be punished by whipping or imprisonment. No sectarian minister or other minister of religion shall keep open his place of meeting between sun-set and sun-rise. Religious teachers taking money from slaves shall pay a penalty of twenty pounds for each offence, and in default of payment, be committed to the common gaol for a month.*

None of this stopped Mr Burchell. He was fearless. He continued to have public collections at services even though he was at great risk of being discovered by the constables. He used the money he collected from the slaves to make benches for the church and to repair the roof. He said that he refused to obey a law which was aimed at persecuting a few men who had come to Jamaica to spread the Good News of Jesus Christ. The magistrates called the parson several times to a meeting at the courthouse to scold him for his practices. Mr Coates and another member of the Assembly, his good friend Mr Grignon, accused the minister of prostituting young slave girls in order to get money for his church. Mr Burchell was outraged. He explained to the magistrates that the slaves gave money willingly, but Mr Grignon was vexed and did not believe him. He told the minister that he and his religious brothers were not welcome in Jamaica any more:

> *You have intruded yourselves on the island, unsolicited and unwelcomed. So long as you proceed on your own resources, you are licensed on the principle of toleration; but we have passed this law, that you may not raise an income here for carrying on your purposes, and to prevent your further increase amongst us.* *

The magistrates kept summoning Mr Burchell to meetings, but nothing stopped the minister from doing the work he knew he was called to do.

The authorities continued their harassment of the mission churches. On Christmas Day, a group of drunken militiamen stormed into a Wesleyan chapel in the Parish of St Ann to drive the worshippers out. They rode their horses into the church building during the celebration of the Last Supper and told the parson that the horses would like to receive Holy Communion. When the minister refused to cooperate, a militiaman dismounted, grabbed the sacred Hosts and proceeded to feed them to his horse. '*If these wretches can come to the table of the Lord, so can my Spanish stallion.*' The slaves were frightened by the presence of the soldiers and their horses in the House of Prayer. The congregation quickly fled, leaving the parson standing alone at the altar. The men in red uniform then left, laughing and drinking the glasses of grog they had brought with them. The rumour was that a Reverend, Mr Bridges, was so vexed with the sectarian ministers that he had ordered the militia to storm the chapel.

This reverend was the rector, the chief Anglican priest of the Parish of St Ann.

~

I met Nyame down by our favourite place at the Montego River. She brought the baby and bathed her naked in the cool water. It was February month. The African Tulips were in full bloom.

'De preaching ting gwine get you in trouble, Sam.' She sat on a rock with Juba between her legs.

I was standing near to them beside the river edge. 'How you mean?'

'Too much reading of the Bible confuse up yuh head.' She looked up at me, half smiling.

'Me have no choice, Nyame.'

'Don't tell me foolishness, Sam. You can give it up any time you want.' She looked down and away from me, gently pouring water over the baby's head.

'It not so simple.'

'Is you mek it confusing. If you continue with de preaching, dem gwine beat you and lock you up.'

'Then dem will haffi do that cause I not stopping.'

'Why man so fool-fool I would nebba know in me whole lifetime.'

'I haffi do it, Nyame. God call me fi free de people.'

'Sam, you don't hear what me saying to you. Dem gwine shoot you dung before you can do dat. You have a girl pickney now. You mus get some sense inna yuh head.' She raised her voice and the baby started to cry. 'Sh, sh, hush baby, hush. Even de baby know sey you nah have no sense.' She lifted Juba out of the water, wrapped her in a cotton cloth and snuggled her to her breasts.

'Me waan you fi marry me, Nyame.'

'Then you mus act like a husband.'

'Me doing it so we can be free from de stinking slavery. Me waan fi tek you as me lawful wife and me waan give Juba a home she can call her own, so when she grow big, she can be proud of herself. Don't ask me fi stop, though, Nyame. A beg you, me waan fi go forward.'

'Then how me gwine sure you will be safe? Dem gwine kill you, Sam, if you don't careful.'

'We mus tek de chance.'

I hugged her close to me, feeling the warmth of her breasts. We both held the baby tight, rocking our bodies as silent as we could.

Nyame looked at the baby. 'She pretty, eh?'

'Yes. Me told you she look sweet like you.'

'De massa say dat Juba is not a proper name. Me mus call her Catherine.'

'Why Catherine?'

'Him say is fi him mada name.'

'What him mada haffi do wid it?'

'Me nah know, Sam.'

'We will call her Juba.'

'Me don't have a good feeling, Sam.'

'Don't fret yuhself. Everything will go fine.'

~

After a prayer meeting in the bush one Sabbath, I met with six of the native church leaders deep in a large cave upriver from the water mill on Belvidere Estate. The time was ripe for action, for us to start planning for our freedom. Dove, head driver on the plantation, was in charge of guarding the entrance. He sat on a rock close to the mouth of the cave with a machete under his right thigh. Six of us sat on the damp ground in the interior which was brightly lit with torches: Gardner, head waggoner from Greenwich Estate, Johnson from Retrieve, Reid from Cambridge, Tharpe from Catadupa, and Taylor, a saddler from the Bay. All men except Taylor were head slaves on the Great River estates.

Gardner spoke in his confident way. 'Me preaching at Greenwich, me preaching at Seven Rivers and Hazelymph and de people coming in numbers so big me feel de buckra gwine find out and punish de whole of we.'

'Dem a tek in de Christian message.' Johnson was a close ally of Gardner. Both men were strong and fearless.

'And de time soon come when dem gwine look for more than dat.' Gardner drew a line in the dirt with a stick.

'Me wanted fi we to talk tonight, brothers.' I looked across at the five men, their shadows flickering on the walls of the cave. Dove was within earshot, still guarding the entrance. I felt the night was dangerous with buckra's spies searching about.

'It's good you bring we together, Daddy Sharpe.' Reid sat next to me. He was a burly man and a very strict slave-driver. The other two, Taylor and Tharpe, nodded in agreement. Taylor was quieter, a religious man who was a member of Minister Burchell's church in the Bay. Tharpe was a Daddy also — Father Tharpe we called him — an excellent preacher with a bold presence.

Dove moved in from the entrance of the cave to join us for a short while. 'As long as you not gwine preach to we, Sam.' Dove did his own preaching with a group of slaves on Belvidere Estate but he was a man of few words and acted miserable most of the time.

'All of we are good preachers. We learn good from Moses

Baker and Parson Burchell.' I spoke earnestly. 'We all have a calling fi spread de Good News of Massa Christ. Jesus want us fi free our brothers and sisters from slavery.'

Taylor kept his head down when he spoke. 'How we gwine do dat, Sam? The seven of we and de whole of Jamaica inna slavery.'

'We haffi start somewhere, Brother Taylor.' I had to make sure that the men did not give too many excuses.

Gardner looked straight at me. 'We can go all bout de place and tell de people of de Good News. They will listen to we. A know dat fi sure.'

'All of we here except Brother Taylor is a head driver. So, if each of we visit different estates and talk to de driver, then him can call de slaves dung to a prayer meeting in de Bay, then. . .'

'Then de word will spread far and wide,' Johnson finished off my words for me.

Then each man took turns speaking as if in a prayer.

'And we will give power to de people,' Gardner said.

'And Jesus will become fi we massa,' Tharpe said.

'And de buckra will haffi run go weh,' Reid said.

'Cause we kyaan serve two massa, jus one,' Taylor said.

Dove spoke up. 'And who gwine keep watch so we don't all get kill?'

'Why you ask a fool-fool question like dat, Dove? Thomas Dove, of course, gwine keep watch.' Gardner picked up some dirt from the cave floor and threw it at Dove.

Dove raised his machete and swished the air with it. 'Watch you raas mouth.'

'So that is the plan.' I wanted to put a close to the meeting. 'We will reach about fifty estates through St James, Hanover, Westmoreland, St Elizabeth and Trelawney.'

I saw Dove pull a bottle of rum from a bag he had hidden in the cave.

We all stayed back for a while, chatting and joking late into the night.

NINETEEN

April 18th, 1832

Mr Bleby sits in his spot on a chair under the prison window. He has visited me in prison a couple of times, curious about the content of my diaries and about my views of the slave rebellion. He has a deep sympathy for our cause and a genuine distaste for Mr Grignon, and Reverend Bridges whom he finds rude and boasy. Nevertheless, he is of the opinion that whatever attempt we may have made to resist the authorities would have ended in disaster. He may be right, but he is wrong when he tells me that I should await patiently the time when the Lord will bring about a change in our condition. He thinks we slaves were deluded, that we believed false information and became the pathetic victims of wild rumours.

'You continue to write your daily memoirs, Sam?' He speaks to me like I am a pickaninny.

'Yes, Minister.'

'Have you completed some chapters which you may want to share with me?'

'Yes, Minister. You may read these.' I hand him a batch of papers.

'I shall treasure them, Sam. You have not yet written of the actual rebellion, but tell me, Sam, you and the rebels set fire to expensive buildings. Did you not?' He speaks in an accusing way.

'The whole thing got out of control, Minister. You know this.'

'Indeed, it did.'

'We wanted a peaceful stoppage to work.'

'And Mr Knibb tried to explain to you that this would not work. I met also with my congregation to dissuade them from this madness.'

'Yes, but it was too late. Everything was too late. We were very angry by then. Nothing you or Parson Knibb said could have stop it.'

'What made it worse was that the rebels gained momentum because the planters went into a panic.'

'They were afraid, Sir, and so they should have been, slaves rising up with machete and gun and burning trash houses. The planters gave us an advantage by leaving their estates. Some of us thought the buckra leave Jamaica in the hands of the Black people.'

'You did not really believe that, Sam?'

'It seemed that way, Minister. There was no way of telling. Not a White man in sight anywhere. Pure freedom.'

'That is not freedom, Sam. You destroyed everything in your tracks. Some Negroes told me they were threatened with their life if they chose not to join the rebellion. Is this true?'

'People went mad, Minister. It was the taste of freedom.'

'Mayhem.' He moves nervously on his seat.

'Call it what you want, Sir. We thought we broke the chains, Sir, and that felt sweet.'

He looks over at me in an inquiring way. 'It did not seem to be an organized revolt.'

'We did not intend to revolt, Mr Bleby. That is why.'

'But many had weapons and seemed prepared to fight. Did they not?'

I hate when he asks "Did you not? Did they not?" It is as if I have no choice but to agree with him.

'Yes, but they got a lot of the weapons after the burning started. We were not organized, Minister Bleby.'

'How did you feel, Sam, when all this was happening?'

'Hopeless. My plan had gone wrong. I prayed and asked the people to pray but that was useless.'

'There were many atrocities, Sam.'

'I know and I repent for those.'

'Did you really believe that freedom was coming?' He asks it in such a way that I should answer, "Of course not, Minister Bleby".

'Yes, Sir, from what I read and heard, the government was holding back.'

'Do you bear the responsibility, Sam? You spread the word far and wide. You brought newspapers up from the Bay and read them to the people and they believed what you told them.'

'Yes, because I was telling them the truth, Minister.'

'It was not entirely true, Sam. You know that.'

I do not understand this man. He is telling me what I know and what I do not know.

'I did not trick the people, Sir.'

'I spoke with Gardner in gaol before his execution.' He shifts his body again in the chair.

'How was his state of mind, Minister?' I feel as if he is trying to make me feel the full weight of my guilt.

'He wanted for his life to be spared. He said that you were the director of the whole rebellion.'

'I have never denied that, Sir, not once.'

'And that you had every man take an oath that he should fight and do his utmost to drive the White man out of Jamaica. Your plan, he said, was to have a governor appointed for each parish.'

'Before you make a judgement, Mr Bleby, you needed to be

there yourself when I spoke to the people.'
'Surely you must have known, Sam.'
He expects me to guess the thought he has in his head.
'Known what, Minister?'
'That the King was not going to send you freedom?'
'To be honest, I was not sure, Sir. It seemed to me that he was. I know from everything I read in the papers that Jamaica was holding back the free paper from us.'
'Parson Burchell left for England before the rebellion. Did he not?'
'Yes, Sir, in the month of May.'
'This must have given you some freedom to do what you wanted, Sam.'
I feel he is scolding me now.
'Remember, Mr Bleby, I am a slave, not a freed man.'
'Tomorrow is your trial, Sam.'
'Will there be anyone arguing in my defence?'
'I have not been privy to any information. Are you aware that the authorities have punished the missionaries?'
'Yes, I know of this.' I am tired of his questions. I feel he is attacking me and pushing me to say things I don't want to.
'They jailed Mr Knibb, Mr Burchell and others.'
'Yes, I know. Some were calling it the Baptist War.'
'Which is hideous, for the Baptists did not cause it.' He is quick to defend Messrs Burchell and Knibb.
'I not blaming the ministers, Sir. Many slaves who organized and fought the battle were Baptists.'
He looks away from me but I see a slight smirk on his face.
'We were concerned. The authorities were promising slaves their freedom if they would testify against us in the courts.'
'They would not betray you, Minister.'
'Most have not.'
'The magistrates would order them to be hanged anyway,

Minister, so what would be the use?'

'Regardless, as Christians, we must always tell the truth.'

'I always tell the truth, Sir, but I don't think they going to let me talk in court.'

'In a court of law, the defendant has the right to speak.'

'That is if you White, Mr Bleby.'

'Even if you are not. You need not to be concerned or afraid.'

'I'm not sure of that. How many slaves you think they bribe to talk gainst me, Minister?'

'There will be witnesses for the prosecution, Sam, but I do not know of any bribery.'

'If any of my friends, who swear with me that night at Tucker's house, are at court tomorrow, they will not go against me, Mr Bleby. I know that.'

'The charges are serious, Sam, and the penalty is death by hanging.'

'But dem will heng me anyway, Sar, whether me tell dem de trut or not.'

'We must always tell the truth, Sam.' He pronounces every word carefully as if he wants to correct my speech.

'I know that if it happens tomorrow that they testify against me, it mean that the buckra did threaten them. We swear, Minister, we swear on the Bible to keep together as one.'

He uses a scolding voice. 'But these are false oaths, Sam.'

'Not to me, Sir, and not to them.'

'May God be with you, tomorrow, Sam, and let His will be done.'

'That is all we can ask for, Mr Bleby. May the good Lord bless you and keep you.'

He calls for the guard, picks up my sheets of paper and gives me a blessing.

1828

My preaching of the Word spread through the countryside. Three days a week I visited estates and held prayer meetings in the slave villages. Many followed up with my invitation to come to service on the Sabbath at the Baptist church in Montego Bay. Minister Burchell was delighted at the new inquirers who sought membership in his church. He continued to be very strict about admitting converts, just like he had been with Nyame and me. They had to profess a deep faith in Jesus Christ and receive recommendations from other members about their good character before they could be received into the fold. With each passing day, I felt the rewards of living a righteous life. It made me feel happy in my soul and it gave me a sense of hope that freedom from slavery would come one day soon. Our new Massa was a just God who shed His blood to deliver us from evil.

My joy became complete when Nyame agreed to marry me. The marriage was a promise I could make to her that I would not lust after no other woman and that our flesh would become one through the love of Jesus. We made a solemn vow to live a sacred life in union with each other. Nyame made her own personal pledge to love me, but she was not sure about the Christian part of it.

Mr Burchell was supposed to ask permission from our owners if he could marry us but he never bothered with that. He just went ahead and did it. We married one bright Sunday morning in the month of December in the Baptist chapel in the Bay. Mr Burchell asked us, and another minister who served as witness, to hold back after the eleven o'clock morning service. He had prepared a bouquet of white Christmas flowers which he gave Nyame to hold. He placed a short white veil on her head and asked her to kneel with me before the altar.

There we exchanged our vows to love one another till death do us part. My young bride looked like an angel of God. She smiled so sweet, making her face shine bright. God bless Parson Burchell for bestowing such holiness on us.

~

I first met Mr William Knibb at the Baptist Mission the same year I married, 1828. He was a very good Baptist friend of Minister Burchell.

He had originally come to Jamaica as a schoolteacher to take the place of his brother, who died after spending only a few months in Kingston. Minister Knibb was a good-hearted man who loved us slaves with a true feeling. His sympathy drew us Negroes close to him. His eyes were warm and kind. His skin was white like Mr Burchell's, his hands slender and his nose pointed the same way. Some said that even though he was White he had the heart of a Black man.

He resided in a place out of parish called Ridgeland but he visited these parts often.

'The souls are countless, Thomas. In my travels through Rio Bueno, Stewart Town, and Falmouth, I count close to 5,000 who want to hear the word of God.'

'The latest reports say that with our nine Baptist missionaries we have converted over 12,000 souls. The calling is great indeed, and so rewarding.' Mr Burchell had a more positive tone in his voice.

'The statements from the committee of inquiry are blasphemous and damning.' Mr Knibb's voice was angry.

'Is this the inquiry instituted by the Assembly?'

'There is madness in the land, Thomas. Reverend Bridges says that we prey on the unstable minds of ignorant Negroes.

Reports are that our principal object on the island is to extort money from our congregations, that we preach sedition from the pulpit, and that we are the cause of the general unrest among the slaves.'

'There is such deceit and mistrust, William, a distortion of our true intentions to preach the Christian message.'

'They believe our motive to be that of public mischief, which is preposterous.' Mr Knibb's complexion turned pale and he became wobbly on his feet as if he was about to faint.

'Is anything the matter? Would you care to sit?'

'It must be the infernal heat, Thomas. I have noticed I have not been in best of health of late. Perhaps if I take up residence on the north shore of the island, my health would improve. I fear sometimes that I will have three orphans before the year is out if I do not take care of my health.' He held on to a chair to prevent himself from falling. The main room at the Baptist mission was simply furnished, with a few chairs and a table for eating.

'Do have a seat, William. May I offer you a cup of tea?'

'Thank you, no. I must soon prepare to return to Ridgeland.'

'The Lord will spare your life as long as it is His will that you bring new souls to him. We will not stop, William. We have fervent believers like our class leader here, Samuel Sharpe, who would never surrender his Christian faith. We are growing in numbers, William. The missions as you mentioned are thriving, in Rio Bueno, Stewart Town, Falmouth, Lucea, Savannah-la-Mar and Ridgeland. Every week we are increasing the numbers of those baptized at Crooked Spring and at the Bay. On the Sabbath we now have 2,000 and more coming to worship in the Bay. We have so many inquirers that it is not possible to meet the demands of the ministry even with the assistance of our class leaders.'

Mr Knibb looked over at me when Minister Burchell mentioned my name but I do not think I made a lasting impression upon him. In the years following, he denied to the authorities any knowledge of or familiarity with me.

'Congratulations, Thomas, to you and Lusty on the birth of your daughter.'

Mr Knibb began to speak in a more spirited way.

'Thank you, Sir. We were delighted in her safe delivery and I dare say she has repaired some of the losses we suffered from the death of our little boy.'

Mr Knibb suddenly seemed distracted. 'It never ceases to amaze me what a pleasant aspect the kingdom of Satan has. This land of Jamaica is so beautiful with its hillocks and pastures, so reminiscent of the parks in England.'

'It is God's Kingdom, William, not Satan's.'

'So much toil, my dear Thomas. The good Lord is testing our faith to the utmost.'

'And this is good.' It seemed Minister Burchell was trying to lift his spirits.

'It is difficult to spread the Gospel in these times of unrest. The slaves are anxious. One of yours told me that "free paper was come" and when I asked him what made him think so, he said that Massa is flogging him every day now because he would soon be free and have no more master. I tried to tell him that Massa was not telling him the truth.'

'I doubt whether the slaves trust their masters' word anyway.' Mr Burchell smiled in a cunning way.

'But, Thomas, the slaves do believe that King William is sending them their free papers. Who is driving these ideas into their heads?'

'Details of the abolitionist movement are widely known, William. Word spreads very fast from master to slave and from one slave to the next. The messages may become distorted.'

'In the meantime, flogging and imprisonment are rampant. One slave owner I know flogged his slaves because they did not want to buy and sell in the market on the Sabbath. We have followers of Christ forbidden to go to worship. We need some direction on these matters, Thomas. I have written to the authorities for some advice.'

'The only way is to stand by our beliefs, William. There is no other way.'

'Are you familiar with the column by Dorcas in the *Jamaica Courant*, his tirades against me and other ministers of religion?'

'Yes, indeed, it is said that he is none other than the rector of St Ann's, the Reverend Mr Bridges.'

'The bush daddies are not helping our cause either. Slaves who have been expelled from my ministry have started their own congregations and are preaching freedom to their followers. I believe these Black Baptists hate us as much as the planters do.'

'This is not altogether true, William. What say you, Daddy Sharpe?' Mr Burchell looked over at me but I did not think it my place to respond. 'Here in St James I have church leaders who are preaching an orthodox message of Christianity. The mission is large, Brother Knibb. We have a distance of some 80 miles between stations. Perhaps you would consider joining us. Your faith and goodwill could bring salvation to many.'

~

Mr Burchell's wishes came true, because before long, he had new parsons ministering close to Montego Bay. Mr Knibb moved to Falmouth in 1829 after the death of Mr Mann, who had taken ill with fever. Mr Burchell's good friend, a Presbyterian minister by the name of Waddell, also set up a church nearby in Hampden. The new parson was afraid when he first arrived in the island. He told Mr Burchell that people called Jamaica 'hell upon earth' and that when White people came here they abandoned all religion to live a life of badness. Mr Burchell told him there was some truth to his statement but not all of Jamaica was like that.

The Waddells resided near to Rose Hall on Cornwall Estate. The proprietor, Mr Samuel Barrett, showed kindness to the family when they first arrived by providing shelter for them in the overseer's house on a neighbouring property. The Barretts were unlike other buckras because they refused to use the cart whip on their slaves. They were good friends of the missionaries and came to their assistance during hard times.

When I visited Reverend Waddell's mission, he told me of his trials adjusting to life in Jamaica. He had problems transporting his worldly belongings from the Port of Falmouth when he arrived by ship. The wharfinger charged him hefty fees which were more than the worth of his belongings, and to make matters worse, when he hired a cattle cart to carry his effects to his new home, the driver made at least ten stops along the road. At each checkpoint, the minister was required to pay a tariff master. His residence was only a short distance of twelve miles from Falmouth Bay but by the time Reverend Waddell reached his destination he was practically out of money.

'Tradesmen in Jamaica make a good living, Minister.'

He became flushed in the face. 'It is not an honest living. It is extortion and robbery.'

'They make a living off welcoming *trusting* buckra from England, Minister. Dem is jinal, Sir.'

'I am not sure I fully understand, but I do know that my wife and I have been swindled.'

'So it goes in Jamaica sometime, Minister.'

Despite his initial setbacks, Reverend Waddell was eager to make his home a place of worship. On the first Sabbath, he stepped outside into his yard and began to ring a loud cowbell to signal people to come out for service. Seeing no response, he descended the hill and proceeded into areas where the Negro houses were, all this time carrying and sounding the big bell. He had even cleared the furniture from out of his house to accommodate a large number of worshippers but his efforts were of no use.

'Sundays in Jamaica, Minister, are days for us to tend to our provision grounds and to foodstuffs at the market.'

'But I am told thousands show for service in the Bay.'

'They will come to know you, Minister.'

Very few assembled that first day of worship. Those who gathered were the old, the sick and the blind. He administered to them and I am sure the Lord blessed him for his good works.

Reverend Waddell was patient and his mission grew almost as big as the Baptists'. He spent five days of the week visiting the surrounding estates and preaching the Word of God. He did this at shell-blow and in the evenings at dinner time. After long days in the field during crop time, hundreds flocked to his house where his family held reading classes for slaves. Young and old sat at tables, and when they became sleepy, they rested on the floor, only to waken again for more schooling.

Reverend Waddell asked me to assist him and his wife. We sat for many hours, reading and repeating phrases from the Bible until such time as the faithful began to see and understand the words on the written pages. Many of Moses Baker's followers came too, anxious to learn to read about John the Baptist. The minister received warnings from neighbouring planters that it would be dangerous to teach the slaves to read, but he did not pay them any mind. He was a good minister.

The overseer's house soon became too small to hold the numbers of slaves, so the Waddells received permission to use the old Rose Hall Estate which was empty except for rats, rat-bats and owls. On the Sabbath, the main hall of the old Great House filled up with persons of every age and colour. The minister gave thanks to God that they could all worship under one roof. But the White people who attended the services did not take too kindly to his sermons. They told him that he brought mockery to the land because he preached equality between slaves and freed persons. Mr Barrett was the only one who encouraged the minister to preach the gospel, because he wanted his slaves to be taught discipline, for them to learn how to stop from carrying on bad, swearing, stealing and fighting.

Minister Waddell was shocked at the idea that the Negro slaves did not marry. He told them that if they committed themselves to a Christian path they would need to abandon their wayward ways.

Even his own personal slave, Ellis, did not understand. He was a young strong male, popular with the women.

'But what happen to me woman dem, Minister?' Ellis was downhearted.

'When you are married, you will choose to live with only one female for the rest of your life.'

'That not good, Minister. Me already have pickaninny from different woman.'

'Well then, you choose the oldest woman who bore you the first child, and you make her your wife.'

'No, Preacher, it kyann go so.'

'And why not so?' Minister Waddell was confused.

'Well, to tell you de truth, Preacher, most of we like de young woman dem.'

But the parson persevered in his teachings, and with time, after many sacrament classes, Ellis and his first woman, and other men and women alike, were converted to the new Christian ways. They embraced the Lord Jesus Christ and what seemed previously to be a tribulation was now a joyous sacrifice.

Ministers like Mr Waddell and others went about their work with such zeal and goodwill but they seemed to be ignoring what was really going on in the heart of the slave.

We wanted freedom.

I realized from reading the newspapers that the local government was telling us a whole lot of untruth. The *Royal Gazette* reported that the conditions of slaves were improving in countries which had adopted resolutions to prepare slaves for freedom. In some cases, the local officials were even pressuring for slaves to have the right to purchase their own freedom without the consent of their owner. Reports from Trinidad showed that the measures adopted by His Majesty's Government for the amelioration of slaves were being followed in the correct way. The Negroes were conducting themselves well and the planters were not complaining about them working fewer hours. In Jamaica, we saw nothing of these changes. The magistrates kept re-enacting the old slave laws, doing their best to harass the preachers and flog the slaves.

But the time was soon coming when all this must stop. The government in England was becoming impatient with local legislatures and we slaves were growing anxious for our free paper.

In May of 1830, Minister Burchell told me that the Anti-Slavery Society in England had put forward a proposal for immediate emancipation. It was not long after this that word spread in every hill and valley in Jamaica that the King was preparing the free paper, and that the buckra in Jamaica was intending to hold it back from us.

TWENTY

April 19th, 1832

I recognized Mr Coates as soon as I entered the courtroom
even though he was dressed like a court judge with a strange
wig on. Two other men, dressed just like Mr Coates, were

252

seated next to him at the front of the room. I learned their names to be Mr Downer and Mr Plummer. To one side on three benches sat twelve White men who were introduced as the jury. The clerk read the names out loud. I recall the first few: Thomas Coy, William Tinkler, Hugh Perry, Joseph Gill Jump. For the prosecution, there were several slave witnesses, most of whom I recognized: Joe Martin, a mulatto, and Robert Rose, a Negro, both from Cambridge Estate; Edward Barrett, a mulatto from Seven Rivers; Edward Hilton from Mountain Spring; John Davis from Westmoreland; and another Negro slave, James Clarke.

Two slaves, George Reid from Cambridge and Ann Thomas from Ginger Hill, were present for my defence. They sat on the left-hand side of the room behind me. I was surprised by the number of slave witnesses, because I believed that their testimonies, until very recently, were of no use in court proceedings. The slaves' owners and other buckra, including Mr Grignon, were also present. I was looking for more familiar faces but I could see none. My owner, Mr Sharpe Esquire, was not there and neither was Mr Knibb nor Mr Bleby. And no family was there, but that was to be expected. Owners do not like having too many family members of slaves together in the same room even in regular time, much less during a trial.

Two guards sat me down on a chair facing the three men in wigs. My hands were in chains and I was dressed in prison clothes. They did not clean me up for the trial. The two White men stood on either side of me, each with a musket clutched to his right side. They must have thought I would try to escape. Mr Coates instructed one of the guards to bring me to the bench. I was told to place my right hand on the Bible and swear to tell the truth, the whole truth and nothing but the truth. Mr Coates bobbed his head like a lizard, his slit eyes flicking from side to side. The reading of the charges began this way:

> At a Special Slave Court held at the Court House in the Town of Montego Bay in and for the parish of Saint James in the said Island, the Nineteenth day of April in the second Year Reign of our Sovereign Lord William the fourth by the Grace of God of the United Kingdom of Great Britain and Ireland, King, and of Jamaica Lord Defender of the faith and so forth for the trial of Slaves before John Coates, Robert Thomas Downer, and Henry Augustus Plummer, Esquires Justices Assigned to keep the peace in and for the said parish.*

I was surprised that they praised the King so much because I thought he was seen as the enemy who had betrayed them and willed the ruin of Jamaica. I did not realize either that Mr Coates had so many important titles, especially 'the keeper of the peace'.

I was told that I was a man of evil mind and that I was being charged with 'rebellious conspiracy for the purpose of stirring up Negroes and other slaves to commit acts of insurrection and rebellion for the purpose of obtaining by force my own freedom and that of my fellow slaves'. The prosecution told the jurors that they could not obtain the names of slaves who would testify to my conspiracy to incite rebellion. Despite that, they were accusing me anyway of being unlawfully present at night meetings for the purpose of ministering oaths so that my fellow slaves would renounce obedience to their owners.

Joe Martin, the mulatto from Cambridge Estate, was

questioned first for the prosecution. His owner, Mr Scarlett, tried to lead him on with questions, but Joe was smart not to give away too much information. No one made any objections to Mr Scarlett leading the witness. Martin said he knew me and had seen me only the once on a Friday at Retrieve where he said I swear the people at a meeting. But then he told the court he saw me again during Christmas on the Tuesday at George Reid's house. He said I did not tell them anything more than not to work and that I was not carrying any arms. He mentioned how I urged some people to go up to Ginger Hill and Ipswich but the party had to turn back because of the rain. He did not know what day that was. Nothing happened at Ginger Hill that day and he reported I went afterwards to Content to visit with my wife. He saw me the following day by myself at Cambridge. He could not remember the day but a party met at Cowpark. I was the captain. He said the party went to a place called Struie, where we fired at some militia and he saw a White man killed. I commanded a party and so did Gardner. He never saw me again until the day of the trial.

James Clarke's testimony followed but it was all based on hearsay. He reported what he had been told about a battle from others who had been with me. He told the court that he never heard me talk about freedom because he was never present at the meetings, but then in the next breath he said he heard me tell my company that freedom was long due to them and if any man fell back he would be shot. I recall these words being spoken but I know I was not the one who said them.

Rob Rose was next. He was one of the slaves who took the oath with me before the rebellion. The evidence contradicted the one Joe Martin gave, but I do not think that mattered. The jurors' minds were made up.

Mr Scarlett:	*Do you know the prisoner?*
Rose:	*Yes, Sar, me know Sam Sharpe.*
Mr S:	*Were you with the prisoner the weeks before Christmas last?*
R:	*Me did see him at Retrieve before Christmas and me did meet him couple time at prayer. In Johnson house, de first time, and at Tucker house, de next time. Me tek de oath. Sam put de Book pon de table and ask me fi tek de oath and me did say yes.*
Mr S:	*What did the oath say?*
R:	*De oath was if we would agree fi set down and me did sey yes. And everybody inna de house did sey yes too. Him say we nah fi trouble nobody or raise no rebellion inna Jamaica. Him say we must set down all day Wednesday and Thursday.*
Mr S:	*When did you next see him?*
R:	*Me see him de Sunday night when him come up to Cambridge and we did eat supper at George Reid house. Then him go weh next day to Content and me did go wid him. George Reid come back inna de evening and spend de night.*
Mr S:	*And then, when next did you see the prisoner?*
R:	*Me tink it was de Thursday wid a crowd of people wid arm and machete.*
Mr S:	*Was Sharpe commanding the crowd?*
R:	*Me nebba see him command nobody.*

Rob Rose continued his story by agreeing with Joe's testimony that he went with me to Ipswich but turned back because of the rain. He saw me another day come through Cambridge, but when asked by Mr Scarlett about whether or not I was armed, he said that he was not sure. He talked of the same battle at Struie where a White man was killed. He did not say that I killed him. He concluded his testimony by telling of another occasion where he saw me at Retrieve with a large party but said that Johnson was in charge, and when the group moved to Hazelymph, he and I went off to Cambridge by ourselves.

James Sterling's and Edward Barrett's testimonies followed. Both denied that they had ever seen me use the fowling piece. They never saw me 'give it', Barrett said. He said they called me 'Schoolmaster Sharpe' and the people looked up to me. When Martin was cross-examined he testified that he never heard the people call me 'Captain'. He heard them call Gardner 'Colonel'.

It must have been confusing for the jurors because the information the witnesses gave was all mixed up and contradictory. When Clarke was cross-examined, he said that I had come back down to Cambridge the day after going up to Whittingham Estate. Yet, Martin testified it was the same day I went there and that I went home after that. Rose also told the court that I had told fellow slaves in the meetings that we should not burn any houses and we were not to fight. Sterling confessed that when we met back at Cambridge I held a meeting and that this was a prayer meeting only.

Mr Grignon was the White gentleman who led the cross-examination. It seemed he had grown even shorter and that his breeches were fitting tighter. The cross-examination was very brief. Mr Grignon did not ask any questions to challenge what the witnesses had said previously and he certainly did not say anything in my defence.

I want to know what other reason the court would have to appoint Mr Grignon to cross-examine witnesses than to make sure I was convicted?

Two witnesses for my defence were brought forward, George Reid from Cambridge Estate and Ann Thomas from Ginger Hill. Neither one was asked more than a few questions. Reid said that he did not see me administer any oath, and to the other questions, he said he did not know the answer. Ann Thomas's testimony was one statement:

'Me know Sam Sharpe, me was at Retrieve when Sharpe come up there.'

That was all for the defence.

I was not asked to speak.

It is not clear to me how the jurors came to the verdict or whether Mr Coates, Mr Downer and Mr Plummer merely made the decision on their own. Whichever way it was, the judgement was arrived at very fast. I have no training as a lawyer but it is obvious to me that the witnesses did not give very convincing evidence. Some of the testimony was not true, but the magistrates would not have known this because they did not give me or a defence attorney a chance to talk. I am sure Reverend Burchell told me that I am entitled under law to my own defence.

If I had been given a chance to talk, I would not have denied the charges but I would have explained to the court that my motives were not borne of malice but of the desire to gain human dignity, to remove from us the shackles of slavery. I would have prayed aloud to the court to ask the Lord to look down upon us sinners, to say that all of us, Black and White alike, are sons of Abraham, that whosoever believeth in Him shall not be ashamed, for there is no difference between the Jew and the Greek, for the same Lord overall is rich unto all that call upon Him.

I thought that it was the Governor's duty to appoint the most respectable gentlemen of property to run the sessions in each parish. This was a complete muddle-up. Perhaps he could not find anyone who was not biased against the rebels. So many men of property, including the three gentlemen, Mr Coates, Mr Downer and Mr Plummer, who presided over this court, had lost their residences and estates. There was no question that they wanted to find me guilty, guilty of acts of outrage and insubordination. I was considered by all to be the General Ruler, the director of the whole, and nothing was going to change their minds.

I am condemned — condemned to be hanged by the neck until I am dead. The court valued me at sixteen pounds ten shillings, a piddling amount for a male slave of thirty-one years.

TWENTY-ONE

April 22ⁿᵈ, 1832

Each day, I read over and over again the Psalms of David from the Good Book which Mr Bleby has obtained for me. They feed and comfort the soul.

The cell feels smaller now that I have received my sentence to be hanged. I want to free myself from the closeness of these four walls. They stifle me for I cannot escape their stench of sweat and urine.

I am now doomed to the gallows.

I never did manage to travel out into the ocean on the big ships I used to watch from Cooper's Hill. I never did build the house on the hill for Nyame, my girl pickaninny and me. And I never did get to work for an honest wage as a freed man.

Now I have my eternal soul to nourish. Soon all my worldly desires will count for naught.

I shall make my last walk to the gallows proud and strong. The crowd will never have the satisfaction to see me afraid. My executioner will hang me by the rope until I am dead, but I shall not waver.

Minister Burchell used to love to recite Psalm 43 whenever he felt the Lord had forsaken him. I pray now like David for the joy of God to enter my soul. The Heavenly Father is the God of my strength. I ask Him to send me His light and His truth so that He may lead me, lead me to His holy hill. And then I shall go unto the altar of God, the Almighty God, He *who gives me exceeding joy. I speak to my soul in the words of the psalmist:*

> *Why art thou cast down, O my soul?*
> *And why art thou*
> *disquieted within me?*
> *Hope thou in God; for I shall yet praise Him,*
> *who is the health of my*
> *countenance, and my God.*

I have faith in the Lord. He shall not forsake me. My flesh is fragile and its state temporary but my soul shall dwell forever in the House of the Lord.

I know I shall rather die than be a slave.

1831

Drought scorched the land. Slaves toiled harder than ever in the sun-hot and the earth did not yield any produce. The fields caked up so bad that not even the oxen were strong enough to plough through the soil. Tribulation was all about. Food was short and the planters could not keep us slaves healthy. Some sold off what they could, gave up their properties and returned to England.

General unrest by the slaves made matters worse for the planters. We read in the papers about resolutions of the Anti-Slavery Society making way for immediate emancipation. The buckra in Jamaica were well vex and they did not hide what they were feeling. They talked in their houses, so we could hear everything. George Reid of Cambridge Estate said that his master told him that he would soon be a free man and that he would have to pay all his expenses out of his own pocket. Mr Morris, owner of one of the biggest plantations, Kensington Estate, told his slaves that they too would soon be free and that they would have to pay for their own allowances of food and clothing. At Flamstead, the busha told the penkeeper that when war broke out between the Whites and the Blacks, he would be the first one he would shoot dead. Another slave master was reported to have said that freedom had come from England but he would shoot every damned Black rascal before he should get it. All the massa across the land talked in such a way that we came to believe that we would soon be free. "The Lord and King have given we free but the White gentleman in Jamaica keep it back."*

In this time of great oppression, the ministers of religion became more frustrated and exhausted. Minister Burchell often told me in private that he considered slavery an enormous evil, a violation against God and man:

Slavery! Accursed slavery! That infernal system! From my inmost soul, Sam, I detest and abhor it! I must confess I am tired of living in its midst; though I sincerely love the work in which I am engaged. *

The minister was tired and I feared he would soon abandon his mission in Jamaica. He said his lungs were almost destroyed and that he was in need of relaxation and a cooler climate. Minister Burchell had worn himself out. Even though he had class leaders who looked after the inquirers and reported to him, he himself travelled far into the bush to spread the Word of God. His journeys were more than 100 miles per week.

He moved into a house out of parish in a place called Gurney's Point where he was supposed to relax, but instead of resting, he continued to minister to the people, gathering 500 and more on the Sabbath. He became wearied in body and mind to the point where he could bear the burden no more. His church had grown to more than 5,000 members and his Baptist friends in England were not sending relief fast enough.

The constant boderation from the magistrates added to his grief. They accused Minister Burchell of stealing money from us slaves to build his big beautiful churches. The truth is he could barely collect enough moneys just for the upkeep. The pastor had a system whereby he sold tickets to the active members, who were able to renew them every three months if they continued to show that they were leading a life according to the Gospel.

We slaves loved the ticket system. We were proud to show the ticket every Sabbath when we attended chapel service. It carried our name and the signature of the minister, and on the edge of it, there were sayings printed like 'Pray for your Children' and 'Pray for the Grace to live near God'. The ticket was our tag to salvation, to the freedom of our spirit. The cost of the ticket was ten pence per quarter, a subscription of only halfpenny per week. Most of us could easily afford this with the earnings we received from our provision grounds.

The minister told the authorities that the charges were voluntary and that he did not receive even half of what he should have collected. Despite his explanations, they continued accusing him of extortion. They said the parson was in the business of selling 'passports to heaven'. The White men did not like Minister Burchell because he was too friendly towards us. They used every excuse to persecute him. When the rebellion broke out, the buckra became so disgusted with the pastor that he needed to guard his own life.

In the early part of May, Minister Burchell preached his last sermon in the Bay to a crowd of more than 500.

'My dear brethren, you have come before the table of God

to ask for His forgiveness. And He shall grant it to you, for any one of you who asketh in His name shall receive. The Lord is good and ready to forgive, plenteous in mercy unto all those who call upon His name. "For God hath not appointed us to wrath," my dear ones. He has appointed us to obtain salvation through our Lord Jesus Christ who suffered and died on the cross, so that whether we wake or sleep, we should live together with Him.

I am saddened to say that because of my labours my constitution is rapidly giving away. My heart is heavy with the news that I must announce to you today. I have thought on it in agony for many weeks but now believe it to be the Will of God and the right decision for me to depart from my flock once again. I shall be leaving soon for England where I hope to regain my strength so that I may return to continue my much-loved work among you. You have no need of fear or tribulation for your hearts dwell in the House of God where we can always find refuge. "The Lord shall comfort Zion; he will comfort all her waste places; and he will make her wilderness like Eden and her desert like the garden of the Lord; joy and gladness shall be found therein." The greatest commandment, my friends, is love. Jesus told us to love one another as He has loved us. Blessed is everyone who feareth the Lord and walketh in His ways. There is but one God and He is everlasting. Walk in the ways of the Lord, my friends, and you shall be saved.

Remember what I have told you, my brothers and sisters in Christ. Many will try to persecute you and make you feel low but "there is neither Jew nor Greek, there is neither bond nor free, there is neither male nor female: for ye are all one in Christ Jesus." When the fullness of time was come, God sent forth his Son, made of a woman to redeem us, those of us who were slaves under the law. "Wherefore thou art no more a servant, but a son; and if a son, then an heir of God through Christ." So be not saddened, my friends. Ye shall know the truth and the truth shall make ye free. "If the Son therefore shall make you free, ye shall be free indeed."'

One of the elders of the church, Sister B was her name, stood up and walked up the aisle to the altar, grabbed Minister Burchell round the waist with one hand and started waving the other hand back and forth over her head. She bounced the pastor so hard he had to hold on to her so he would not fall. Sister B was a large Jamaica market woman.

'Praise the Lord for the minister. Say after me, brothers and sisters, Praise the Lord.'

Praise the Lord.

'Praise be to the Lord for the parson.'

Praise be to the Lord for the parson.

Then she started to hum a tune and swing her hips to and fro, carrying the minister with her rhythm. She signalled to the organist to play the music.

> Everybody: *O shout, O shout, O shout away,*
> *And don't you mind,*
> *And glory, glory, glory in my soul!*
> Sister B: *And when 'twas night I thought 'twas*
> *day thought I'd pray my soul away,*
> *A glory, glory, glory in my soul!*
> Everybody: *O shout, O shout, O shout away,*
> *And don't you mind,*
> *And glory, glory, glory in my soul!**

She sang on, this time using a different chorus and tune which the organist easily followed. The faithful joined her in song.

JESUS! blessed Name
Jesus, still the same
I will sing it more and more,
Till we meet on heaven's shore. *

She moved a short distance from the minister but still held
on to him, lifting his hand high up, swinging it back and forth
so all could see his movement. 'We will miss you, Parson, but
we know you will come again.' Then once more she burst
into song:

When the King come back from the far-
off land,
And the trumpet sound to meet Him;
Oh! the joy that thrill through the
raptur'd land
Of the saints as they rise to greet Him.
Everybody: *O hasten, Lord that happy day,*
The Kingdom of Thy glory;
For our spirit yearn for Thy blest return,
As we tink on the gospel story. *

Minister Burchell was overcome with emotion. His frail
body swayed to the music and tears fell down his cheeks, but
then he managed to compose himself. 'My friends, the Spirit
of the Lord is among us. "Where two or more are gathered in
my name," saith the Lord, "There I shall be." I shall not
abandon you, my brethren. Mr Gardner, a young Baptist
brother from England, will guard my flock while I am away. I
shall return from England soon, and by the Grace of God,
shall see you free. You must be obedient in everything you do
and let your soul be subject to the higher power of God. Be
patient also. You need to be patient so that "after ye have
done the will of God, ye might receive the promise." I want

you to look for a sign from heaven. At Christmas, a star will fix itself to the corner of the moon and then you will know that God's Will shall soon be done. But you must be spiritually minded and live a life of peace and of patience. Love thine enemies and do unto them as you would have them do unto you. Do not shed their blood. Life is sweet but it is hard to give back and hard to give. Above all, be courageous, my friends. Stand fast in one spirit and with one mind, strive together for the faith of the gospel, "for God hath not given us the spirit of fear; but of power, and of love, and of a sound mind."'

It was a sad day saying goodbye to Minister Burchell but a happy one too. We knew that he was returning to England to improve his health and that he was going also with the mission to bring back for us the free papers from the King. He said that many were fighting for our cause in England to draw this hateful thing of slavery to an end. Before leaving, he confessed to me that when he first came to Jamaica, he had a burning desire to tame the savages of a God-forsaken land but over the years he came to realize that the inhumanity resided not in us slaves but in the men of his own kind. That was a brave thing for the minister to say to me.

On the day they sailed for England, I met Minister Burchell, Miss Lusty and their child at the wharves with a gift of fruit, mangoes, otaheite apples, starapples and bananas, wrapped in a osnaburg bag.

'I wish you safe travel, Minister.' I handed the package to him.

'You needn't have brought these, Sam.' He looked as if he was going to cry.

'Massa, we say, *"bowl go, packy come"*.'

'I have not heard that before.'

'It mean that when you give, you will always receive back in plenty. I bring these gifts from the estate for you and the Missus. I want you to have them for your journey.'

'Your kindness never ceases to amaze me, Sam. The Lord has blessed this mission.'

'The Lord bring blessings to us, Minister, by sending you to Jamaica.'

'I do believe it was His Will that I be here.'

'You must come back, Massa. The people expecting you. They think you only gone for a short while.'

'I shall return as soon as I am well, and I will fight for the cause of freedom when I am there.'

'I know you will do that for you is our friend. God's blessings to the Missus and to your pickaninny, and safe travel.' I shook hands with Miss Lusty.

'We must go now. And God's speed be with you, Sam. You are a good man. You must continue to do the work of the Lord. I do hope we shall meet again.'

'If not here, then in the Spirit World, Minister. I will be a free man before we meet again.'

'I do hope so.' He held me by both shoulders and drew me to him for an instant. I could see tears in his eyes as he and his family boarded the small boat which took them out to the big ship in the harbour.

I had now lost both my ministers. Moses Baker, who they say was almost 100 years old, had died the year before up at Crooked Spring. He was a strong man till the end, a firm believer in the Baptist way, and a strict judge of anyone who did not obey the laws of his religion. He taught me how to be righteous in the eyes of the Lord. May his soul forever rest in peace.

~

The more the abolitionists in England fought for the cause of freedom, the worse the planters treated us. The buckra here in Jamaica were scared that we Black people were going to take over the land and that they would be forced to go back to England to leave their properties in ruin. They were certain that we would never be able to manage on our own because we were not much different from the orangutans who roamed the forests of Africa. Reverend Bridges even believed in the 'humanity' of the slave trade because it "afforded the savages of Africa an opportunity of becoming acquainted with the civilized institutions of Europe which they could never enjoy in their own land."* If he had known Mama, I suppose he would say she should be grateful for being taken from her family in Africa. After all, she learned all those good behaviours from Mr Crawford.

By summertime, the buckra were so incensed with the situation in England that they began to hold public meetings. In every parish, they passed resolutions to be sent back to the House of Lords in England. Those of us who did not attend the meetings were able to read in the *Courant* newspaper about the ranting and raving that went on. Some of the planters even wanted to break ties with the King to join up with the Americans, who loved slavery even more than the British.

Dorcas, the same writer Reverend Knibb had talked about, kicked up the most fuss of all. He sent warnings to all the Whites in Jamaica that a big storm was coming:

*If you would not have your blazing canefields to be your watch-fires, the shrieks of your wives and children your alarm-bell, and your burning houses for your beacons, - attend to the warning voice of - Dorcas.**

He believed the slaves were plotting to burn down the estates. I knew of a small group of rebel slaves but no large-scale organization existed at that time. His writings caused a commotion among the Whites, resulting in harsher treatment of slaves and greater unrest.

We were also led to believe that the King was giving special orders to the soldiers:

> *It must be alarming, when whispered, that our brethren, THE BRITISH SOLDIERS — who have been ostensibly stationed for our protection, who are liberally paid by us, the expense of whom forms the chief drain upon our exchequer — HAVE RECEIVED SECRET ORDERS TO REMAIN NEUTRAL, OR TO ACT AGAINST US, IN THE EVENT OF A DISTURBANCE.* *

We did not realize until then how much the King was upset with the Governor. The King was instructing him to prepare us for freedom. So if the gubna was not going to obey the orders, then the British soldiers would be sent out to fight on our side. This gave me the assurance that we should move forward with plans to stand up to the government. There was growing support for action among the slave population. Three thousand slaves in the Baptist mission alone had learned to read, so all these and more were learning about things fas fas and talking bout their saviour, King William of England. Thousands and thousands came to learn that the regulars of the British army were to be our support in case of trouble. The momentum was growing.

~

The town hall in the Bay was packed for a meeting. At the front of the hall sat twelve White men behind a long table. The rest of the room was filled with White, Coloured and Black men of many classes — property owners, tradesmen and slaves. Despite the high ceilings and tall windows, the hall was boiling hot. The crowd was restless and loud, chatting even while the speeches were going on.

The men at the front took turns speaking to the gathering. They blasted the British Government for making Jamaica change its slave laws. Even though the Custos, Mr Barrett, was present, Mr Grignon seemed to be the person in charge because all the other men who spoke addressed him as the delegate who was to take the resolutions back to the Governor. Little Breeches, who was seated at the centre, was so short I could hardly see his face from over the top of the table. Mr Coates was there too, the last one to speak. I had met him at the tavern in the Bay but I did not know then that he was the gentleman who would pass sentence on my life. He reminded me of a green lizard, slippery with a scaly skin. I would never want to provoke him.

If you ever poke a green lizard with a stick, it will chase you down, jump on you and bite you.

Mr Lizard addressed the crowd. 'It has become clear to us all that our friends in England are doing little to protect our interests here in Jamaica, once the prized jewel in Her Majesty's crown. They are forcing us into making the inevitable choice of procuring protection from some other nation. They leave us little choice. The Parliament of this Kingdom is designing laws which are contrary to the sacredness of property we hold so dear in our slaves. We shall refuse to proceed any further in ameliorating the slave code unless the British Lords are prepared to talk to us about compensation for the loss of our property. We are in full support of resolutions passed in other parishes in Jamaica which state that *"when we see ourselves scorned, betrayed, devoted to ruin and slaughter, delivered over to the enemies of our country, we consider that we are bound by every principle, human and Divine, to resist."'** The White people in the crowd burst out with a loud clapping.

'Resolutions have been placed in the hands of the Governor but we have heard nothing in reply. We must appeal to His Excellency, the Earl of Belmore, for action, action now so that we do not have a bloody rebellion on our hands. His reports to England state that the slave population is collectively sound and well disposed. And what then of us, my friends? Are we to stand by idly and watch our properties reduced to naught? I think not. For the sake of self-preservation, my friends, we must work to protect what is rightfully ours. We lawfully acquired our slave property and we are being compelled now to surrender it. This will lead to the utter ruination of both master and slave. We shall not have it. I tell you, we shall not have it so.'

The crowd dispersed, noisier and angrier than ever. The buckra were shouting at the slaves in the crowd, calling us names like *wretches*, *knaves* and *scoundrels* and telling us to report back to our owners lest we be put in jail and given hard labour. 'We can still do with you what we want, including flogging your women.'

Despite efforts from His Royal Majesty's Government, the slave laws in Jamaica had not changed much. The free Coloured were the ones in a more privileged position because that year they were granted equal liberties to the Whites.

As we freed ourselves from the jeering of the crowd and left the town hall, the slaves talked among themselves:

'So dem vex wid de buckra massa in England.'

'Iin-hiin, cause dem a send we de free paper.'

'And we Black people gwine rule de country.'

'So dem catch dem fraid.'

'Yes, brother, and de Redcoats dem a get instruction from de King.'

'Iin-hiin, fi sey dat dem mus help we if there is trouble.'

'What a tribulation for buckra massa.'

'Me dear sa. Is fi we time now.'

'A tell you.'

'Pastor Burchell sey him will try fi bring we de free paper.'

'And suppose him don't come back?'

'Him will come, man. And if him don't come by Christmas and de star de a fix itself side de moon, then is fi we time.'

'Some people sey fire a go bon.'

'Iin-hiin, but Minister Burchell tell we sey we mus not shed blood.'

'And Daddy Sharpe sey dat too.'

And so the talk went on through the towns and villages.

From August on — the months when we dig the cane holes — word of freedom spread fas through the land, so fas that many could no longer heed the words of Minister Burchell. They became impatient, angry at massas for making them toil under the cart whip in the hot, hot sun. 'Remember, my friends, be spiritually minded and live a life of peace and of patience. Love thine enemies.'

The minister's words were soon forgotten.

TWENTY-TWO

April 26ᵗʰ, 1832

They have determined the end for me. I must leave this place against my will. My constitution is strong, I have no illnesses, physical or mental, yet they will still kill me. I have fought valiantly for the cause of freedom and exhorted my fellow slaves to stand up to busha.

We are not chattel to be bought and sold at the market place. We have endured enough and the time has come for us to throw off the chains. What evil is there in this? The destruction of the temples of God and the cruel hangings of slaves are evil. In these there is iniquity, but in telling my fellow man that we shall be vassals no more, I can see none.

My soul screams out in anger at the shame of having my body destroyed at the hands of the hangman. What will he care? He is merely doing his job, executing one convict after another. But though he can hang my body from the gibbet and throw it away in the bush for the crows to eat, he will never harm my soul. My spirit will not die and the dream of freedom will never die. That same hangman, who, on the fateful day of May 23ʳᵈ, will put the noose around my neck, he himself will be free, free from the chains of slavery when the time comes.

I need to talk to somebody. I want to hear laughter and to feel the warmth of human company.

The prison cell sends a chill through my body.

I seek food for my soul from the Good Book. I shall remain strong to the end, steadfast in my hope.

I piss in the corner of the cell. The wretched place stinks like hell.

Twenty-seven days remain, time enough for me to finish telling the story of my life. I am surprised that they have given me so much time. It is the custom that within a half hour of being sentenced to death, the prisoner is taken to the gallows. Maybe they want to see me suffer out the remaining days, or with time, they are hoping that I will betray the missionaries and my friends. But they have already killed off most of the rebels. There is nobody left to betray. They have hanged them, shot them and dashed dem weh in the bush. Not one received a Christian burial. The authorities say it is an act of mercy to kill us off. The general, Sir Willoughby Cotton, was reported to have said, 'Severe measures are unpleasant, but occasionally not only necessary but merciful in the sequel.'

I must gain the strength to finish the narrative of the Baptist War.

Second half of the year, 1831

After a long period of dry time of toiling in the bitter sun-hot, the rains finally came. They fell so hard that the rivers and fields flooded and the people got sick from epidemics of smallpox and dysentery. The myalmen tried to cure the sick but too many died, especially the old and the very young. Church membership increased, the slaves coming from all bout to hear if the parson had any good news of the free paper. But there was none and so the slaves became more anxious and more stubborn.

The head drivers had no problem getting people to turn out for secret prayer meetings in the bush. The slaves were restless and in need of direction. We now had followers on the estates — Bellfield, Adelphi, Moor Park, Crooked Spring, Unity Hall, Retrieve, Hazelymph, Duckett Spring, Cambridge, Argyle, to mention but a few.

After prayer one Saturday night at Retrieve Estate, the leaders stayed back to meet privately with a group we had specially invited to hear of our plan. My closest allies were there, Dove, Gardner, Reid, Tharpe, Taylor, Guthrie, Linton, a Brown man who was the head slave at Hermitage Estate, John Morris, also a mulatto and head slave at Duckett Spring, and Johnson, who was the driver at Retrieve. Those who testified at the trial, including Edward Hylton, were also there; James Clarke was absent. I had also invited freed Brown men who used to attend my prayer meetings and who became sympathetic to our cause: Mr Mackintosh and his son, Largie, and a man called Campbell.

We crowded into Johnson's house. As head slave, he acted like an overseer at Retrieve Estate. His owner gave him a big house with furniture and food for his wife and children. Johnson was a tall, muscular man, attracting to him all those whom he met.

I stood by the doorway and addressed the group, beginning in a soft, smooth voice to get their attention. As I spoke, I became more animated and felt the people move with my spirit.

'De King is on our side, my brothers. Him give de soldiers orders not fi fight gainst we. So dat mean him nah gwine give no assistance to buckra if we decide fi tek we freedom. What dat tell you? It tell me sey de King is ready fi give we de free paper. Our beloved preacher, Minister Burchell, sey him will return from England to bring we de good news of salvation and de good news of our freedom. But we must be ready. We must have a plan. If de government hold back de paper, then we haffi tek fi we freedom. We mus tek our freedom for de time is right, my brothers. De time is right for we is saved, we is saved in de blood of Jesus, and under de Divine Law, we is all sons of Abraham, heirs to de promise of de Kingdom of God. Yes, my brothers, all o we fi one in Jesus. Praise be to His holy name. I say to you, if de Son of God shall make you free, then you will be free indeed. Praise be to Massa Jesus. It is de truth, my brothers. De gospel of Matthew tell us in chapter 6, verse 24 dat, "No man can serve two masters." Jesus is fi we Massa for him shed Him blood for we, Him shed Him blood so we can be saved. Praise be to de Lord Jesus. Praise be His holy name.

We have worked nough days and years aredi. We shall work no more as slaves, my brothers. It is de life of de dog. Dem flog de dog and drive him out a yard. "We won't tek no flog no more."* We gwine free at last, my brothers. You hear what a telling you? We gwine free at last, my brothers.'

A few men began to raise their arms and clap their hands. 'Is trut you a tell we, Daddy Sharpe. Fi we time come.'

'Yes, my brothers,' I felt their closeness in the room. 'De White man have no right fi hold we in bondage, just like we have no right fi hold him prisoner. Paul tell we in Galatians chapter 5, verse 1, "Stand fast therefore in the liberty wherewith Christ hath made us free, and be not entangled again with the yoke of bondage."'

'We gwine free, Daddy Sharpe. Is fi we time now,' Linton shouted out from the group.

'But we must tek care, brothers. Minister Burchell sey we mus have patience, sey we mus wait for de free paper to come from England,' I cautioned them.

Johnson spoke out. 'The buckra dem nah gwine hand it over. Me sure of dat.'

'This is true, Brother Johnson. Little Breeches and de Whites are holding secret meetings in de Bay. Me know dat because me stand up outside Mr Watt door and listen to what dem haffi sey. De high buckra dem sey dem waan fi kill all de Black man inna dis country. Dem plan fi spare de life of all of de slave woman and pickney but dem gwine keep dem in slavery same way. So, you right, brother, dem will try fi hold we back. Dem a mek *studiation* fi kill we Black man. Dat is why we must have a plan.'

Dove spoke up in an angry tone. 'So what kind of plan gwine stop dem from kill we, Daddy Sharpe?'

I was surprised to hear him talk at a public meeting.

'Remember what me tell you. We must be patient. De King is pon we side. If de free paper don't come by Christmas, and if we wake fi see a star fix itself next to de moon, then we must tek action. We must refuse fi work. We must set down after Christmas. We will demand a honest wage which we will set at two shillings and six pence per day. Then de massa will listen to we cause he will need fi we labour. It is de start of de cane harvest, so de massa need we fi work. But we will refuse fi work unless him pay we. Dat is what we will tell him.

'De buckra will catch dem fraid for dem will tink sey we gwine bon down de cane fields. Dem will tink we gwine slaughter dem wife and children and bon down dem house jus like de slaves do in Haiti. Dat is because dem think we mad, dat we is blood-sucking savages. But we must show dem what we want. We don't want their blood. We want fi we freedom and fi we dignity. We want fi we pickaninny to be born free, my brothers. We want fi plough fi we own land, to hire fi we own labour, to stand up and respect de White man and expect de same in return.'

Dove stood up to address the crowd. 'If we stop work, dem will shoot we. Dem will put we out at de muzzles of de gun and shoot we dung like pigeon. We will fall like dead pigeon pon de ground. Dem will throw we inna de bush and john-crow will nyam we to de bone. Don't fool yuhself, man. Dem nah gwine set we free.'

'We must keep our dream of freedom, Brother Thomas. We must block out de vision of death for dat will draw us dung into a dark hole. We must swear to one another, like our African brothers do, to bond together and to be faithful so dat we nebba look back, nebba give up fi we claim to freedom. We not doing dis fi weself, my brothers. We doing it fi we woman and pickaninny, fi those who work under massa whip and fi those who dead aredi fi freedom sake. We shall be free, my brothers. If de spirit is free through Jesus, then de body must be too. John tell we in chapter 8, verse 36, "If the Son therefore shall make you free, ye shall be free indeed."'

We talked long into the night and at the end of our meeting, joined hands, prayed the Lord's Prayer, and sang:

> *Come in, Kind Saviour,*
> *No man can stop we.*
> *Walk in, sweet Jesus,*
> *No man can stop we.*
> *See the wonders Jesus done*
> *O, no man can stop we.*
>
> *Raise up, sweet Jesus,*
> *Raise we up.*
>
> *Praise be to God.*
> *Praise be to His holy name.*

We promised one another that we would not falter, that we would spread the Word of God and tell the people of our plan. A man named Edward Ramsay said he would help pass the news to the estates. Our plan was to set down the day after Christmas if the freedom paper did not come. We would not speak to any buckra but keep everything in secret. I kissed the Holy Bible and passed it around for others to do the same.

December month approached. There was no sign of Minister Burchell and no talk of the freedom papers coming from England. Gardner, Dove and Johnson became agitated, fearing that our plan of peaceful resistance after Christmas might lead the planters to take up arms against us. They began the dangerous task of collecting stocks of machetes and firearms which the head drivers stole from the estates. They stockpiled ammunition at Greenwich Estate, where Gardner was the driver.

Gardner expected to gather more arms during Christmas when the owners routinely went down for visits to the Bay. He also rallied the support of men on neighbouring estates to be in charge of organizing companies. Their job would be to guard their own properties, resist the Whites and make reports to him at Greenwich which became the new military headquarters. Gardner also appointed Dehaney, who was to operate in the Salter's Hill area, and Tharpe, at Catadupa in the country between Retrieve and Croydon estates. Both these men were committed to the cause. Dehaney was a yellow-skinned Negro, a burly man with a broad chest and more than ordinary share of muscular energy. Tharpe was smaller but still had the appearance of a leader and chief. According to Gardner, he was a great ruler and horseman, feared by the White man.

I stayed up late one night at Gardner's house at Greenwich. His owner, Mr Christie, treated him as if he was a White man. His place was bigger than the regular slave hut. It had more rooms and furniture, even a proper bed with mattress. We sleep on the bare ground inside the slave hut. He had tables, chairs, a cooking pot, plates, knife, fork, and buckra-style bowls, no slave-style calabash, which was the usual kind of dish we used for serving food. The massa even supplied him with his personal stock of rum. As a Baptist, Gardner was not allowed to take alcohol, but that night, the preacher had drunk a few ounces well.

'How de plan gwine work, Sam? De people don't know wah fi do. We don't even give dem a time fi stop wuk. How we all gwine stop same time unless you have one raas loud mouth that can reach clear cross de country? Wah bout de people in de rest a Jamaica? What dem know bout dis?' He took a shot of rum from his glass.

'You not supposed to drink, man.' I tried to stay calm and not say anything to incite him.

'Dat is wah Parson Baker used fi sey, but to tell you de truth, Sam, me see a whole heap a minister dem try a lickle of de Jamaica cane juice.'

'Never mind that now, brother.'

'Is you bring up de topic, brother man, not me.'

I wanted to ease his fears. 'What we need to do is to make a plan that will work.'

'What kind a plan, Sam? Don't we already go all bout de estates fi tell de head slaves sey dem must set down after Christmas? Here, me think you need some grog fi sharpen yuh wit. You getting forgetful, brother man.' He reached for the rum bottle to pass to me.

'Not now. Yes, I agree with you, we need a stronger way to organize it.'

'Oh, raas, man.' The rum was setting in. He looked across the table, pointing his finger in my face. 'Is you start dis, Sam. Is you haffi finish it.'

'What choice do we have, Gardner? If they don't bring us the freedom paper, then we stop work. Me not going back to the slavery times.'

'And buckra massa will place him arm around yuh shoulder and sey to you, "Oh, Sammy, my boy, you fine young slave. I love you so much. You have worked so hard for me all these years."' Gardner imitated the White man by talking proper, '"It is time now that I should pay you. I shall pay you handsomely for your work. I shouldn't mind losing money on my crops." You need a shot of dis rum, Sammy, fi clear yuh head. You mad no raas, yuh head all a mix up, mix up.'

'You making fun of me, brother.'

'A not making fun, Sam. You know full well wah de massa gwine sey.'

'I know.'

'"You f__in wretch. Get up off the ground and go work in the field as I tell you or I'll string your ass up on that tree and shoot you myself."'

'It may not happen that way. Besides, Minister Burchell may return from England.'

'And what if he does? They will shoot him too.'

'The power of God will prevail, brother.'

'Yes, but we must tek care of weself.' He stood up suddenly and removed his shirt. 'Look pon me, Sam.' He pounded his chest and then flexed the muscles in both arms. 'Look ya, Sam, we is a strong people and we haffi look after weself.'

'You a drink too much, man, sit down and quiet up.' I was not sure that this was the right time to bring up the topic but it was bothering me too much to keep it to myself.

'I don't agree with what you have been doing.'

He looked over at me, startled with his eyes bulging. 'What is dat now, Sammy?'

'Training an army.'

'You do yuh praying to God and me will tek care of de rest.'

'That won't work, brother. We must act together, as one. Otherwise, there is no command.'

'Then, we wait. We wait and see.' He sat back down. His eyes looked straight into mine. 'Me won't use de guns if we don't have to. If dem shoot at we, then we tek up arms. Dat me promise you.'

'That is the only way it should be.' I reached over the table to offer him a handshake. He grabbed my arm, pulling it hard towards him so my upper body leaned over the table. He was sweating hard.

'Why we, eh, Sam? Why de Lord choose fi we to live in disya hell?' He leaned closer to me and with one hand quickly took hold of my neck-back and pushed my face down on the table. With the other hand, he slowly poured a shot of rum over my head.

I pulled myself away. 'What you doin', brother?'

'Don't de rum feel good?'

'The only way it will be good is if we are brothers and do this fight together.'

'Amen, my brother. I am ready.'

'Who and what do you have?' I asked him.

'Johnson train bout 150 men and dem have some fifty gun wid dem. Me and Dove set up members to form a Black Regiment which will work out of Greenwich. Dehaney organize a group over by Salter's Hill, and Tharpe in and about Catadupa.'

'We're not soldiers, Gardner. The big guns will tek us down.'

'Well, you tell me how yuh prayer dem gwine do it.'

'We have a blood pact. Remember? We have each other's word as brother to brother. We go to arms only if we have to.'

'You a do it again, Sam.'

'What?'

'Preaching. You want more rum pon yuh head?'

'We have another big meeting at Retrieve before Christmas. We will mek sure we are ready then.'

'Remember, Sam. No matter how things go in de end, me love you, man. There is no bigger cause than fighting fi freedom. Is you, Sam, you is de one who bring me to dis, you and yuh preaching.'

'May God be with both of us.'

'Me will drink to dat, Daddy Sharpe.'

A couple weeks before Christmas, Gardner and I held the meeting at Tucker's house on Retrieve Estate. This was our last chance to make sure things went right. I spoke to the group:

'On the day after Christmas, a star will fix itself to one corner of the moon. This will be a sign that our slave labour for the White people must stop.

'You are the headmen. You are in charge, my brothers. You are the ones the busha trust. You are the ones who carry out his orders. But you will tek his orders no more. The time has come for you to take charge for yourself, to tell your people that they will be free and that they will work no more. Now is the time to be delivered from Babylon. The hour will soon arrive when we shall taste the milk and honey of Canaan. This is your hour, the one for you to command.

'On the day after the holiday, that will be the Wednesday morning, busha will come to tell you to set the slaves to work. That same morning, my brothers, you will tell the slaves his command but you will also tell them for the very first time not to obey his orders. You will not go to work that day. You will tell your master that your people have been set free. What a glorious day that will be, my brothers, when we shall break from our chains to be free at last. Praise be the name of the Lord.'

Everybody called out, 'Praise de Lawd.'

Say again, 'Praise de Lawd.'
'Praise de Lawd'

Johnson spoke out. 'Praise be the name of Daddy Sharpe.'

Praise be the name of Daddy Sharpe.
'Praise de Lawd.'
Praise de Lawd.
'Praise de Lawd for Daddy Sharpe.'
Praise de Lawd for Daddy Sharpe.

'Thank you, my brothers, and God's blessings to you. We be free. We be free, my friends. We be slaves no more. Glory be that day. Oh God, that it come true.'

Johnson spoke up. 'But suppose it don't work, Sam. The women are chicken-hearted. We gwine need their support.'

'It will work, yes, if you tell them that they and their pickaninny will be free forever. They will do as you say, not as the massa says. You must set down. You must not trouble nobody. Raise no rebellion. Set quiet and be peaceful. If the massa don't like that and him waan go down to the Bay to sound the alarm, then you must stop him. You must tek his gun and his horse. You tell him you will not hurt him, you will not harm his wife and his children, you will not burn his house. But he must let your people go. The time has come, tell him. Our King has already sent the freedom papers. His government is hiding them, but massa must obey his King and set we free. We must tek the sacred oath once more that we as brothers will set down and not work on that glorious day to come.'

Dehaney and Johnson passed around a cup for all to drink. I swore on the Bible and passed the Holy Book around for others to kiss and to hold. We all took an oath and said, yes, we would set down the Wednesday, the first day of work after the Christmas.

> *And the Lord said, I have surely seen the affliction of my people which are in Egypt, and have heard their cry by reason of their taskmasters, for I know their sorrows.*

'You have been baptized in Christ Jesus, my brothers. You were dipped into the river by Moses Baker and cleansed of your sin. You have the protection of the Spirit against all evil. We must tek the obeah away. We must heal the land and drive away forever the evil of slavery. A great deliverance will take place. We will sanctify ourselves in the name of the Lord. Go now in the peace of Jesus.'

~

A few days later, the slaves at Salt Spring gave a message that they were not going to take the whip no more. George Guthrie from Spring Mount gave me the information. It was the 15th day of the month when the attorney at the estate, Mr Grignon Esquire, was coming for a visit. He needed to make a check regularly because Salt Spring was a large estate with over 250 slaves. Guthrie said Massa had his usual cross look on his face, half hidden under his broad-rimmed hat. His head slave, Blacka, a short, burly man, drove him up in the gig that day. The slaves did not like the driver for he always carried a cart whip which he used on them at his master's command.

As they approached the estate house, they happened upon a young female slave with a few sticks of sugar cane in her hand. Mr Grignon told the woman to throw down the cane because she had taken far more than the allowable amount. She refused to obey her master and started to carry on, sucking her teeth and cussing bad word. Mr Grignon promptly told the driver to lash the woman with the horsewhip, but Blacka too refused his master's command. Just then, the slaves saw another driver come up. He raised up his machete at Mr Grignon, telling him to leave the woman alone for she was his wife.

The massa then catch him fraid and went to another part of the estate where he found all the slaves lying down, chatting and drinking in the boiling house. The slaves told him they had worked long enough and from now on they wanted money for their work. The poor man was beside himself. He mounted the nearest horse in a panic and galloped away off the property as fast as he could. The slaves at Salt Spring did laugh hard that day to see Little Breeches a ride off by himself down the hillside.

Next thing, a White constable rode up the hill with instructions to arrest the drivers, but the slaves grabbed hold of the man and threatened to push him into a vat of hot boiling sugar. The slaves took his horse away, so the policeman had to find his way by foot back down the hill to the Bay, running faster than fowl, tripping and falling on the rockstones as he went. What a tribulation for Little Breeches!

Next, the militia, with their big guns and horses, came up to the estate to deal with the situation, but by then the rebellious slaves had escaped into the nearby bush, and the others who remained agreed to go back to work the mills. Even though it appeared that Mr Grignon had finally won the little battle, the slaves felt they had beat him out because they ran Massa from the estate that day.

News of the Little Breeches affair spread through the countryside.

> 'What a way Lickle Breeches gallop go weh pon him horse.'
> 'Everybody a tek up machete and laugh after him.'
> 'What a sinting.'
> 'Mussi him breeches too tight mek him gwaan so.'
> 'Bwai, a tell you man, mussi so it go.'
> 'Even Blacka sey no to Massa and him is one a him faithful slave.'
> 'Is a big problem fi Lickle Breeches, man.'
> 'Me know, sar, is true. How him gwine mek sugar now?'
> 'De slave dem nah gwine wuk fi free no more.'
> 'Dat is a good ting, man. Freedom soon come.'

~

On December 22nd, the Governor released a proclamation from King William to be announced to the slaves throughout the land of Jamaica. Posters were put up in public places and masters were instructed to read the contents to their slaves.

> Whereas it has been represented to us that the slaves in some of our West-India colonies and of our possessions on the continent of South America, have been erroneously led to believe that orders have been sent out by us for their emancipation.

> And whereas such belief has produced acts of insubordination, which have excited our highest displeasure. . .

We do hereby declare and make known that the slave population in our said colonies and possessions will forfeit all claim of our protection, if they shall fail to render entire submission to the laws, as well as dutiful obedience to their masters.*

So, we did not know whether the King changed his mind about the free paper or whether it was to come sometime later. It sounded as if he was not pleased with the reports he was receiving from the governors. We did not know whether the Governor of Jamaica was making up some lie and writing pretend posters around the country or whether it was really the King sending the message. Whatever it was, we were enraged. Someone was tricking us and holding back the paper. This situation made our plan more dangerous, because now we were not sure if we had the support of the King's soldiers. We knew that we could not depend on them. We had only ourselves.

The holidays worked to our favour. The Negro Saturday fell on the day before Christmas and the Governor granted us two more days off after Christmas. Many of the White families took advantage of the four days and went down to the Bay to be with friends. This left the plantations in charge of the head slaves and a few remaining overseers. With little or no supervision, the rum flowed more freely than ever that Christmas.

We were nervous and troubled, betrayed by the King's announcement and unsure if Minister Burchell was going to arrive in time.

We wanted to keep everything secret, but slaves broke the news of our plan to the missionaries. Minister Knibb was sending deacons of his church through the country to tell us that we were mistaken, that no freedom paper was coming from England and that we must go back to work on Wednesday. We did not like his message. We were cheated, convinced that buckra massa had paid the minister to tell us these things.

The Tuesday, two days after Christmas, was the day set for the opening of the new Salter's Hill Baptist chapel which was being moved from Crooked Spring. We came from all parts for the occasion. Salter's Hill is a beautiful, cool place about ten miles down the road from Kensington, not too far from Hamstead, closer to the Montego River. The chapel was built on top of a steep hill, and from inside the building, I could see through the window, far out across the valley to mountains blue in the distance. The chapel was filled mostly with slaves, over 1,000 in number. Minister Knibb came up from Falmouth by horse along with a new minister, Mr Whitehorne, also from Trelawney. Mr Gardner, who was replacing Minister Burchell, and another young preacher, Mr Abbott from Lucea, were also there. It was to have been a cheerful occasion to praise God for a new place of worship, but the crowd was restless and angry and in no mood for celebration.

After Mr Gardner preached from the Bible, Mr Knibb took the pulpit. His hands were shaking, his face sad and angry at the same time:

> *My dear hearers, and especially those who attend regularly on the means of grace, and who belong, either as members or inquirers, to the church, pay great attention to what I have to say. It is more than seven years since I left my native land to preach the Gospel of Jesus Christ to you; and when I came, I made up my mind to live and die to promote your temporal and spiritual welfare. Till yesterday, I had*

hoped God had blessed my poor labours, and the labours of your dear minister, who loves you and prays for you, and who is now in England for his health. But I am pained — pained to the soul, at being told that many of you have agreed not to go to work any more for your owners; and I fear this is too true. I have learned that some wicked persons have persuaded you that the King of England has made you free. Hear me! I love your souls, and I would not tell you a lie for the whole world; I assure you that it is false, false as hell can make it! I entreat you not to believe it, but to go to your work as formerly. If you have any love to Jesus Christ, to religion, to your ministers, or those kind friends in England who have helped you to build this chapel, and who are sending a minister, do not be led away. God commands you to be obedient; if you do as he commands, you may expect his blessing, but if you do not, he will not do you good. **

Everybody was silent for a long time. Not a word. Just an angry silence. Then the comments:

'De parson now tun pon we like buckra massa.'

'De man mussi mad to raas.'

'Why him come to we now all of a sudden fi talk bout freedom?'

'Buckra massa mussi bribe him fi tell we bout dem ting de.'

'One time him sey we kyaan serve two master and now him a come ya fi sey is fi de Will of God fi serve buckra massa.'

'And if we don't obey God command, then Him gwine punish we.'

'A foolishness dat.'

'De man mussi mad to raas.'

'Me woulda kill him raas if him try fi mek slave a me again.'

The minister stayed many hours trying to reason with us, but we were too angry to listen.

One of the elders confronted him. 'You teach we sey dat de spirit shall make we free. And it is dis freedom we want, Preacher. Daddy Sharpe mek we swear pon de Bible sey de day after de Christmas festival, we must 'top wuk, for now we is free and have one master only and dat is Christ Jesus.'

'The Spirit will make you free, my brothers, but you must also be obedient to God's will.'

'Dat nah mek no sense, Minister.'

'It means you must be patient, just as Minister Burchell told you.'

'Busha sey dat freedom soon come, and before it come, we must tek de beating and wuk hard fi him.'

'You must not listen to busha. When last has he told you the truth? Your freedom is not near, I tell you. You must go back to your houses and tomorrow wake and go to the fields.'

'You a tell we pure lie, Minister. If you a joke wid we, we gwine drive you out a yard.'

As we walked our separate ways from Salter's Hill that night, none of us knew then that that would be the first and only time service would be held in the new chapel.

Shortly after sunset on that same Tuesday night, the 27th day of December, 1831, flames shot high up into the air. Fire and smoke could be seen across the Parish of St James. It was the trash house at Kensington Estate, set ablaze by a few drunken slaves led by a man named John Dunbar. This marked the beginning of the slave rebellion. Our plan for peaceful resistance, which we had worked so hard for, went wrong all in an instant. *Alarm filled every breast; anxiety sat upon all faces.* *

Part IV
THE BUSH

The destruction of the Roehampton Estate in the parish of St James in January 1832

TWENTY-THREE

January 1832

I take the liberty here to insert journal reflections based on events pertaining mainly to my family and life at Cooper's Hill.

My worst fears have come true. The great turbulence in Jamaica has erupted into open rebellion by the slaves against their masters. The land in St James is ablaze and the country in chaos. I am further alarmed by the rumours that our slave, Samuel Sharpe, is the leader of the revolt. There is sheer madness in the land, fires, massacres, loss of life and property. We live in very troubled times.

Our residence is sufficiently close to the Bay that my family has not been placed in any immediate danger. We have loyal slaves who will alert us of any impending threat. My husband wishes to move in with some friends in the Bay but I do not think this is necessary. God knows what would happen to our homestead should we abandon it.

My husband continues to enjoy reasonably good health and to show benevolence to all those whom he meets. Mr Sharpe is a man who has always been fond of society. He enjoys the company of men who come to visit our home to play cards, smoke cigars and exchange views on the current state of politics. Our life is not prosperous but we have enjoyed most of the amenities of a good one. He has earned a modest living by operating a small business in the Bay. All of this has now been threatened by the rebellion. We are extremely vulnerable and may soon have to depend on the kindnesses of others for our welfare.

We were not able to procure the services of a reliable bookkeeper after Mr Crawford left. So my husband made the decision to hand over to Henry the responsibility of managing Cooper's Hill. Henry has grown to be surly and wanton in his ways. He drinks to excess and asks no pardon for his behaviours. He is irascible, swears without cause and entertains women of all sorts. I often think that some of the Negroes are far less depraved. I have requested that he take up lodging in the bookkeeper's home for I do not want the children exposed to his behaviours on a continuous basis. I can not imagine what old age will bring as it is said that faults that are somewhat bearable in youth are abhorrent in later years. I wish I had more influence to teach him finer manners.

I blame Mr Crawford for Henry's wayward ways, for setting a bad example when Henry and Anna were young children. I have not heard a great deal of Mr Crawford's whereabouts, except that he is in the Parish of Westmoreland where he frequently changes employment, unable to win the good graces of his employers. I expect that with the onset of the rebellion, he will join the militia to defend our country in this time of mayhem.

Anna was not able to tolerate life here in Jamaica. After she completed her schooling, she remained in England and married a gentleman of some means, of gentility and property. I am glad for this because she deserves the cultured life that English society can offer. I receive letters from her every month or as regularly as the post from England will allow. I do miss my dear Anna terribly. I love her as my own. Very few persons can detect a fault in her because of her many virtues. She seldom thinks of herself and shows concern always for the welfare of others. She tells me of her regular visits to the poorhouses in London. God bless her heart.

It is easy to grow nostalgic for Anna. The walls of our home at Cooper's Hill are decorated with portraits which she has drawn. The one of my husband is particularly lifelike. Unlike Henry and me, Mr Sharpe possesses the patience to have sat long hours while she painstakingly sketched his portrait.

Our eldest born, Samuel, is now eighteen. He is a handsome boy, tall, blond like his father, but with a stronger constitution, healthy and immune to the tropical diseases which beset so many of the Whites on the island. I do believe that White Creoles are of a hardier stock than our English-born counterparts who suffer dreadfully when they venture to the West Indies. Samuel will make a faithful husband one day to a fortunate young lass and he will be a responsible and loving father to his offspring.

Elizabeth will be sixteen years of age in March. She is a bonnie child, of a gentle disposition, innocent and free of any ill humours that might taint the soul. She has received excellent schooling in England but, as is to be expected, finds it difficult readjusting to Jamaican society after exposure to her British peers of high breeding.

We have chosen to educate Jane Gray in Jamaica because of the expenses we have incurred in schooling for our two eldest children. Jane is just a child and already talking of marriage to an older man, a Rev. Thomas Sharpe, of no relation to the family. She is far too young to be thinking of betrothal but I fear this is unavoidable. Creole children in Jamaica are exposed to the adult life at a far earlier age than their British counterparts.

Our younger boy, Thomas Joseph Gray was born in

November 1820. We named him after my father. He is at that age which seems to give him licence to be unruly and disobedient. I need to keep a close watch on his free-spirited nature. In Jamaica, this trait can lead children into dreadful mischief in later years if it is not curbed from infancy.

Our youngest is but an infant, Frances Gray, born in February 1830. I treasure every moment of her life and guard her carefully lest she succumb to illnesses like those whom I have already lost. Four of our infant children died, some only weeks or months old. Any mother who has lost a child will know the pain and distress I have endured.

I wonder why the Lord has chosen this fate for me. I feel a heaviness of spirit especially on those days when it pours incessantly. I feel confined and trapped within. The wind is too great to permit anyone to venture out, not even to sit on the piazzas. The house becomes damp and my clothes and linen musty. The pages of our books curl with the heavy moisture. At night, we suffer from infestations of flying roaches and other insects. Some of the critters find their way through the mosquito net into my sheets. Scorpions also appear to be more prevalent in the damp weather but they mostly nest under large rocks on the property. They are venomous and I have known of children to die from the bite.

I no longer have the company of Nana. She suffered long from various illnesses, and towards the end, had such swellings in her feet and legs that she was almost totally incapacitated. The doctor said that it was due to neglect in treating chigoes. Her condition worsened as she gained more weight. She could not walk very far without being out of breath and eventually her heart weakened as a result of the great strain upon her body.

It was a cool April morning when I was awakened by

screams coming from the kitchen. I found Bessy and Hercules bending over Nana. They carried the heavy corpse to the great room and rested it gently on the sofa. I gently closed the eyelids and said a private prayer in my heart for God to bless her soul. Nana was a good servant. She kept to herself, did her work faithfully and caused no contention. She was affectionate towards the children, and nursed them and cared for them as if they were her own. I trusted her like family and came to realize that there was a special place in my heart for her.

After Nana died, Bessy's expectation was to become the head Negress of the household. This I could not tolerate after years of her insolence and disobedience towards me. I would not have her in a position of authority which would give her licence and liberty to continue to act in her ill-mannered way. I persuaded my husband to have her sold to another owner. I learned later that she bore a child whom she claimed was Henry's offspring. I doubt the veracity of her claim for she has a conniving nature and would have many motives for establishing a link to this family. I purchased two new female slaves for service in the house. They need considerable training and supervision but are working out tolerably well.

My cousin, John Thorpe, came from England to spend a month with us at Cooper's Hill. I enjoyed his company immensely. We spent hours talking about family and friends in England and how different life was here in Jamaica. In the evenings, we played cards, games of chess and backgammon. He brought me as a present a copy of the published work of Jane Austen, her most recent novel, *Emma*. I became so engrossed in the book that while I read it, it transported me entirely to another place and time. The character of the protagonist Emma reminds me of Anna, never thinking of herself and always wanting good for others.

Mr Thorpe and I stayed many days indoors but ventured on occasion to Montego Bay. During his visit, we took a lengthy journey to St Jago de la Vega to stay with Mr John Lunan and his family. Mr Thorpe dressed tropically for the great adventure. He looked handsome in his broad-rimmed white hat which he used to shade himself from the bright sunlight. We also acquired for him suits of white clothing which many of the planters wear to keep cool in the excessive heat of the day.

Our trip to Spanish Town took two days because of the treachery of the mountain passes. Exhausted from the strenuous journey, we stopped overnight at a tavern in the town of Moneague to give ourselves, in addition to the horses, a well-needed rest. Moneague has a pleasant air. The pastures in that section of Jamaica, in the Parish of St Ann, remind me of the green meadows of England.

The views on the approach to Spanish Town were spectacular. We traversed through a deep gorge with precipices on each side of a river called the Rio Cobre. John was astonished by the sight of naked children breastfeeding from their nannies on the banks of the river. The women sat with bare bosoms suckling two at a time, each child of a different age.

The heat in Spanish Town proved to be too severe for John to bear so we cut short our stay, and when we returned to Cooper's Hill, he fell ill with the malignant fever. The doctors recommended that he make immediate plans to return to England. I was surprised and disheartened by his sudden illness. He is a man of about eight or nine, and thirty, of a strong constitution. I could not help but think, and I am ashamed of myself for doing so, of the satirical portrayal of 'Johnny Newcombe' who would fall victim to tropical diseases soon after arrival on the island. Our plan was to have stayed some two weeks with our very good family friends, the Lunans.

I was embarrassed for him because on occasions such as balls, the young freed Coloureds would make John amorous offers: 'Massa, please tek me back to England as yuh wife.' My dear John was beside himself, flattered on the one hand by so many proposals but at the same time bewildered by a host of Black women soliciting favours of the lewdest kind. I think my cousin was relieved when he finally boarded the ship for England.

The fears of a slave rebellion and the growing animosity of the planters towards the sectarians had been festering for some time but have now become realities. Many English families have abandoned their estates and returned home. Land values in Jamaica have plummeted and Cooper's Hill, which was not prosperous at the best of times, is no exception. In a peculiar way, my husband and I have become accustomed to our way of life here. It would be difficult for us to be persuaded to resettle in England.

There are whispered reports of slaves poisoning their masters. I am told there are few remedies to the poison of the plants, especially the wangla which the murderous slave cooks in the soup to serve to the master. Other sources of natural poison on the island are the gall of the alligator and the juice of the bitter cassava plant extracted before it is boiled. I am fortunate to have a trusted group of slaves, but there will be no comfort in this if the rebellion becomes so widespread that all loyalties to the master are eroded.

All White families have been put into grave danger.

I have sent word to Sam Sharpe to say that I should like to speak with him. I have heard it said that his followers call him Daddy Sharpe. I understand how he would have many supporters for he has all the qualities of a great leader. He is intelligent and charismatic, loyal and kind, but I think he may have been deceived into believing that freedom may be won by way of the sword. If the reports I read are all true, then it is clear that he has violated the laws of this country and of this government.

Slavery seems such an abhorrent thing when one feels such deep human compassion for those who are enslaved.

I wish to discourse with him.

Mrs Samuel Sharpe

TWENTY-FOUR

May 4ᵗʰ, 1832

I am so dirty and I stink bad. I cannot see my reflection but I imagine how ugly I must look with my hair knotted up. When I was in the service of Maas Sam, Nana made sure I was scrubbed clean every day. The Missus, she said, never liked to have the slaves smell bad.

Mistress Sharpe has come to visit me in prison. She looks older and has lines in her face but her hair is still jet black, fastened as always in the back with red pins.

'They have allowed me to come visit with you, Sam.' She looks happy to see me.

I feel embarrassed about my condition. There is nowhere for her to sit. 'It's lovely to see you, Missus.'

'I will call the guard for a seat.' It is as if she can read my thoughts. She leans over to speak through the bars to make her request.

'I apologize for this filth, Mistress Sharpe.' I hang my head.

'I did not expect it to be the Governor's house, Sam.' She chuckles.

I am not accustomed to Mistress Sharpe making jokes. James brings a stool into the cell, and she sits.

'What a mess I got myself into, Missus.' I sit myself down on the dirty bedding and look up at her perched on her seat.

'We have all had a difficult time of it, I am afraid.' Her voice is soft in a sad way.

'I'm sorry to hear, Mistress Sharpe.'

'I wish you could call me something else. It sounds hideous at times.'

'What is that, Ma'am?'

'Mistress.' She pauses a while. 'Never mind that. The times are dreadful. The rebellion has brought us almost to ruin.'

'Things are bad all round, Ma'am.'

'Yes, your master's two brothers, Mr Charles Sharpe and Daniel Bernard Sharpe, both lost their residences and estates. Burned to the ground. I had wanted to speak with you when the rebellion began. I had even sent word for you to visit.'

'I never get any word, Ma'am, and even still, I don't think I would a want to do that. Why you did want to see me, Ma'am?'

Her voice drops low down. 'It is all too late now, Sam. It is all over. The damage is done.'

'How is your family, Missus?'

'Mr Gray's relatives, of course, suffered dearly with the loss of their plantations.'

'I meant your own family, Ma'am. You and Massa.'

'Samuel is a young man now almost nineteen, and studies in England. You knew that our dearest Katherine died at age five.'

'Yes, Ma'am, I'm sorry.'

'Elizabeth and Jane Gray are growing to be fine young women, sixteen and fourteen, now. Frances Gray is our youngest.' Her face goes pale and her voice turns to a whisper. 'Since Katherine, I have lost three little ones.'

'I'm sorry, Ma'am.'

'The English call Jamaica the graveyard of the Indies.'

'Plenty people dead here fi true, Ma'am.'

'I hope you are not making a joke of this, Sam. I have come to see if you need anything. I have heard about your trial and sentence.'

'I need now to prepare my soul for the hereafter, Ma'am.'

'Elizabeth and Jane are making a white suit for you to wear on your last day.'

Her eyes are soft. She never looked at me like this before.

'That is a lovely gift, Missus. Tell them for me, Ma'am, that I am thankful to them, that I feel blessed by their kindness.'

'It is their way of extending their affection towards you, Sam.' Her face regains its colour. 'You served long for us and even though you worked for other proprietors, you belonged to us.'

'I hardly knew them, Ma'am.'

She doesn't seem to hear me. 'Curious thing.' She stares at the wall with a blank face.

'What is that, Ma'am?'

'We say we own you, but you became like family after a while. It was the same with Nana.'

'I hear she did pass on.'

'Yes, Nana had not been well for a long time. She was a dear soul.'

'What happened to the sweet girl, Bessy?'

'We needed to sell her. It became too complicated with Henry in the house, and besides that, she became pregnant.'

'All the young girl want them pickaninny fi White, Ma'am.'

'Well, perhaps this is so. I was never sure who the father was.'

'And Master Henry, Ma'am, he is fine?'

'We shall not speak of him. To think that I used to tell him to keep his distance from you lest he learn bad habits.'

'We are used to that, Ma'am. The master always thinks the slave is a wretch compared to his own child.'

'Well, don't mention it to anyone, will you, but I think you to be a brave soul.'

'Thank you, Ma'am. I would not know who to tell anyways, Ma'am.' I want to grab her attention for she has a faraway look on her face, 'Mistress Sharpe.'

'What is it, Sam?'

'Did you ever hear anything more of Miss Mary?'

'Do you mean the owner of "The Stag" establishment?'

'Yes.'

'It is a very sad story, Sam.'

'What happened, Mistress?'

'She was found one morning in her bed. They think it was poison.'

'Why would anybody want to do that?'

'We are not sure. Some say it was her own doing.'

'That is horrible Ma'am.' I suddenly feel weak.

'Yes, but she was a lost soul. Rumour has it that her children were taken from her and she was not allowed to bring them with her to Jamaica.'

'I always thought something was wrong.'

'Yes.'

'She was miserable to me but she was a good woman still. God bless her.' Moments of silence pass between us. She looks distracted again. 'Mistress Sharpe.'

'Yes, Sam.'

'I want you to know that despite everything I never did mean any harm to you and your family.'

'We all became affected by the rebellion in one way or another. What a waste of life!' Her voice sounds angry.

'What is that, Ma'am?'

'A waste of life that you should die.' Her eyes look kind. I feel she is being tender towards me.

'That is sweet for you to say, Missus. We had a plan and we thought freedom was coming, but it turn out wrong for us.'

'*Wrong for us too, I am afraid.*'

'*But those who got shot down or hanged or beaten to death, I will make sure they didn't die for nothing.*'

'*And how will you do that?*'

'*By walking bravely to the gallows.*'

'*I think you saved Mr Burchell's life by turning yourself in to the authorities.*'

'*Is he safe now?*'

'*Yes, I believe so, in America, thanks to the kindness of Custos Barrett who advised him to leave the island.*'

'*That man was always kind to us slaves.*'

'*Yes, and our family friend, Mr Lunan, has also been sympathetic to the needs of the slaves. I believe he had a strong influence on Mr Barrett.*'

'*Mr Manderson was also a caring gentleman.*'

'*He is now a magistrate and member of the House of Assembly. He did much for Mr Burchell. And I believe your imprisonment may have helped the Baptist cause. The magistrates finally found you and this diverted their attention from the missionaries.*'

'*I turned myself in, Ma'am.*'

'*Yes, of course, I know this.*' *Her eyelids flutter as if she is nervous.*

'*I praise God their lives were spared.*'

'*The planters wanted blood, Sam. Banners were posted on the doors of the courthouse to rid the island of the sectarians*':

> *But the prophet which shall presume to speak a word in my name which I have not commanded him to speak, even that prophet shall die," —* DEUTERONOMY, *chap. xviii, v. 20*
> *May this be the fate of all such as*
>
> BURCHELL!*

'Who was responsible for that?' I asked her.

'Let us not speak any more of this. Certain gentlemen of property convened a meeting at the courthouse with the said purpose of passing resolutions to this effect.' She stops for a moment and looks at me in a mistrustful way, puckering up her mouth. 'I talk to you as if you are an intelligent man, Sam.'

'I understand what you are saying, Ma'am.'

'Mr Sharpe always said you were intelligent. I never saw it at the start.'

'We say, Ma'am, "black fowl can lay white egg". Maybe you wasn't looking for it.'

'I'm not entirely sure of what you mean, but when we are young, the world is seen through very narrow lenses.'

'I am glad you came to visit me, Missus.'

'I have enjoyed it too, Sam. If only more of us could learn to treat one another with respect.'

'We is all brothers in Christ, Ma'am.'

'If we truly believed this, we would not be in the mess we are in.'

'Would you be so kind as to tell me something, Ma'am?'

'Yes, Sam. Well, it would depend. What is it?'

'Why Mr Sharpe never testify for me at the trial?'

'Yes, this must have seemed odd to you. He pleaded on your behalf but he was forbidden to take part because of our bad debts. I have heard it said too that they think him too partial to the cause of the Negroes.'

'You must give him my regards and tell him that I love him like my brother.'

'This seems somewhat morbid to say, Sam, but he has applied to the magistrates of the town for your body to rest at Cooper's Hill.'

'That is good, Ma'am, for there I shall rest in peace.'
'May you forever rest in peace, Sam.' She reaches out to
hold my hand. She never touched me before like that. 'I shall
work with Reverend Bleby to publish your memoirs.'
    'I am almost finished. I need to write a few more chapters
to make my peace with Christ.'
    'I must go now. I am surprised that they have let me stay so
long with you. Know one thing, Sam — that we hold no
grudges, my family and I. You must let me free you from that
guilt. All blessings to you.'
    'God be with you, Ma'am.'

December 27th, 1831

The fire at Kensington served as a beacon for the slaves
on nearby estates, a sign from God that the battle had begun,
that redemption was coming. Blue Hole Estate was the second
to be set ablaze and then it spread after that. Each fire saluted
the other in the fight for freedom. People were shouting in
jubilation, conch-shells and cow-horns blowing in every
quarter, 'Kensington pon fire! Palmyra pon fire! No more
watchman, no more driver! Brimstone come! Bring fire and
bon Massa house!'
    The fires spread and there was no stopping the madness.
One plantation after another went up in flames. Not only the
trash houses but whole fields were burning, quick to light
because of the dried leaves during crop time. At least ten estates
burnt the first night. The horizon lit up with the brightest
flares I had ever seen. Craziness came over the land. The White
people gathered their horses and gigs, and women and children
were taken as quickly as possible down to the Bay to seek
refuge on the ships waiting in the harbour. Slaves ran in all
directions, some too alarmed to do anything but to go and

hide in the bush, while others took to rebellion, tiefing and burning all that they could find. The overseers could not give orders to their head drivers because the slaves had taken up their machetes and left the estates. Livestock ran wild because of the fires, cattle and horses breaking down walls and trampling through the cane pieces. The great houses were abandoned, all order on the estates lost with no chance of recovery. Our plan had come to ruin, for now there was no chance of peaceful resistance. We were at war.

My first instinct was to protect Nyame and the baby. I thought of Mama too and wondered where she was. When the fires broke out, I was on my way from the chapel at Salter's Hill back up to Croydon. So I turned back down towards Anchovy way. I was concerned about Nyame's safety because the rebellion was spreading fast, moving closer to Content Estate. When I arrived, I found Nyame to be alarmed and frightened, but she and Juba, thank God, were safe. The slaves at Content had so far remained where they were. Nyame's father had left to join a group of insurgents that was travelling up to Shettlewood and Belvidere area. He had been a strong supporter of our plan and held regular night meetings to recruit members to join the movement.

'Me come check on you to see if everything all right.'

'The people dem gone mad, Sam.'

'It wasn't part of the plan. Me must go up to Greenwich tonight to meet with Gardner.'

'The night is full of danger. The soldiers will pick you out and shoot you down.'

'They're not about, Nyame.' I held her chin up so our eyes could meet. 'Dem fraid more than we, Nyame. Is fi we time now.'

'You promised there would be no violence.'

'That is why me must leave you, to talk to Gardner and Dove before it get more out of control. Remain here at Content, but if there is a problem, go 'cross to Cooper's Hill. The mistress there will tek you in.'

~

The White people must have got word of trouble prior to Christmas because we heard the militia had been put on alert before the fires started: the Westmoreland and Troop of Horse regiments from the Saturday before Christmas, and the Western Interior, St James and Trelawney regiments from the Monday. It was especially dangerous up by Shettlewood where Little Breeches was in command.

Slaves were part of the plan to set fires. I found out later that large-scale meetings had been held at both Retrieve and Richmond Hill earlier in the evening to talk about ways to start off the rebellion. Nobody had consulted me.

As I approached Greenwich, I found Gardner and Dove speaking to a big group of followers gathered from neighbouring estates. At least 500 male slaves with their women and children had assembled and anxiously awaited instructions. Also grouped there were freed Coloureds and Blacks who had fled the towns between Montego Bay and Savannah-la-Mar.

The place was secure. Gardner had set the camp on a part of the hill which had good defences against possible assailants. He had placed trained marksmen in the tall trees overlooking the estate. His men had built platforms on the trees, giving them a perfect view of the road and valley below. At the rear of the camp were steep hills where Gardner and his army had cleared tracks for an escape should there be a sudden attack. The colonel was more than ready.

His voice was strong and commanding. 'Dem block we dung by Shettlewood Barracks, cutting off de road both ways, one way to Sav-la-Mar and de other to de Bay through de Great River Valley. Me send Hurlock through Cambridge dung a de Bay to bring us back some intelligence. So we waiting fi him to return. In de meantime, mek sure dat you each have a weapon. De children and older slaves will stay back at camp. Others of you will go into companies led by de colonels. When we get information bout de enemy location, we will set up ambushes along de road and use de armament fi bring dem dung. Is fi we time now, brothers. We mus have de courage of de prophets, of David who Yahweh deliver from de enemy:

> *I have pursued mine enemies, and destroyed them,*
> *And turned not again until I had consumed them.*

> *And I have consumed them and wounded them, that*
> *They could not arise; yea, they are fallen under my feet.*

Gardner's words were bold and threatening. He spoke like a maroon warrior, someone they feared, someone they could trust to lead them into battle.

'And what says Daddy Ruler, General Samuel Sharpe?'

I was taken by surprise. I moved nearer to Gardner and spoke to the crowd, being careful not to contradict him. 'The alarm bell has rung, my brethren, and freedom is near. Our brothers could wait no longer. So we must have a new plan. We kyaan turn back now. We must claim the land and capture massa house but we must not bring dem to the slaughter.'

Gardner broke in on me. 'Amen, Daddy Sharpe. Our Jerusalem has come, friends. De time is here when our enemy will raise fortification around us, when dem will encircle us and hem us in. We must go to de fight, Daddy Sharpe.'

I raised my voice so all could hear. 'There are many in neighbouring parishes who don't know of our plan, but when they see the fires, dem will start to rebel against their masters. We must tell our brothers and sisters that we shall not shed blood. We shall be free, but the only time we must tek the life of buckra is when we defend weself. If we kill the White man and rape him women then we will not be free. We shall be prisoner and slave forever more.'

Gardner took charge again. 'Listen to me, my brothers. Me will keep you safe. There is danger and we must act swiftly or else dem gwine tek we prisoner. Captains, me want you fi scout de estates tonight and bring back word as fast as you can if there is any resistance. Carry any weapon you can find, musket, carbine, pistol, club or stick. And don't forget yuh machete. When you come upon de head slave at de estate, tell him to warn de attorney or any other White people dat we coming fi tek over de property and dat dem must leave. If de driver start fi cuss you and him get ignorant wid you, then come back to Greenwich and we will back you up wid more weapons. Tell all de people you meet dat we have thousand of man here at Greenwich and de great battle against de Whites is about to begin.'

Gardner continued to make his plans for war. 'We will happen upon a place and decide when to fire at de militia. You will wait for de command from one of de colonel or captain. We will always place our position on top of a hill so dat we can see everyting good. We will go out in squads, each headed by a captain. Me tell you again, you will tek orders from yuh captain or colonel and nobody else. When you reach pon de estate, you must run weh de massa, him wife and children and tell dem fi gwaan dung a de Bay. You must empty de house of arms and other article de Negroes might want, including de furnitures. Then burn de house and other building around but save de blacksmith and de cooper house. We will need dem later to supply us wid bullets and arms. Always wait for a command. After we done wid de estates, we will go next to capture de towns and villages. Other squads will go along de main road fi fight in ambush so dat we can tek dung de militia as dem try fi come up from Black River, Sav or de Bay.' He paused and not a sound was heard from the crowd. He then turned to me and said, 'Now, Daddy Sharpe will lead us in prayer.'

'We beg you, Heavenly Father, to send down your Spirit on us, to give us the knowledge to do what is right. The Lord said unto Joshua, "I will not fail thee, nor forsake thee." And the Lord said unto Abraham, "Fear not, Abram: I am thy shield and thy exceeding great reward." The Lord who redeemeth Israel now leads his people forth. Guide us, O Lord, in thy strength. You are the almighty, the all-powerful. Praise be to your holy name. Your praise shall continually be in our mouth. O magnify the Lord with me and let us exalt His name together. "The Lord redeemeth the soul of his servants: and none of them that trust in him shall be desolate."'

The rain came in later that night and we found what shelter we could from the cold.

December 28ᵗʰ, 1831

At cockcrow, everything was quiet, but with the dawn of light, the battle cries began.

We received word of troops gathering over by Shettlewood. In order to clear a passage through the northern parts of the parish, Gardner thought it necessary to go up against the militia forces. The core of his military was the Black Regiment under the command of newly named Colonel Johnson of Retrieve and Colonel Charles Campbell of York Estate. Both men were warrior-like, Coromantees, with strong physiques and a deep passion for the cause of freedom. They commanded a group of about 150 men with only about 50 guns among them. I was concerned that Little Breeches was going to be too strong for them. The slaves were not trained in the use of firearms and they were afraid to use them. Besides, the weapons were old pieces which they had stolen from their masters: muskets and fowling-pieces, carbines and pistols. Johnson and Campbell were my friends and I did not want to see them hurt.

Gardner set up a ranking of slaves in charge of his unit. They called me General, the one who was to give all the orders. I was the Daddy and Teacher turned Ruler and General. The next-in-command was Gardner, with the rank of colonel, and below him Dove, lieutenant colonel. Many of the stronger leaders he made captains of bands: M'Cail from Prospect Plantation, Campbell and Johnson. He also had lieutenants and ensigns: James Fine, Thomas Simpson, and some freed Brown men, M'Intosh and Largie, and a female named Wilma M'Donald.

Gardner looked like a real military man dressed in his red jacket, cocked hat and feather, riding back and forth on a white steed which he had taken from Greenwich Estate. His uniform had black sleeves with red stripes up the seams and his pantaloons were blue. Some uniforms had been stolen from estate houses but others were made by women who stayed back at camp during the day.

I remained at Greenwich for part of the day to organize groups that went out under the command of captains. Scouts returned at intervals to report on operations. Bands went out through the countryside encouraging slaves to abandon the estates so they could set fire to the trash houses and empty and destroy the great houses. Large cane fields, yellow with the ripened sugar cane, were set ablaze.

The head drivers and skilled slaves were mostly on the side of the rebellion but many field slaves did not want to harm massa's belongings. On estates where there was no driver, the slaves became confused and frightened. They formed their own groups to block out the rioters. Others became afraid and fled to the bush. The looting and the burning of estates continued all that day, mainly in the south, Cambridge, Richmond Hill, Catadupa through to the main road to St Elizabeth. Fires were also set close to the troops at York, Hazelymph and Belvidere in the hopes of scaring them off.

Jamaica, a land once green and fertile, was being burnt. I was fearful and could not help thinking of the words of Job, that 'they that plow iniquity, and sow wickedness, reap the same.'

We must have frightened away the planters, because there were no White people to be seen on the estates except for the odd busha who stayed back to try to restore order. Some owners came back up from the Bay to try to put out the fires, but by that time, the destruction was too far gone. It seemed that the buckra were afraid to come out on the roads because of our ambushes, and especially at night they remained in their houses, for the dews always made them sick. We knew the bush so much better than they, all the pathways, rivers, gullies and hills. And of course, the Black man always has an advantage in the night because of the colour of his skin. No wonder they were scared of us.

December 29th, 1831

I met up with a large group on the road between Hazelymph and Cambridge. They were armed with guns, machetes, lances and sticks, but I was carrying no weapon that day. I commanded the company moving south along the road to Ginger Hill, riding on a horse in the middle of the line with fifty or more men marching front and back, forming columns, two by two.

The scouts, who were posted on the hilltops through the region, sent us word that the militia were arriving from St Elizabeth and heading towards Ginger Hill. The White men had collected together farther south to wait for the right time to approach. A group of slaves from Retrieve, Richmond Hill and Belvidere had captured Ginger Hill the day before. We needed to offer some help to our brothers at Ginger Hill now that we had learned the militia were approaching. We positioned ourselves along the road where they would pass, to make an ambush. But they never showed. We learned they had turned off the road to Ipswich.

Buchannan, the head driver up at Ginger Hill, had shown the overseer, Mr Annand, to the home of a freed Black man in the area, warning him that it would be too dangerous for him to stay in his house. Buchannan told the busha that the slaves had refused to go out to work the day before because Jamaica was now free and all the estates between Ginger Hill and Montego Bay were burned down. When the White man tried to reason with Buchannan, he was told it would be useless to resist because 'it was not the work of man alone, but that they had assistance from God.'* The rebels emptied out his house and set fire to the buildings the same night we came up.

I paid a visit to Mr Annand that evening. I told him to swear that he would never stand between us and our rights.

The man looked frightened, sitting in a chair in the middle of a small room with about five or six Black men around him holding machetes and guns.

'I do not wish to take the life of anybody, Mr Annand. I will not take the life of anybody who does not stand between me and my rights. I know that freedom is our God-given right, Sir, and freedom is what we will have. *Letters have long ago been sent out from England to this effect but the people of Jamaica have kept us as slaves without any authority for doing so.* * Do not be frightened, for these men will not harm you. The scriptures tell us, Sir, that no man can serve two masters. We are believers in this Christian faith, and all those who believe in Christ shall be saved. If the Son of Man therefore shall make us free, then we shall be free indeed.'

I sent a few men on to Ipswich to warn our brothers that the militia were diverted there, but it started to rain and so they turned back. I went the other way, down to Content to stay the night with Nyame.

~

We suffered terrible losses at Montpelier that evening. Gardner explained that he put Colonels Campbell and Johnson in charge of about 200 men. They commanded the company with great courage and passion. Just after nightfall, they approached the estate in four columns of fifty men.

Gardner told the story of the battle of Montpelier, 'We manage first fi burn de trash house at New Montpelier before de militia run us. A couple of de men got wounded in de fight. Then, Haughton, de head driver at Shettlewood gather up a whole heap of rebels fi help we. Him line dem up, slaves from Ramble, from Alexandria, from Silver Grove, from all bout. Him line dem up all in a row and mek dem swear pon de Bible that as long as there was any one White man left in de country, dem shoulda fight fi dem freedom. De men joined ours, so our numbers increase quite a bit.

'It was about an hour after dark. One group was under de command of Johnson, who led his company to de Negro houses as ambush. Three other division come up by de main road. Dem call it de King Road. As we come close, me hear one of de colonel dem give de signal to halt and then run. We start fi dash all bout in de bush and some of de men get confuse. Me was surprise for me couldn't hear no shots from either side. We was too Black fi dem fi see we inna de night. Then some of our men start fi mek noise, blow horn and shell and cause a racket inna de place. Suddenly we get de order fi shoot from behind de stone wall by de cane piece. De musket dem blast out inna de night and then me catch sight of de militia. Me don't think we kill too many still. But nothing could stop we now. We march through de gate and keep firing at them. A party of about twelve men get scared and start fi run back. Dem fire pon we but miss wid every shot. Me tell you, Sam, de bullet dem fly past we and nebba trouble one of we. Me swear to you. Me don't know what happen to Dove. Him was supposed to be in command but de men sey dem did see him go a hide behind de stone wall. We charge straight through to de still house and Johnson group was meking an attack by de trash house. There was some man-to-man fighting and one Brown man get chop up wid a machete.

'Then we mek a mistake. Me tink it was Blacka, one of Johnson lieutenant, who break weh and move towards de trash house carrying a torch. *Whoosh!* Just like dat. Me tell you, Sam, de whole building go up in flame. Me tell you, Sam, me tink me was going dead right then and there. We come to be in full view of de enemy. Then dem start fi shoot and, Sam, what a tribulation, fi we men start fi drop, one by one. Dem shoot dung bout forty of we, including brothers Johnson and Campbell. Dis set up one panic. De command was lost. Some lie dung dem head inna de dirt, other man tek de chance fi jump de wall, but dem too met wid death. Dove and me try fi call for an orderly retreat but it was too late. De only ting we could do was fi keep up fire to cover some who manage fi get weh.

'And dat was de end of de battle. Is a funny thing, me nebba see not even one White man shoot a gun, only de Black man dem. De White militia line demself up in a square and de Coloured men did all de shooting. Campbell did hurt bad but we move him and tek him weh wid us. Johnson did too close to where de militia was standing. So we had to leave him dead body deh pon de battleground.'

'How many dead in all?'

'Ten men. Two of them was from Montpelier, James Richards and Giles Miller. James did marry to a young female named Jenny Ellis. You shoulda hear her bawl when she get de news. She was so proud of James. Him did belong to de first gang and him did work hard like an ox. Him did own a cow, two hogs and four chicken and him have two acre of provision ground where him grow plantain, cocoa, yam and corn. But everyting mash up now, she sey, cause of de rebellion.'

'We have gone mad, Gardner. There is blood on our hands. This was not the plan.' I felt saddened by the slaughter of Johnson and the other men.

'One thing me know for sure, Sam, is that we kyaan turn back. We haffi go wid de battle and tek charge. Otherwise, it's slavery time again. You know me see yuh mama at Montpelier?'

'You never mention nothing bout that.'

'Me swear it was she. She was wid de slave Haughton round up from Shettlewood.'

'But she supposed to be in Accompong.'

'Me know it was she, yelling and shouting "fire" just like de others. You should a see her fighting, man.'

'God bless Mama.'

Later I prayed in private a version of the 54th psalm of David:

> Save us, O God, by thy name, and judge us by thy strength.
>
> For strangers are risen up against us and oppressors seek after our soul. . .
>
> Behold, God is our helper. . .
>
> He shall reward evil unto mine enemies: cut them off in thy truth.
>
> I will freely sacrifice unto thee: I will praise thy name, O Lord;
>
> for it is good.

But the night brought little comfort with its sounds of pillage and murder.

TWENTY-FIVE

May 6th, 1832

The authorities have given Mr Bleby permission to visit me one last time. I expect that they do not want visitors too close to my execution day for that would stir up too much sympathy for the leader of the rebellion.

He comes dressed today in civilian clothes, very formal with a ruffled white shirt and necktie. He carries a small bundle of papers tied with a ribbon.

'Sorry I not dressed too decent to welcome you, Minister.' *The cell stinks now more than ever.*

'These are infernal conditions they keep you in, Sam.'

'Not to worry. It soon be over.'

He takes a seat on the stool which the guard has provided.

'I have read the chapters you gave to me.' *He pulls the ribbon loose.*

'Do you think you will be able to publish them?'

'They need some revision, Sam, but we shall see. Your owner, Mrs Sharpe, has expressed an interest in readying your work for publication.'

'I shall be grateful if you do this, Mr Bleby.'

'There are personal details that may be of no interest to the reader.' *He flips through the sheets of paper.*

'I shall be thankful for whatever you able to do. I shall leave it to your best judgement.'

'Why are you so eager that your writings be published?'

'For I want people to know how we struggled for freedom.'

He stares at me in a way that makes me uncomfortable, as if his eyes are piercing into me. 'Tell me more of the uprising, Sam. Is it not true that you incited others to fire and rebellion?'

'What does it matter now, Minister? I go to the gallows soon enough.'

'Yes, but it shall be recorded in history for future generations. We must get it right, mustn't we, Sam.'

'I write it like I know, Minister.'

'Reverend Smith tells me that Gardner was so reluctant to become involved that he once had to slip out the back door of a meeting room. He had wanted nothing to do with the rebellion but you sent him large numbers of men to command.'

'When did he say this?'

'When he was being interviewed in prison at Savannah-la-Mar by a Reverend Smith.'

'There may be mistakes in how people report things, Minister.'

'As best I can recall, the rector quoted Gardner's words as, "Oh, Sir, if I had had any good friend to tell me the real truth, as I now find it to be, I never would have been brought to this."'*

'I never misled him or any of my other friends, Sir. The chief priests and captains bribed him as they did Judas Iscariot. They are lies, false as hell.'

'How do you know this, Sam?'

'I thought I did hear that the Chief Justice promise him and Dove that their lives would be spared if they help Mr Knibb find out more about the rebellion. That is what Mr Knibb tell me.'

'Yes, this is true, but improper procedures were followed for his trial. Your friend was hurried to the gallows in violation of the instructions of the Governor, who has always demanded that he first see all capital sentences before they are executed.'

'Well, *they tek their sweet time with me and they still gwine hang me.*' *I find myself bending over with a sharp pain in my stomach.*

'*What is the matter?*'

'*No matter, Minister. It must be some colic.*' *I pause a while, rubbing my side to relieve the hurt.* '*They will not change their mind, you think, Minister?*'

'*About what?*'

'*Reverse my sentence?*'

'*I think not, Sam. There is no right of appeal.*'

'*I knew the answer, Sir, but there is no harm in asking.*'

'*No harm whatsoever. Do you think you managed things badly, Sam?*'

'*Why you ask this, Minister Bleby?*'

'*Gardner indicated that the plan did not work because of the want of a chief who could plan for the best and convey orders with perspicacity and dispatch.*'

'*Those are harsh words, Sir. I rather not talk ill of the dead. God rest his soul. Gardner was a fierce rebel and a blood friend I knew ever since I was a child.*'

'*Do not misunderstand me. He said you were the ruler. You swore every man all round, from the Parish of St James, Trelawney, St Elizabeth, Hanover and the upper parts of Westmoreland. He said the oath was that every man should fight and do his utmost to drive the White and free people out of Jamaica. If you succeeded, a governor would be appointed to every parish.*'

'*You don't think that was a good plan, Minister Bleby?*'

He seems uneasy, shifting his body on the stool. '*The only way to save your eternal soul, Sam, is to beg forgiveness for your sin.*'

'*What sin, Sir?*'

'*The sin of inciting others to rebellion.*'

*"'If I have done wrong in that, I trust I shall be forgiven, for I cast myself upon the atonement.'"** *

'But how do you reconcile your role in being the leader of the rebellion?'

'I counselled the people, Minister. I was their teacher. We prayed always for the guidance to do the right thing.'

'This was not a divine mission, Sam.'

'How you know that for sure, Sir?'

'God does not work in these ways.'

'Do not be too sure, Minister Bleby. His ways are mysterious.'

'What did you do all those days and nights before you turned yourself over to the authorities?'

'I not sure what you asking me. It was my Garden of Gethsemane.' I feel worn down and disturbed by his line of questioning. *'I need some sleep, Minister. I am tired.'*

'I must leave you, then.'

'You must know, Sir, that destruction of property and murder formed no part of my plan. I wanted no man injured. Our only object was to obtain freedom.'

'Not many understand this.'

'I regret we caused so much pain, but I cannot atone for my fight for freedom.'

'May God give you strength, Sam, and the reward of eternal life.'

'Thank you, Minister, and the grace of God be with you too.'

December 30th, 1831

Campbell died on the Friday, the day after the battle at Montpelier. His wounds were too deep for him to recover. We buried him on the hillside at Greenwich, sprinkled white rum on his grave and sang praises to God for his great courage. Gardner conducted the ceremony.

For a short time, Gardner lost his passion to continue the fight, but when he heard news that Little Breeches had run away from his position at Montpelier to go hide in the Bay, he took up his sword and once again mounted his white horse. We heard reports that the militia was dumping large boxes of ammunition, food, clothes and army equipment into the river. When they went to haul away their possessions, they discovered that the neck yoke was broken off from the wagons. The slaves had been up to mischief.

News spread that the White man catch him fraid and Black man rule the country. Mr Grignon's retreat made way for the rebels. From Lucea straight across to Orange Valley, back up to Ginger Hill and beyond to YS Falls became our land. Buckra was hiding himself along the coast at Round Hill and Montego Bay. Not one White man was to be seen in the mountain parts. So, the looting and burning grew out of control. There was no turning back. Massa's food and belongings were strewn about the lawns of the estates and the slaves helped themselves to the liquor, salt pork, butter, peas, barley and some fancy foods they had never even tasted before. The slave villages and places of worship were kept intact, but many of the great houses, the workhouses and the cane fields were burned down.

We walked the roads like we was free. Freedom had come at last. Praise to the Heavenly Father who had seen it right to redeem his people.

We were on our own now. The planters had joined the militia, the freed men, both Coloured and Black, were fighting as the enemy, and the missionaries were being rounded up. We needed to find a way to govern ourselves, but there was no order and no plan.

The slaves burned the old Montpelier works buildings as soon as they realized Little Breeches had retreated with his regiments. A handful of the Montpelier slaves, including Charles Tharpe and George Miller, tried to defend their massa's buildings but there were too many slaves from other estates wanting to do damage. Under the command of two captains, Hine from Springfield and Duncans from Easthams, they cut up shingles from the rooftops to make firewood and lit torches from the fires in the kitchens and slave houses. They then ignited Massa's house, Busha's house, and the works buildings. Amidst the ruins was the body of a White man in a coffin abandoned there by Mr Grignon. The slaves dragged the corpse out of the box and threw it in the fire. They also discovered the body of their fearless leader, Johnson, lying face down in the front yard. For him, they dug a hole in the ground and gave him a Christian burial right there in the middle of all the confusion.

With the blowing of the shell, the jubilation started at seeing a big estate like old Montpelier burn to the ground. With renewed vigour, bands moved through the country later that day to set fire to neighbouring Shettlewood, Seven Rivers, Belvidere and other estates in the Great River Valley. Thousands of slaves on these estates watched their massas' houses and mills go up in flames.

We rejoiced also because we thought the King's men had landed to break our chains of slavery. The black ships had arrived in Black River Harbour. We soon learned that the ships had landed the regulars to come out to kill us, not help us. Along with the White soldiers, the ships carried gunpowder, the black sand destined for the slaughter of the rebel slaves.

Hurlock, the man we had sent to the Bay to spy for us, reported that regular troops of the British Army were also arriving there. 'The gubna declare martial law which mean sey de King's army is in charge and de soldier mek all de rule dem. Dem gwine kill we and heng we with nobody fi save we.'

Hurlock was a short and slim man without the heavy bulk of a male Negro. He had shifty eyes and a twisted smile that came out of the corner of his mouth when he spoke. 'Me go all bout de town and talk to de soldier dem. One day me dress like a woman, de next day, me is a man carrying water pon me head. Me fool dem every time. Me tell dem all de news from de rebels. Me tell dem sey bout 10,000 man attack Mr Grignon up at Montpelier.'

'Me open up me yeye dem wide so me could frighten dem. Me sey to dem, "De rebel dem is dangerous, Sar, trust me. Dem a carry big gun and machete, and dem will kill any White man dem see. Mek sure unu lock up yuh wife and pickaninny inna de house for de rebel dem gwine come fi tek you weh."'

The men who were with me laughed at Hurlock's story.

'And how they look when you tell them, brother?' George Reid asked.

'Me tink dem did piss up dem pants.'

'You should a tell them we have 50,000 strong and if dem know what was good for them, dem should board de big ship and tek dem woman and pickaninny to England.'

'Dat would be good but dem tell me de regulars soon come. De soldier dem arrive pon de ship call *Blanche* and another dem call *Racehorse* and dem soon gwine bring de big gun up de mountain top fi kill all a we. Fi dem headquarters is at Parson Burchell church. The Baptist chapel in town turn into barracks, to raas. De whole of de Bay inna panic. Dem have bucket of water ready in case we come fi set fire to the town and all de rest of de people dem a lock up inna dem house.'

We had an opportunity to take Montego Bay but it messed up badly. One of our men, Charles McLenan of Springfield, had gathered a large army and was to join forces with Tharpe, who called himself the King of St James. The two leaders were rivals and could not agree on who should take charge. McLenan gave up command and returned to Montego Bay, leaving Tharpe too weak to mount the attack with his own men. We had lost our chance. The soldiers had arrived in the Bay, and were going to bring their big guns up into the hills.

When the regulars decided to move into the interior, we were ready for them. We ambushed them along the roads, firing shots and throwing rockstones. When the gunpowder of the White man became too great, we ran like all hell into the bush. On one occasion, we lost fourteen men who were picked out and shot like pigeons in flight. The enemy was advancing in increasing numbers up from the Bay and we were feeling the pressure of the invasion. We were much more afraid of the regulars than the militia, because the former had no discipline or conscience.

In the south, our scouts informed us that two companies of the St Elizabeth Regiment were approaching YS but we were confident that given the numbers we had at Ginger Hill and Ipswich, we would be able to fight them back. Before setting out, we prepared a big feast of roast suckling pig and liquors so we could celebrate our victory when we returned. Our troops set out that evening, but never got to taste the food and drink. The militia descended on us at Ginger Hill and Ipswich. They wreaked havoc, killing about thirty of our men, taking an equal number of prisoners and destroying stockpiles of firearms we had hidden in the houses.

It rained heavily that night, and as we retreated into the bush, we became cold and sick from the wet. This was our first major defeat, pushing the Black Regiment back into Belvidere and Greenwich. We had lost control of the road to Black River and needed now to regroup to find new vantage points. We were up against big odds. And the enemy was to become fiercer, as we heard the Maroons from Accompong were to join their command the following day.

The sense of danger forced our men into the offensive. The following day, December 31st, the Black Regiment, under the command of Colonel Gardner, gathered a company of about 150 men, slaves from Greenwich, Chester Castle, Belvidere and Hermitage. They burned Argyle to the ground.

Our headquarters at Greenwich, our last stronghold, was being threatened with the advance of the militia. We received word that the Negroes in the village at Struie were in danger. I made the decision not to stay back at camp that day but to take a party up to Struie to assist with the defence of our post there. Men from one of Gardner's parties had come up from the night before and lay in ambush, ready to pounce on the militia advancing from Westmoreland. The rebel operation was successful. We had a good vantage point at the top of a hill, my party on one side of the road and Gardner's on the other. Two scouts perched up in a tree and as soon as they gave a whistle, we were to fire. We remained half hidden in the bush, and just as the militia turned the corner, we heard the signal. Our men fired and I saw one White man drop in the road. The others retreated, not only because of the strength of our fire but because of the superior position we held on the hill. One of ours ran after a straggler and chopped the man with his machete.

By the first day of January, the general's troops were making headway in the north. They secured Round Hill at the mouth of the Great River and moved up from there into the interior to occupy Montpelier and the Great River Barracks which the rebels had so valiantly captured from Little Breeches. This threatened our hold on the big estates in the valley.

That following day, the general released from jail about 100 prisoners whose job it was to deliver a proclamation telling us that we must beg pardon from the King. Mercy was to be shown to the slaves who surrendered, but the leaders of the rebellion would have to pay with their lives. It was announced that some wicked persons had told us lies about the King making us free and about our masters withholding the freedom papers. The general was coming with big forces, the notice said, to crush the rebels and punish the guilty. We must surrender immediately and be pardoned. Anyone found with a rebel would be put to death without mercy.

A few slaves gave themselves in to the authorities, but most of us did not trust the message. We believed we were to be killed even if we did surrender. Slaves fled in panic into the mountains, all the way south into the Parish of St Elizabeth. A group tried to send a delegation to Accompong to get the support of the Maroons but those warriors would have nothing of it.

Our spies informed us that the soldiers were going to be placed in areas where they could surprise a whole bunch of us together. Our only tactic for survival now was to split up, forming small parties so they could not discover us as easily and blow us all away in one fell swoop with their big cannons.

The following morning saw a second proclamation. This time it was a reward for bringing in the main rebel leaders. A 300 dollar ransom was offered for each of us, Gardner, Dove, Johnson and myself, and His Majesty's pardon to anyone assisting in apprehending us. Their intelligence was able to find out who we were, but it came up short on Johnson. It was going to be difficult for them to get ransom money for him unless somebody dug up his grave. The proclamation described me with fancy titles:

> General Ruler Samuel Sharp or Tharp, alias Daddy Ruler, director of the whole and styled also, Preacher to the Rebels.

I was not sure how they arrived at the name Tharp. Maybe they were mixing me up with Tharpe from Catadupa or Tharpe from Hazelymph.

The reprisals against us started almost immediately. Executions became commonplace. When questioned by the soldiers, prisoners openly confessed that White people had told them that they were to be free at Christmas and that freedom had actually come out from England but was being held back. These confessions meant nothing to their captors. Officers were convinced of the guilt of the prisoners and the unsuspecting slaves were shot through the head. No trials. In one case I witnessed, a man was arrested while cooking one of the estate hogs. No questioning, no mercy. He was executed before me on the very spot where he was standing. It seemed the army's intent was to capture the rebels but return as few as possible to the estates.

We started to lose ground. The general was moving columns up from the coast on the east side in Trelawney and on the west in Hanover. We were blocked too from moving into St Elizabeth and Westmoreland to the south and down the Great River to the north. We soon realized the grave danger we faced of being surrounded, trapped on all four sides. Panic set in.

TWENTY-SIX

January 4th, 1832

Attack on our headquarters, Greenwich. Our scouts sighted the King's troops advancing from the north and the St Elizabeth and Westmoreland militia from the south. Both forces converged on the headquarters at Greenwich. Gardner determined that with the numbers left there, we were too weak to put up a fight. We retreated from our stronghold down behind the big house and hid ourselves in the bush nearby. As a decoy we left an old lady, Miss Matty, who had prepared a special brew for the soldiers.

Almost 100 men, dressed in full military uniform, closed in on our deserted camp. The leader marched in his heavy boots straight up towards Miss Matty.

'Where are all your good friends, old lady?' He pushed the barrel of his rifle under her nose.

'Me nah have no friends, Sar.' Her voice was barely audible.

He slammed her face with the end of his long gun and then shoved it under her chin. 'I'll not ask you a second time, wretch.' His face flushed with anger.

'Dem did desert de camp, Sar, but me did stay back cause of me lame foot.' Her voice became stronger, 'Me have some hot soup here though, Sar, if yuh men dem hungry.'

'You prepared this big pot of soup all for yourself, old hag?'

'It nice and tasty, Sar.'

He grabbed the ladle she was holding and scooped up a portion of broth from the pot. He yanked her head backwards, forcing the liquid into her mouth. Immediately, she began spitting and coughing up the soup.

'You devil! Trying to poison the King's men were you?' The man held her more violently, forcing his way behind her. He grabbed tufts of her white woolly hair, jerked her head back farther, and with a knife, he slit her throat.

We scurried down the steep ravine at the back of the camp through escape routes which Gardner had carefully designed. The soldiers were hot on our trail. I could hear the war cry of Maroons and the pounding of military boots through the brush. Fortunately there was no sound of Spanish bloodhounds, which would have hunted us down and torn us apart. Our only hope for survival at that point was to split up and hide in the numerous caves which lined the bottom of the hill. The cave I entered had a large hole the height of a man, but the interior soon became small and dark with crawl spaces leading to openings on the other side of the hill. The majority of us managed to escape except for a couple of men who were captured by the Maroons before entering the caves. We spent the night at Cow Park which was one of the few posts we still held.

January 5th

The rebellion went underground. The roads were no longer safe for us to travel on. I was trapped, unable to make my way down to Content without being captured. My new home became the bush. We set up temporary camps, scattered across the southern sections of St James. Women, who had returned to the slave villages, helped us out by sending food, water and Bible hymn sheets. Small bands were all that remained of the resistance and these became isolated one from another. In order to communicate, we resorted to fire signals and the blowing of the shell from strategic positions on mountaintops. A few scouts, skilled in finding their way through the backabush, also helped to keep one camp in touch with the other.

Freed slaves and runaways in the towns joined us at night for our raids. We had to be very careful, for even though the buckra could not penetrate the bush that easily, the Maroons continued to pose a threat. They had been sighted in the Chesterfield area and we suspected they wanted to hold us back from spreading west into the Parish of Westmoreland. They were rewarded the regular tariff for each pair of slave's ears they handed over to the authorities.

The battle was now lost.

I urged many to return to the estates, but some refused to go back and instead ran deeper into the woods. Many perished for lack of food and human contact and the Maroons captured those who ventured into their territory.

I prayed for them and for my brothers and sisters in other parts of Jamaica. I prayed that they would have the strength to resist the evil of oppression. I prayed that our enemies would be brought to justice. I asked God to deliver us from evil, to defend us from those who rise up against us. The mighty were gathered against us, they lay in wait for our souls, but the Lord would laugh at them and punish them. I sang praises unto Him who is our defence, the God of our mercy.

January 6th

Gardner tried desperately to build a support of fighters to defend our last post at Struie but he had lost too much weaponry. Besides, the spirit of the men was broken. They were tired, hungry, and intimidated by the power of the White soldiers. Many deserted the camp to roam aimlessly through the countryside.

A few skirmishes continued but they were ineffective in holding off the enemy. At Anchovy, a group of slaves fired upon baggage that the militia was carrying up the mountain. They killed two White men. Gardner received word that at Reading Hill the Western Interior Regiment would be advancing, but the slaves there were defenceless. He could do little to rescue them. His men were badly beaten back, shot down and taken prisoner.

January 7th

All the King's regiments joined forces with Sir Cotton at Belvidere, which they made their new headquarters. Sir Cotton showed authority by marching to Seven Rivers, Catadupa and Lapland, meeting our resistance only at Richmond Hill. We were afraid of the general. He looked like a chicken hawk with his beak nose, pointy chin and feathery hair.

Right across the land, slaves were giving themselves up to the authorities. They still did not believe the promise that if they surrendered they would be pardoned, but they had little choice. Good hiding places were nowhere to be found and supplies were being cut off. Some lives were spared, but most slaves, as they surrendered were shot through the head and left to rot on the side of the road for the john-crows to pick at.

The *Watchman*, which had supported our cause, was now writing articles against us: *Do they suppose they would be allowed to burn down the properties of their owners and go unpunished?* *

Revenge was sweet.

We would not be forgiven for what we had done, and we suffered severe consequences for our actions.

January 9th

A band of our men launched a fierce attack on a company near Leamington where a private named Chambers was chopped to death with a machete. We also managed to hold off a militia offensive near the Flint River where slaves burned down Orchard and Tryall estates.

Troops advancing from Westmoreland were posing an imminent threat to Gardner's hold at Struie. In the face of this danger, I established two new camps on the stretch between Catadupa and Vaughansfield. Gardner remained at Struie. The enemy was pushing us into separate corners with little chance of escape. Our only hope was to move farther east, but this posed the danger of capture by forces at Maroon Town.

We needed to push farther back to seclude ourselves in the mountainous regions. The White man could not travel easily over honeycomb rock. The leather boots the soldiers wore made them slip and fall on the jagged terrain. The natural soles of our bare feet, on the other hand, grabbed the rock with ease and surety. Our main hazard in these parts was the Maroon force who knew the land better than anyone, outsmarting us at every turn.

The militia forces had grown to be mighty now and fearless. Three companies of the Western Interior Regiment marched up to Greenwich under Little Breeches' command. They must have been the same men we drove from Montpelier in December. We hid in the bush and tracked Mr Grignon's movements. He took his troops and heavy artillery, horses, carriages, cannons and infantry through Ducketts and Cambridge. Along the way, the militia scooped many prisoners and shot those who tried to escape into the country around Catadupa and Belmont. The enemy continued their operations in these parts until the end of martial law several weeks later. Any slave who did not immediately come forward and surrender when accosted was shot on the spot.

One such slave was Patrick Ellis. He stood up bravely to his captor and refused to run or surrender: 'Shoot me, Massa, for

I will never again be a slave.'

That posed no problem for the massa. He took him at his word and ordered the fire. The bullets exploded in Ellis's head and his brains spilled out on to the roadside.

The militia hunted us down with vengeance as they would rats in the bush. As far as we could tell, there was no regard for the pardon the general was offering. They thought the only way to bring the Negroes to their senses was to burn every slave house in sight. After all, the wretches had deprived them and their families of their homes and a whole year's crop. What right did they have to keep their own?

The enemy made sure that the message was absolutely clear. Whenever a prize Negro, or someone whom they thought was an instigator of the rebellion, was captured, they would cut off his head and stick it upon a pole in the district where he lived. This was a horrific spectacle, especially for the Africans, who believed that the decapitated body meant that the spirit was no longer whole, that it had no chance of returning to its ancestral home.

The enemy's fire power was stronger than all the thunder in the sky. The soldiers used cannons to destroy our camps and villages. They mounted them on carriages which they drew by oxen up to the mountaintops to position on roads where they thought there was a high concentration of rebels.

Baroooooooooooooooom. I saw one explosion blow a whole company of our men away in one blast. Bodies splattered, pieces flung in every direction, into the bush and into the air.

By month's end, the King's men were flushing us out with rockets, long pieces of metal mounted on stands about three times as long as a man. The White men called them the Congreves. When the heavy warheads were fired, they shot through the air, giving off a red glare and exploding on contact.

The army would seek out the smoke from cooking fires in the bush, position their rockets at the mouths of caves and in the direction of the settlements, make aim and fire, totally destroying the huts and the people inside.

January 12ᵗʰ

At last, a victory for the rebels. Roehampton Estate was burned to the ground. Mr Baillie owned over 200 acres of cane and over 300 slaves. The whole of the sugar works went up in flames.

Nowhere was safe now. Those of us who survived retreated farther and farther into the Cockpit Country. I became isolated from the other rebels and from Nyame at Content. She must have been concerned for my safety but upset at the same time because of the danger I had put myself in.

Despite the odds, our men still managed to be a menace to the soldiers. A company of the King's men was returning to Maroon Town about a half mile from Kensington where they found trees lain across the road. The group of slaves had also cut deep trenches in the road so that the enemy's carts and ammunition could not pass. The rebels managed to get out some shots, forcing a retreat and hitting one of the officers in the head.

January 14ᵗʰ

Dehany's camp was completely destroyed. Two men were killed and five taken prisoner. Dehany managed to escape, setting up new headquarters at the home of his daughter near Vaughansfield. He was one of our main leaders, as strong and fierce as they come, originally assigned by Gardner to control the Salter's Hill area.

To make matters worse for us, the government introduced the Cornwall Rangers. They were not all trained for war but they were a fast-moving group whose job it was to round up as many runaways as possible and return us to the estates without inflicting casualties. The Governor was concerned that the militia was killing off too many of us. I suppose the government's hope was that we would restore order to the plantations and save for them what we could of the damaged crops.

The special guards did not follow orders. They captured many, but the atrocities continued. On one estate that the Rangers came upon near to the Bay, they rounded up the slaves and, for no apparent reason, singled out a young, healthy looking male.

'Did you burn down Massa's trash house?'

'No, Massa.'

'Don't tell me lies, wretch.'

'Me a tell you de truth, Sar.'

'Stand over there.'

'Me don't do nothing, Sar.'

'Did you not hear me? Stand over there by the tree and take off your shirt.'

The slave obeyed the guard.

'But, Massa. Beg you, Massa, me nebba do nutten, Sar. Do, Sar, me beg you. Me did help bring de slave dem back. Me nebba did bon dung de trash house.'

'God damned it, shut your mouth, boy.'

The slave knelt down and clasped his hands as if in prayer. 'Please, Massa. Do, a beg you. Lemme talk to me wife.'

'Stand up, boy.'

The slave obeyed the command.

Then the order went out, 'Fire!'

Two militia fired shots from their rifles into the man's belly and head. He fell lifeless to the ground.

Slaves rushed to him and the wailing began.

The man in charge pushed the mourners away and lifted the corpse. He stuck his finger in the bullet hole in the dead man's head and said to all present, 'Let this be a reminder to you all that this will be your fate if you betray Massa. Now go back to work. There is plenty to do around here.'

January 18ᵗʰ

A similar incident was reported at Lima Estate. Sir Willoughby Cotton was accustomed to showing his clemency by going from estate to estate pardoning the slaves who had been involved in the rebellion. After he had extended this act of kindness to the slaves at Lima, the attorney, Mr John Gunn arrived one hour later, accused the head driver of a crime he had supposedly committed and shot him to death.

Soon after, Lieutenant Gunn led a company of free Coloureds into the hills to Wiltshire Estate above Reading Wharf. There they took women and children prisoner and shot two men. They then made their way up, going towards the estates near Lethe, captured an old grey-haired Negro prisoner and burned 'every shelter for the then houseless wretches.' Fortunately, the slaves were able to escape before Mr Gunn was able to do them harm.

January 21ˢᵗ

Our scouts reported the arrival of more than 100 Maroons at Falmouth. They had come from Port Antonio under the command of Captain Fyfe, superintendent at Charlestown in the Parish of St George. They marched straight up to the army barracks at Maroon Town, from where they were dispatched to search us out in the backcountry of Vaughansfield. When we heard of their approach, we could think of nothing but sudden death. They were worse than the Spanish dogs. They could smell us out same way, run through the thicket better than the dogs, and when they captured us, were merciless in the use of their lances, machetes and other weapons. The remainder of our men knew they were defenceless against the Maroons and so took their chances to escape back to their villages. When the soldiers and Maroons arrived, they found no men, but they viciously attacked our camps, destroyed shelters, ammunition and food, leaving nothing intact. We were now fugitives with no supplies.

January 25th

The St Elizabeth and Westmoreland regiments made a surprise attack early in the morning, three o' clock to be exact. They came up the hill to Gardner's camp at Struie too fast for the watchmen to ring the alarm, but Gardner did not surrender even in the face of possible death. He and others showed themselves in the open and invited the militia and regulars to chase after them. 'Unu tink you bad. Try fi fight me now and see wah happen to you.'

But his men were too weak for the enemy forces. They and Gardner were forced to retreat. Several were captured and held prisoner. The remainder scattered in all directions, many finding caves which the soldiers later managed to surround. This was the end of Gardner's company. The White men went inside with their weapons. Only a few slaves escaped.

I then lost contact completely with Gardner and Dove. I heard that two days later they gave themselves in to the authorities, to a Lieutenant M'Neel. Gardner is reported to have said that he was tired of hiding out in the trees and that he would beg clemency of the Governor. He trusted that the lieutenant would keep his promise by presenting his case.

The enemy scoured the whole line of the Great River from Unity Hall clear up to Elderslie. As prisoners were taken they were transported to the towns to await trial: Savannah-la-Mar, Montego Bay, Black River, Lacovia, or YS. We received reports of militia parties marching through the streets, herding droves of handcuffed prisoners to the courthouse. Most slaves were executed with few questions asked. Any evidence presented in their defence was said to be inadmissible. The witnesses whom the defence brought forward were known by everyone to be liars and rascals. Very little time, maybe an hour at the most, elapsed between the sentence and the hanging. The Governor himself was supposed to give his consent before sentences of capital punishment were executed; how he managed to sign all those forms so fast in so many different towns of Jamaica, all at the same time, remains a mystery. The gaols were full and the hangings must have been the fastest way to make space.

Our spy, Hurlock, told me that he was witness in Montego Bay to slaves being stood up by the Cage, the small gaol in the main square, and summarily shot through the head. The majority who were sentenced to death were usually first tied to the hangman's ladder and flogged with the cat-o'-nine-tails. They were hanged, three or four persons at a time, behind the courthouse where the gibbet was erected. The hangman would leave the corpses hanging in the breeze until the next three came along. He would cut down the hanging bodies as he needed to, and at the end of the day, the workhouse slaves brought carts to transport the dead to be buried in a mass grave in the sands on the outskirts of the Bay, just east of Miss Mary's tavern.

January 30ᵗʰ

The fearless rebel leader Dehany was captured. He had belonged to a man called Mr Grizzle. Dehany was ruthless, chopping any man who opposed his wishes for freedom. The busha at Mocho Estate was discovered in a cave, reportedly shot by Dehany and left there to rot. He told everybody that it was the intention of the Negroes to burn the properties from the interior to the seaside and then destroy the towns. He hoped that the Whites would have the good luck of boarding the ships before it was too late.

The enemy operations lightened as they came to realize that only a few stragglers like myself remained at large.

I went into hiding in the backabush, beyond a place called Mocho where the brush is thick and hard to penetrate. Strap, the slave from Cooper's Hill, was my sole companion. He had joined up with the rebels and had fought under Gardner's command, first at Kensington and then at Struie. When the second camp was destroyed, he asked if he could hide out with me. We found a secluded cave but did not have enough supplies to keep us going. I depended on him to make runs into the slave villages for food. He was clever in the bush, running as quiet and as fast as a puss. With the information he brought back, I was kept informed of the progress of the war.

February 2nd, 1832

The Governor lifted martial law. He sent out a proclamation the following day, giving us who were left ten days to surrender.

> And whereas, there is reason to believe, that numbers are deterred from returning to their duty by a fear of that punishment which their rebellious practices merit, I have therefore thought fit to issue this my Proclamation, promising and assuring to all slaves who have been misled by misrepresentations of cunning and designing persons, His majesty's most

gracious pardon, provided they do, within the space of ten days from the date hereof, surrender themselves at the nearest military post, or return peaceably to plantations to which they belong, and resume their ordinary occupations, quietly submitting themselves, and obeying all the lawful commands of their masters or managers.*

Why was I to believe that he was going to pardon me if he said that the rebellious practices deserve punishment? How was I to know if His Majesty was going to be most gracious? His Majesty had promised us soldiers. And instead, what did we get? A ship full of gunpowder to shoot us down like animals. They wanted me to return peaceably to the plantation where I belonged and submit myself to the lawful commands of my owner.

I wonder if the Governor really thought that I would come running out of the bush saying, 'Massa, Massa, me sorry fi wah we do. Pardon me, Massa, pardon me. Me will be your faithful slave forever more and me will obey all yuh commands no matter what you say or do to me. Thank you, Massa, me so lucky fi have such a gracious gubna.'

The gubna man, Earl Belmore, travelled the road from Montego Bay to Black River and back again but there was no house for him to stay at. They were all burned down. He toured the area through Woodstock to the estates of Greenwich and Hazelymph to Seven Rivers, Old and New Montpelier, Anchovy Bottom and down the hill to the Bay. He stopped at the properties to tell the people that they must go back to work, that he was the gubna and they must do what he says.

February 5th

The once beautiful Greenwich Estate was a wasteland. Buildings were burned down, crops destroyed by cattle, and the horses and farm animals gone astray. The earl addressed the slaves there:

> *I am directing my observations chiefly to the headmen of the property. The distress and misery that you have brought on yourselves by the destruction you have committed, you are now houseless and in a great degree your provision grounds have been destroyed sharing the same fate as the cane fields of your masters.* *

Not a word was spoken. The people looked on him, turned their backs and walked away.

The estates were in disorder. The bushas were nowhere to be found. Perhaps they were still afraid to come back up from the Bay.

Gone were the so-called happy days when we would greet Massa after a long day's work: '*How d'ye, Massa, how d'ye mass buckra?*'* The lively song of the so-called contented Negro was no more. The owners had now to face rude and angry slaves. Even though there was no freedom paper, the 'good old days' of slavery were ruined for buckra forever.

One would think that with the Governor's visit and with the end of martial law, peace would be restored to the land. But this was not so. At the end of January, a group that called itself the *Colonial Church Union* was born. Reverend Bridges was one of its founding fathers. Their mission was to defend the interests of the colony and to show that the Anti-Slavery Society in England was promoting lies. The sectarian ministers, like the Baptists, became their enemy. They were blamed for inciting us to rebellion and for advancing the cause of emancipation.

Immediately after the end of martial law, the new Salter's Hill chapel was the first object of their vengeance. A party of St James militia torched it to the ground. Only one service was ever held there, the one conducted by Parson Knibb the night of the Kensington fires. On the 7th of February, the minister's chapel in Falmouth was also destroyed. The next day, at noon hour, the Baptist chapel at Montego Bay, where Minister Burchell had ministered to thousands, was demolished. The Baptist chapel at Lucea shared the same fate. Chapels at Brown's Town, Savannah-la-Mar, and St Ann's Bay followed.

Despite an official end to the war, unarmed slaves were still being shot down and others taken prisoner and flogged. The legal limit for flogging was still supposed to be thirty-nine lashes. It was reported that one slave received 500 with the cat-o'-nine-tails. Each time the cat-o'-nine-tails licked his back, it was nine lashes he was getting. That made 4,500 wallops that tore the man's back that day.

It would take a long time to rebuild Jamaica. Anger and resentment were felt on both sides. The slave had been deprived of his chance of freedom, and the owner, who was never in support of this claim in the first place, hated him even more for the destruction and havoc he had caused throughout the land. *You think you deserve your dinner tonight, wretch? You stinking ass. You will go hungry tonight, tomorrow night and the night after that.*

Our new fate was one of worse misery.

TWENTY-SEVEN

May 14th, 1832

The Holy War

The Lord forgave those who had allowed themselves to be corrupted and defiled by Diabolus. He pardoned them for their sins. He adorned the prisoners with fresh garments and gave them jewels of gold and precious stones. Everybody in Mansoul rejoiced. There was music and singing in every household because the Prince of Peace had forgiven all who repented. Emmanuel promised that he would possess the castle in Mansoul and set soldiers over the inhabitants to protect them from evil. In reparation for his coming, the people of the town went out to the meadows to gather tree branches and flowers to lay on the streets.

The chief priests of Diabolus were arrested and tried: Mr Unbelief, Mr Lustings, Mr Forget-Good and many others who had drawn the town of Mansoul into acts of rebellion against the great King and his son Emmanuel. They were imprisoned and received the sentence of death according to the law. They were hanged the following day.

And so Emmanuel established a new covenant with the people of Mansoul. He forgave them of their wrongdoings and gave unto them grace and goodness so that they might live in eternal peace.

But danger always lurked within the walls of Mansoul. Lord Fornication, Lord Adultery, Lord Murder, Lord Anger, and

Lord Deceit all escaped capture and hid in the holes and dens around the walls of the town. They planned to be as corrupt as possible and fall upon the unsuspecting people of Mansoul. They decided to work first with an army of Doubters who might be tempted to fall for their cunning ways and rebel once again against Emmanuel.

So Diabolus took advantage of this situation and rounded up his army of Doubters. He appointed captains to lay siege upon the town. Captain Damnation was captain over the Grace Doubters. Captain Insatiable ruled over the Faith Doubters. There were nine in all and above these were the supreme captains, Lord Beelzebub and Lord Lucifer. He assembled a mighty army which the townspeople could not resist.

Diabolus was too strong for the people of Mansoul. Women were abused, men lay dead in the streets. A darkness came over the town. It turned to wilderness.

And so too our enemies have wreaked destruction. The battles of regiments have flattened our slave villages. All hope has been lost. Gangs of Redcoats have walked the towns filling the houses with horror and telling lies against the Prince of Peace.

The Lord did not seem to hear our prayers. We begged Him to forgive us for what we had done wrong. We confessed that we did not deserve His mercy and we called upon His name to save us from damnation. Our captains were defeated on the battlefield by the forces of the tyrant. Our enemies were too strong.

Our wisdom and our power are gone because goodness has departed from us. We have nothing that we can call our own except sin, shame and confusion. Take pity upon us, O Lord.

Take pity on your miserable town of Mansoul and save us from the hands of our enemies.

Even after it was certain that we were conquered, the destruction continued. Our houses were set on fire and our men killed in punishment for rebelling against Diabolus.

But we still look for deliverance, for though we have sinned over and over again, the Lord hath said that He shall turn no man away who cometh to Him. We must not despair. We must continue to hope, to look and wait for a sign.

Another assault must be waged and I am sure we will see then the face of God. Those who oppress us will lose their courage and our armies will trample down the enemy. Our people of Mansoul will regain strength to take up arms against Diabolus.

No more will our dwelling place be the land of darkness and death. There will be a new dawn and we shall see the Glory of God, for He is just.

We shall see the Glory of God because he has redeemed us. He loves us. He has bought us with the price of His own blood which He has spilled freely on the ground. He will turn his anger away from us, the people of Mansoul, and a place will be reserved for us who believe in the Kingdom of His Father.

In Paradise there are marvellous things provided by the Father that have not been seen since the beginning of the world. These things are kept with the Father and sealed up in His treasury until the time when His faithful will come there to enjoy them.

I shall wear a robe of fine white linen and I will be recognized as belonging to the Saviour who has redeemed my soul.

I shall urge all my friends before I die to show Him their love as did the people of Mansoul, and to resist temptation to have their affections taken from Him who has redeemed us all. Even if He is away from them, they must know that He still loves them and carries them in His heart forever.

They must believe that the love of the Lord is constant and they must hold fast until Paradise becomes their eternal home.

February and March 1832

'A not sure we can hold out much more, Daddy Sharpe.'

Strap and I sat at the entrance of the cave. It was early morning and the mist had not yet lifted. It settled deep in the valleys of the Cockpit Country, swirling around as if it was trapped there.

'You might be right, you know, my friend. We a live worse than animal, hide up inna a cave. Dem better off than we, at least dem know how fi get food and water and fend for themself.'

'It's a terrible ting, Daddy, dis slavery business.'

'Freedom soon come, Strap, and then you will have yuh own stable and the finest Spanish stallion in the land.'

'That would be sweet, yes.' Strap still had a youthful appearance even though he was a man of my own age, his body still lean and his face bright and hopeful. 'You 'member Pebbles, Daddy Sharpe?'

'How me can forget, man? Him give me the first taste of freedom.'

'Maybe dat is why me did love ride horse so much.'

'Well, you know what dem sey bout *"walking buckra"*?'

'Yes, dem is de White man who so poor and wretched dat him haffi walk all bout de place cause im nah have no horse fi ride.'

'Well, Strap, when you free, my friend, you gwine be the proudest man in the land, you gwine be a Black man pon a horse.'

'De whole ting mek me sad, Daddy. We was supposed fi get we freedom. What happen to dat?'

'Me tink God did get angry wid we.'

'How you mean?' He looked at me in a worried way, squinting his eyes.

351

'We loss faith, my brother, we break the covenant.'

'Yuh haffi help me out, Daddy. Me nah understan dem talk deh.' His tone was sincere.

'I will die a slave in this country, Strap, but you will not. I will not get fi cross de Jordan fi tek possession of de Promised Land, but you will see it, you will see it one day soon. Trust me on that.'

'You mean you gwine dead soon and me gwine live free.'

'Yes, brother, and me ask the Lord every day of me life not fi destroy Him people, not fi let dem die in the wilderness. We are still His heritage. I pray that God will use Him power to redeem us, not to forsake us, my friend.'

'You is a preacher fi true, Daddy. Me hope you right still.'

We looked at each other and felt a bond of brotherhood.

~

By the middle of February, a whole heap of slaves were reported hanged in Montego Bay. I was far away now from my friends and the leaders of the rebellion. I heard that they were cruelly executed.

Hurlock was one who remained at large for a long time. On the day that he was finally captured, he swam the whole length of the Great River three times before the enemy was able to apprehend him. They finally found him in a cave along the riverbank. As for Gardner, he was immediately executed. He was betrayed by the authorities who did not grant him an audience with the Governor, as planned.

They cut off his head soon after the trial and hung it upon a pole at Greenwich Estate.

Dove they committed to the hulks in England.

I learned that the Baptist missionaries had been arrested in January: Minister Burchell, Messrs Knibb, Abbot and

Whitehorne. An article appeared in the *Courant:*

> The Baptist ministers are now in custody, and as we are satisfied they would not have been taken into custody upon slight grounds by Sir Willoughby Cotton, we hope he will afford them fair and impartial justice. Shooting is, however, too honourable a death for men whose conduct has occasioned so much bloodshed and the loss of so much property. There are fine hanging woods in St James and Trelawney, and we do sincerely hope that the bodies of all the Methodist preachers who may be convicted of sedition may diversify the scene. After this, our hostility, even to men so reckless of blood, carnage and slaughter, shall cease.*

It did not seem right that the ministers should take the blame. The magistrates were hungry for blood and the parsons were their easy prey. The authorities would not stop with the torture of the slaves. They saw it fit to go one step further and to put the clergymen on trial.

By the time the month of March came around, newspapers were reporting more than 160 estates had been destroyed and 1,000 slaves killed in battle. This number did not include those sentenced to death by hanging. Fourteen whites in total were reported killed.

We had shown restraint. If our intention had been to murder our masters, we could have shot them up, poisoned them, chopped them with machetes. None of this happened. We were claiming our right to freedom, not seeking blood or revenge. Perhaps we are not the *'semi-savage race of beings'* that we have often been called. I hope that when people write about this rebellion, they will record the bravery of those innocent slaves who died for a noble cause.

If Sir Willoughby Cotton had not come to fight us with the King's troops, the planters and the militia would never have been able to hold us back. And if word had spread to the other parishes of the capture of land and of towns, then the whole of Jamaica would have freed itself from slavery. I am sure of that.

Towards the middle of March, I left my hovel in the ground and, with Strap as my guide, made it out of the limestone forest and along the paths down to Content Estate. Strap went his separate way. He never told me his plan, but did promise he would look in on Nyame from time to time.

I sighted Nyame at the entrance gate to Content, the same one where I had arranged to meet her that wonderful evening I first encountered love. This time I did not have a horse and this time I was not dressed up pretty in my white shirt, black trousers and shiny buckle shoes. I was drawn down and stinking bad from staying months in the bush.

She looked me up and down and then hung her head low, covering up her face. She was ashamed to see me.

I could not find the right words. 'Nyame.'

'Why you done mek life so hard, Sam?'

'It all over now, Nyame. Dem crush we till we dead.'

She walked over to the guinep tree by the gate and slid to the ground where she leaned against the trunk.

'You tink me don't know dat, Sam? All me could do is hold me baby tight so dem don't come and rape we and chop we up.'

'Nobody gwine trouble you.' I settled down on the ground close to her.

'How you know dat? Don't tell me foolishness, Sam. Dem is at war wid we.'

I felt helpless because I could not comfort her. 'De war over now.'

'Listen to me, Sam. You know why de White man rape de Black gal dem?'

'A know all dat, Nyame. A beg you, don't talk dem ting deh.'

'Is wartime, Sam. If dem kyaan find you fi kill you, then dem tek yuh manhood, de Blackman manhood, away from you by raping yuh gal. You hear what me saying to you?'

'Nyame.'

'You better run galang, Sam. Go weh and hide yuhself cause dem gwine find you and capture you.'

'Me time run out, Nyame. It nah mek no sense trying fi run again. Too much gone wrong.'

'How you mean it don't mek sense?' She was getting vexed with me. 'It mek a whole heap of sense to me. Sam, tell me something, you remember sey you have pickaninny?'

'You not being nice to me, you know dat. Listen to me. Me nebba did want to do nothing fi hurt you or hurt de baby. We are slaves, Nyame. You know what that mean? It mean sey somebody own we. It mean sey me kyaan love you de way me want to. It mean me heart pain me right now cause me kyaan mek you be free. How you can have a situation like this, Nyame, whe somebody can buy and sell yuh own flesh and blood?'

She covered her face again and started to cry. I reached to hold her and this time she came to me. She rested her head on my shoulder.

We sat there in silence for a very long time.

'Me haffi give meself in.' I held her closer to me.

'What you saying to me?'

'Dem gwine kill Parson Burchell.'

'Dat is fi dem business, not yours.'

'It not dat simple, Nyame.'

'Me did tell you from de start. You remember?'

'Sey what?'

'Dat you was tempting fate, dat dem was gwine track yuh dung and kill yuh. And now you telling me you gwine give yuhself over.'

'Me mus tek de responsibility. Is me cause de rebellion. Me know dat as a surety.'

'You never did kill nobody.'

'Me know, but de people listen to me, dem follow me like me was dem teacher and ruler.'

'So then tell me something, Sam. Is why you is fi blame? De free paper nebba did come.'

'Me know dat.'

'Well then?'

'Is de only ting fi do. Dem will track me anyways. Me mus go and surrender to de authorities.'

'So you waan dem fi kill you?'

I felt as if she was scorning me.

'Is better fi dead wid dignity.'

'How dat?'

'Dem gwine run me dung anyways, Nyame. Me want fi save those who dem a blame fi de rebellion.'

'Then let dem do it, Sam. You nah haffi business wid dat. You a get me vex again, Sam.'

I went to embrace her but she pushed me off this time. I could see her perfectly formed breasts through her cotton blouse. I wanted more than ever to hold her and love her.

'Is you meking de choice.' She moved as if to slap me but I caught her hand. 'How you so stubborn, Sam? You a mek me get so mad wid you.' She pulled at my filthy shirt, then held the top of my head with both her hands. 'You a leave me Sam, you a leave me fi give yuhself up to a hengman. Dem gwine heng you. You know dat? Heng you till yuh neck bruk. You hear what me saying to you? She lifted up my head and looked me in the eye. 'Is dat wah you want, Sam? Is dat wah you really want?'

'Nobody want dat, Nyame.'

'Well then?'

'Me mind tell me me must go.'

She stared at me for the longest time in disbelief.

'Me want you to give dis to Juba.' I reached into my pocket.

'What is it?'

'Is de lion me show you once before.'

'De great lion of Africa dat was to bring you good luck. Right?'

'Don't mek fun.'

'You did tell me it would give we strength of spirit and guard we from all evil.'

'It gave we strength fi put up a brave fight. Me want her fi have it and me want you fi tell her of de great dream we have. Those dreams will come true, Nyame.'

'How you know dat?'

'Cause after me, others will fight for freedom.'

'You is a stubborn man.' She was calmer now and more tender. 'De spirit between we is strong, Sam. Dat is why it so hard. Is not right fi you to give yuhself up like dis?'

'Me ask Strap fi do me a favour.'

'Him is de same one who bring de letter to Content?'

'Yes, same one. Him come wid me here today. You remember me promise you me would teach you fi ride but me nebba did tek de time fi do it. So me ask Strap fi teach you. Him will teach you better than me, and when you learn how fi ride horse, you will feel like you is a slave no more. Trust me.'

'Dat is sweet.'

I held her close for the very last time, feeling the curves of her body and the warmth of her spirit. She pressed me tight, breathing her soul into mine.

Before I turned myself in, I wanted to meet my brother William. Nyame found out that he resided not far from Content Estate. When I first saw him, he was confused and disbelieving. He had never heard anything about a brother and was doubly shocked when he found out that I was Sam Sharpe, the rebel leader. He never had any recollection of Mama either. We had no resemblance. No one would ever guess we were brothers. He was slim and tall with finer features, a slimmer nose and smaller mouth. We must have had different fathers. I told him that it was good that we could meet like this because so many slaves did not get to know their family.

I told him that I wanted him to turn me in to the authorities for it was time for me to surrender. I asked him if he would look in on Nyame and my daughter, Juba, from time to time, and if he so desired, find Mama and introduce himself to her. I told him it would give her the greatest pleasure.

He led me first to the home of my owner, Mr Sharpe, at Cooper's Hill. There I visited with the family, except for the mistress who was in England. They greeted me as if I was the prodigal son, inviting me into their home and offering me a fresh change of clothes and a grand feast at their table.

I slept the night at Cooper's Hill.

The following day, Mr Sharpe transported me down to the Bay. William was there to hand me over to a constable who stood guard at the Cage, the small gaol house which stands in the main square of the town.

TWENTY-EIGHT

May 22, 1832

'*A so glad to see you, Mama. They have not allowed visitors for some weeks now. Let me tell you, you look good.*'

Mama sits on a chair in the cell, her eyes strong and her face youthful. The only sign of age is her hair, just like Tacky's was, woolly and white.

'*What me did tell you, Sam, bout how me would manage fine?*'

'*A know. You did always say you would tek care of yuhself. As for looking after myself, me didn't listen to you so good. You realize dat?*'

'*Well, dat is a certainty.*' *She looks at me in a sorrowful way.*

'*Dem gwine heng me, Mama.*' *The horror of it strikes me more when Mama is with me.*

She reaches out for my hand and I gain strength from her spirit. I feel tears welling up in me but I hold them back.

'*Once dem did capture you, Sam, it would tek a miracle fi get you out of here.*'

'*Me did hope de ministers would do something for me.*'

'*Dem did get lock up in gaol same way, Sam. So how dem could help you? Dem was coward still. Dem testify sey dem did preach nutten bout freedom.*' *She pulls her hands away.*

'*Me not sure dem was coward, Mama. They jus see religion a different way. Me think sey dem did want freedom for us*

but dem couldn't do nothing to mek it happen. De massa dem
was too powerful.'

'It's fi yuh time now fi find de strength.'

'Me don't feel so strong, Mama. Me need fi pray more fi get
de strength of spirit.'

Her voice is angry. 'What prayer gwine do now, Sam?'

'The Lord will tell me His wish.'

'And suppose Him waan you fi dead?'

'Then me will accept dat.'

'Suppose him don't waan you fi dead?'

'Then, me will live, Mama.'

'Maybe Him gwine strike dung de hengman.' She twists up
her face as if she is disgusted with me.

'You trying fi mek joke, Mama.'

'Maybe a lickle joke, Sam, but me not laughin after you.'
She is quiet again and moves near to me, slapping me lightly
on the face with both hands, half loving, half scolding.

'You've been a good mama to me.' I do not hold back the
tears this time.

'Me raise you like a mada should raise any pickaninny.'

'How is that?'

'Well, if she is any good, then she would love her pickaninny
as bes' she can and care fi him as bes' she can.'

'And a good father should act dat way too.'

'Yes, and all dat too. De problem in Jamaica is de faada
dem stray too much.'

'Like me Daddy. Me always did want fi know who me
Daddy was.'

'Fi yuh faada nebba stray dat far, Sam.'

'How you mean?'

'Bigga.'

'Wah bout him?'

'*Bigga. Bigga was yuh faada, Sam.*'

'*Lawd have mercy, Mama. Wah you a tell me now?*'

'*Me telling you sey Bigga de breed me.*'

'*But me nah understand.*'

'*Dem would a separate we, Sam, if dem did know.*'

'*What a life, Mama.*'

'*Him was there still.*'

'*Him was good to me, Mama, and me did love him like me faada.*'

   We stop talking a while.

'*So where him is now, Mama?*'

   She raises her voice in anger. '*Bigga is wid him ancestors, Sam. De militia capture him. Dem did flog him mussi 500 time till him dead.*'

'*Bigga was a good man. Bless him and may him soul forever rest in peace.*'

'*And him was strong too. Dem beat dung even de strongest o' we.*'

'*Is true.*'

'*So whe yuh wife and baby is?*'

'*Dem is safe in Content Estate, thank God. Dem wouldn't let Nyame come to the gaol fi see me though.*'

'*Why is dat?*'

'*Dem say me would give her bad ideas.*'

'*Then wah bout me?*' *She smiles.*

'*A not sure, Mama. Maybe you too bad aredi.*' *I look at her to see if she reacts, but her face is blank. We sit a while in silence.*

'*Mama.*'

'*Yes, tell me nuh.*'

'*Me give her de lion fi give to Juba when she grow big.*'

'*Dat is good. It gwine lead her fi do great and mighty tings.*'

'*Dat is wah me hope for.*'

'*You did great yuhself, Sam. You show de people how dem could have power.*'

'*One good thing is dat me will die knowing dat freedom will come.*'

'*Then maybe you haffi die, Sam.*'

'*Why you sey dat?*'

'*So we slave can be free.*'

'*Well, if dat is God's will, let it be so.*'

She says her words firmly. '*Me nebba sey God have anything fi do wid it.*'

'*Me know but dat is how me look on it. You will rejoice de day dat freedom come, Mama. There will be no more tribulation.*'

'*Dat gwine be a day fi celebrate.*' She sounds hopeful and happy. Then just as fast, she changes her tone as if she is spitting out fire. '*Me did kill him, Sam.*'

'*Who you kill, Mama?*'

'*Me did kill Mr Crawford. Him did tun into a walking busha begging fi food round de countryside.*'

'*Me don't want fi hear bout it, Mama.*'

'*You gwine listen to me, Sam. Me telling you me did kill Mr Crawford.*'

'*Then de deed is done. In times of war, Mama, de rule dem change.*'

'*Me did tink it would free me, but now me have him blood pon me hand.*' She looks down at her hands and starts wiping them on her frock as if she is cleaning them off.

'*God have a plan for everything, Mama. Maybe dat was de plan for Mr Crawford.*'

'*Dat is why tomorrow you kyaan escape from de gallow. You haffi walk straight up a de hengman.*'

'*Because God planned it so?*'

'*Dat is wah you telling me, but me not sure me believe you. Me believe dat wah me do is fi me own business and fi nobody else. When me depart from disya world, me will go on trial and then it will be decided whether me join de company of de ancestors.*'

'*We shall all be judged on judgement day, Mama.*'

'*All I know sey is a whole heap of evil must be undone.*'

'*Promise me something, Mama.*'

'*What is dat?*'

'*Dat when I am gone, you will join one of de Baptist mission.*'

'*Fi do wah?*'

'*Jus go and introduce yuhself and tell him who you are. De pastor will welcome you.*'

'*A kyaan promise you dat, Sam.*'

'*You will not be sorry if you do it.*'

We talk some more. I tell her about meeting William and she tells me about her sister Miss Nelly, who has passed on. Her weight was giving her problems and she developed sugar in her foot.

Mama does not hug me when she leaves, but I can feel her strength just as I did on the night down by the slave huts at Cooper's Hill when I was a little boy. A mother's love is very special. It fills the void that is now mine and helps me to confront the inevitable.

I now embrace the loneliness of the night. I pray for strength to face the morrow, my last dawn on this blessed earth. I will offer up my mortal body to the hangman even though my blood still runs vigorous through my veins. I will do this because I would rather die than remain a slave. Before God, my brethren, the stars, the moon, the sun, the sky, the rivers,

I know beyond everything else that it is wrong for one man to own another as his chattel.

I believe that it was God's voice which spoke to me in a vision on those nights in the bush. He told me I should stand up to lead my people out of slavery. I did what I thought was right. I told my brothers and sisters that the pharaohs had held us captive and that we must free ourselves from the chains. I believe now that God will not disappoint us. He will keep his promise. The slaves in Jamaica will soon be free and I must die for that to be.

I loved Nyame from the first day I saw her. She is a woman to me, soft and full of beauty. I love when she flashes her eye upon me. Her whole face lights up. Her skin is smooth like silk and the curves of her body fuller than the ripest fruit. I wish I could see her just one more time to tell her that I love her and that I am sorry for any hurt that I may have caused her. Even though she is not with me, I feel her spirit and know that her love will make me strong tomorrow. My God is not a faraway spirit who lives in the sky. He lives in the heart of my loved ones and fills me with that joy.

I shall now put on the white suit which Mistress Sharpe has made for me and lay down my head for one last sleep. I shall wake in the morn to give thanks to God for the dawn of a new day, my last day on earth. I shall think of the living, of Nyame and of our daughter, Juba, of Mama, of my owners, Maas Sam, Mistress Sharpe and their children, of Master Henry and Miss Anna, of my friend, Strap, of Bessy, and of the brave ministers, Messrs Burchell and Knibb, my White brothers in Christ. I shall remember the dead, Mr Crawford, Miss Mary, Tacky, dear Nana, my father, Bigga, Miss Nelly, my closest friend, Gardner and my fellow slaves who died in battle. And I shall be filled with their spirit, with the spirit of love, and I shall offer my soul up to the Father in heaven at the altar of slavery. I know that then my spirit will finally be free.

Search me, O God, and know my heart:
try me, and know my thoughts:
and see if there be any wicked way in me,
and lead me in the way of everlasting.

I am the resurrection, and the life:
he that believeth in me,
though he were dead, yet shall he live:
And whosever liveth and believeth in me shall never
die.

This marks the end of the narrative of my life.

I thank Reverend Bleby and Mistress Sharpe for agreeing to review and publish these writings. I trust that when they edit my journals, they will be true to my spirit.

I have made my mistakes but have lived my life to the fullest by using the talents God has given me.

I am indebted to those who have shown me kindnesses.

I love you, my brothers and sisters. You deserve so greatly the dignity of being free.

Fare thee well.

EPILOGUE

TWENTY-NINE

S am Sharpe was executed at high noon on a bright, sunny day, the 23rd of May, 1832. He was the last of over 300 rebels to be hanged.

Mr Sharpe and our children attended the execution held in the central square in Montego Bay. Reverend Bleby was also present. With his permission, I include here his eyewitness account, which he published some years later.

Mrs Samuel Sharpe

Twelve o'clock noon, May 23rd, 1832

The crowds gathered along the street of the marketplace in Montego Bay close to where Sam was to be executed. People leaned out of the upper windows and crowded the doorways of the houses which lined his way to the gallows.

He set out for his last walk under the guard of the Eighth Regiment, commanded by Lieutenant Crawford. His hands were tied behind his back and he walked erect, holding his head high and looking about the crowd as if he were searching for familiar faces. When he saw those he recognized, he bowed his head in recognition. His eyes were peaceful and calm. He looked handsome in his white suit which the women of the Sharpe household had sewn for him. It gleamed in the midday sun. His face was bright, as if he had achieved some glorious victory.

The guard started a brisk march from the gaol house but Sam requested of the commanding officer that he slow down his pace so that he might walk his last stretch with as much dignity as possible. When he came to the spot where the Sharpe family was standing, he paused, making the guard stop in his tracks. He looked at his owners and bowed his last farewell.

As Sam approached the gallows, the Anglican rector, Reverend Mr McIntyre, greeted him. He granted the prisoner permission to speak with Mr John Manderson and Mr James Gordon. These two gentlemen had helped the missionaries when we were apprehended after the rebellion. To them, he said:

> *Gentlemen, I have rebelled against the laws of the country and am now about to make a sacrifice of my life as an atonement. I have been disobedient to my master who was nearer to me than I was to him. But my mind was slippery and I was misled. I hope the younger branches of my family will make atonement to him for my guilty conduct, and my offences will not be visited upon by any of my fellow creatures.* *

These words surprised the gentlemen because they were of the opinion that Sam Sharpe had felt no remorse for sedition and acts of rebellion.

The rector then asked him if he wished to pray. Sam knelt down at the foot of the gallows and prayed to the Almighty. He praised God and asked for His mercy, reciting by memory verses from the psalms of David:

> '*Quicken me, O Lord, for Thy name's sake: for Thy righteousness sake bring my soul out of trouble.*
>
> *Praise ye the Lord. Praise ye the Lord from the heavens: praise him in the heights.*

Praise ye him, all his angels: praise ye him, all his hosts.

Let every thing that hath breath praise the Lord. Praise ye the Lord.'

He looked up at the gallows and then back to the crowd. He hesitated, then walked quickly and nimbly up the stairs.

When he reached the top step, he paused, placing the left foot first upon the scaffold, and pressing it. He then brought the right foot on a line with the left, placing the heels of the feet about twenty inches apart.*

Before the hangman did his deed, the deputy marshal asked if he had any final words.

Sam Sharpe spoke from atop the platform of the gallows, his voice reaching out to all gathered in the square:

I have transgressed against the laws of the country and government, and with great violation, and I come to be a sacrifice for it; but I will soon appear before a judge that is greater than all. I don't know that I am prepared to face my God, but I depend for salvation through the Redeemer, who shed His blood upon Calvary for sinners. The White missionary who is gone off, and who left his native land for our good, had nothing to do with it; and I have violated him too, for if I had heard what he said, I would not have come to this. Let me beg you, my brethren, to attend to your Christian duties, for it is the only way for you to go to salvation. *

All I wished was to be free. All I wished was to enjoy

the liberty which I find in the Bible is the birthright of every man. I have a humble hope through Christ of eternal life; but I cannot say exactly that I am going to heaven. *
I now bid you farewell.'

In a few moments the executioner had done his work and the noble-minded originator of this unhappy revolt had ceased to exist.*

May his soul forever rest in peace and perpetual light shine upon him.

I witnessed the execution; for, having had so much intercourse with him, I was anxious to see how he would demean himself, when actually confronted with the stern and solemn realities of death and eternity. I could not dispute the justice of the sentence; nor could I challenge the wisdom of the government in carrying it into effect, so far as the preservation of slavery was concerned. He had certainly been a daring violator of the existing laws; and had unquestionably occasioned a fearful destruction of life and property. He was such a man, too, as was likely, nay, certain, had he been set free, to commence another struggle for freedom: for he felt acutely the degradation and the monstrous injustice of the system, and was bent upon its overthrow. But I could not help feeling deep sorrow and indignation — as I turned from his death-scene, and brushed away the tears which the contemplation of his tragical fate called forth — that such a man as Samuel Sharpe, who possessed a mind which under proper influence and direction was capable of noble things, should be thus immolated at

the polluted shrine of slavery.*
Samuel Sharpe was the most intelligent and
remarkable slave I had ever known.*

The sun disappeared behind the clouds and a darkness came
over the land. Saddened by his loss, we all left the town square,
which some likened to Golgotha, the place of a skull.

Reverend Henry Bleby,
Methodist Minister

~

My husband and I had made a formal request to the
magistrates that Sam Sharpe be buried on our property at
Cooper's Hill. It was agreed that we could transport the body
there provided Sam be buried that same day before sunset.
Another condition was that there should be no ceremony.

As preparations were being made, Mr Coates arrived on
the scene and stopped the proceedings. He indicated that
constables should be sent to the magistrates and word brought
back to him to verify, if indeed, that had been the agreement,
to have the body buried at Cooper's Hill. Mr Sharpe refused
to be humiliated in this fashion and withdrew his request to
entomb Sam's body on his property. The president of the gaol
ordered then that he be buried 'beneath the sand of the race-
course beach, the usual Golgotha of rebellious slaves.'

They buried him in the sands of the seashore,
as one wafted with the common human race.
The pure waves long sang his requiem.
The unbroken sun-beams long bathed with lustre
his lovely place of rest.*

And so it was that Sam Sharpe was laid to rest.

Thereafter, Jamaica suffered dreadfully from the vengeful actions of the Colonial Church Union, which effectively put a stop to the religious practices of the sectarian groups. But these groups were not obliterated. The Baptists, Moravians and Presbyterians continued to fight valiantly for the cause of emancipation.

Reverend Mr Thomas Burchell returned to the island in September 1832. 'My health seems perfectly restored, so that I hope to render some assistance in advocating the cause of our much calumniated mission, in clearing from reproach the memory of our poor murdered people in Jamaica.'*

His people were ecstatic at his return. I am sure that Sam would have greeted him in like manner, 'Is it Massa Burchell fi true? Him come back, him come back fi true.' By June of the following year, 1833, the British Parliament passed the following resolution:

> That it is the opinion of this Committee that immediate and effectual measures be taken for the entire abolition of slavery throughout the colonies under such provisions for regulating the condition of the Negroes as may combine their welfare with the interests of the proprietors.*

On Friday, the 1st day of August, 1834, all persons duly registered as slaves in His Majesty's kingdom were granted the status of apprenticed labourer, free at last from the chains of slavery.

It was announced in Jamaica that a holiday, lasting until Monday, would commence on Thursday night. On Friday, every chapel was open for Divine worship.

I went to the Baptist church in Montego Bay that day and offered thanks to God for persons like Samuel Sharpe, whose piety, patriotism and self-sacrifice helped to bring about the emancipation of his people. These pages are published in his loving memory.

Some say that his body was exhumed from the race-course beach and entombed beneath the pulpit in the Baptist church in Montego Bay.

Those who have been moved by this account of his life may pay him homage by visiting his tomb in the Parish of St James.

Mrs Samuel Sharpe
August 1834

ACKNOWLEDGEMENTS

I should like to acknowledge the following persons who assisted in the project:

Georgianne Kennedy, my loving wife and best friend, without whose moral support and superb editing skills I would not have been able to complete this project.

Our three daughters, Amanda Mary, Sarah Elise and Julia Claire, for their great love and for encouraging their dad throughout this project.

Ian Randle and Christine Randle for agreeing to publish my manuscript and Kaci Hamilton for her guidance through the editing process.

The renowned Jamaican artist, George Rodney, for his drawing of Sam Sharpe on horseback. My daughter, Sarah, for her portrait of Sam Sharpe and for her illustration of the lion.

The late Shirley C. Gordon, author and historian who published several works relevant to the emancipation period in Jamaican history. She spent precious time in the months before her death to review this narrative.

Professor Kamau Brathwaite, who took the time to complete an extensive critique of the manuscript, providing me with valuable insights. I greatly respect his opinions not only because of his literary expertise but also because of his extensive knowledge of the Sam Sharpe story.

Valerie Facey, publisher, art historian, researcher and friend who took a personal interest in the project, provided invaluable resources and encouraged me in the publication of the manuscript.

Marylou Soutar-Hynes, poet and educator whose literary skills and Jamaican perspectives I appreciate so much in her review of the manuscript.

Ruth Walker and Ingrid Ruthig, editors, Walkwrite Writing Services, Toronto, for their detailed and thorough appraisal of the work.

Swithin Wilmot, Senior Lecturer of History and Dean of the Faculty of Humanities and Education at the University of the West Indies, high school friend and mentor, whose friendship and exceptional knowledge of Jamaican history I prize so much. My deepest thanks for providing historical leads, the most colourful anecdotes, visits to historical sites and access to records.

Sharon Chacko, artist and social historian, and longtime friend whose literary talents and historical perspectives helped to authenticate the narrative. My heartfelt gratitude for reading and reviewing the manuscript.

Celia Kennedy, loving sister, for her moral support and keen interest in the project, for finding relevant historical and religious resources.

Pearlie Beckford, of Discovery Bay, St Ann, for her many anecdotes of rural life in Jamaica, in appreciation of her extensive knowledge of the oral history of Jamaica.

Jennifer Walcott, trusted friend, whose literary talent and deep knowledge of Jamaica were so valuable in providing a critique of the manuscript.

Alex Meyer, Director of Quality of Course, a writing school based in Ottawa, for providing me with encouragement and editorial feedback in the early stages of the project. She gave me the confidence and impetus to proceed with the project.

Verdic Design Inc., Bridgewater, New Jersey, for creating the original concept for the book cover design.

Mary Swab, Senior Cartographer from Mapping Specialists Ltd., Madison, Wisconsin, for creating the maps.

Rachel Manley, for taking the time to read the book and write a review for the cover.

GraceKennedy & Co Ltd., Kingston, Jamaica, for their generous donation of copies of this book to the Jamaica Library Services.

Thanks to the librarians at The University of the West Indies Special Collections, the National Library of Jamaica, the researchers at the Island Records Office for their assistance in providing resources.

Fred Kennedy

GLOSSARY

Jamaican Words	English Meanings
ANANCY	Central character of African fables. See References, Chapter One.
AREDI	Already.
BACKABUSH	Remote back country.
BACKRA	White man; boss; master.
BALD-PATE	A medium to large blue pigeon with a white head.
BANKRA	A square cornered basket made of palm thatch with a lid and handle.
BLACK UP	Very drunk; inebriated.
BOASY	Boastful.
BON	Burn.
BRAATA	A little amount of the same, added for good measure.
BUCKRA	Alternate spelling for backra.
BWAI	Boy.
CASSADA	Cassava, popular root crop, in two varieties, bitter and sweet. The former is poisonous.
CAT-O'-NINE	Whip.
CHIGOES	Insects which get under the skin where they lay eggs, causing infestations.
COCOBAY	A kind of leprosy or elephantiasis.
COTCH	To lodge oneself or to lean for support.
CREOLE	Descendant of European Settlers in the West Indies.
CROP-OVER	The end of the sugar-cane harvest.
DADDY	Name given by slaves to religious leader.
DEAH, DEH	There.
DISYA	This here.
DUNG	Down.

DUPPY	The spirit of the dead; ghost.
FAADA	Father.
FACETY	Impudent, bold, rude.
FUS	First.
GALANG	Go along.
GALLIWASP	Lizard similar to the iguana.
GOOMBAY	Drum formed of a hollow block of wood covered with sheepskin.
GUINEP	Tree, *Melicocca bijuga*, brought to Jamaica in 1756 from Surinam.
GUBNA	Governor.
GUZU	An act of obeah or witchcraft.
HAFFI	Have to.
HET	To bother oneself.
HIGGLER	A seller of small produce especially in market; originally, an itinerant peddler.
IIN-HIIN	Yes. similar in meaning to North American colloquial 'uh-huh'.
INNA	In.
JINAL	A clever, crafty or tricky person.
JINALSHIP	Character trait of being a jinal.
JOKIFIED	Jocular, prone to jokes.
JUK	To prick, pierce or poke.
KYAAN	Can't.
LAWD	Lord.
LICKLE	Little.
MAAGA	Lean, thin, scraggy (used often in a derogatory sense).
MACCA	A prickle, or prickles of any sort, on plants, animals.
MADA	Mother.
MYAL	A form of witchcraft through which the evil of Obeah may be undone.
MYALMAN	Person who practices myal.
NEBBA	Never.
NEGA	Negro.
NYAM	Eat, with connotation of roughly and

	inelegantly.
OBEAH	Form of malignant magic or witchcraft, widely known in Jamaica, of African origin.
OSNABURG	Thick, coarse cloth used for slaves' clothing.
OTAHEITE APPLE	Tree introduced to Jamaica in 1793, *Eugenia malaccensis*. Pear-shaped fruit, bright red with white pulp.
PACKY	Container made from calabash.
PATU	Owl; two types, Jamaica and White Owl.
PICKANINNY	Child, very young child (early nineteenth century spelling).
PICKNEY	Alternate spelling for pickaninny.
PINDAR	Ground-nut or peanut; *Arachis hypypogoea*. Pindar cake: confection with brown sugar and pindar nuts.
RAAS	Vulgar expression meaning buttocks or ass.
RAT-BAT	Common name for bat in Jamaica.
RENK	Dialect slang for angry, being in a bad mood.
SA, SAR	Sir.
SAMBO	The offspring of a mulatto and a black person.
SENSAY	A variety of chicken having sparse, ruffled and uneven feathers.
SHAKA	Musical instrument, rattle made of calabash with seeds of a vine called John-crow beads, *Abrus precatorius*.
SINTING	Something.
SOMADI, S'MADI	Somebody.
SUSU	Gossip.
TUN	Turn.
UNU	You (generally plural).
WAH	What.
WAAN	Want.
WANGLA	Plant, *Sensamum orientale*, used in obeah practices.
WEH	Away.
WESELF	Ourselves.
WHE	Where.

WHOOPINGBWAI A ghost believed to roam about at night, making a whooping noise.

WUDPIKA Creole spelling for woodpecker.

WUK Work.

YA Here.

YABBA Heavy earthenware vessel of any size.

YAMPY A small variety of yam having fine white flesh.

YERRY Creole variation of 'hear' in its various meanings (listen, obey).

YEYE One of many creole spellings for 'eye'.

YUH Your.

Sources:

Allsopp, Richard. *Dictionary of Caribbean English Usage.* Oxford: England, 1996.

Cassidy, F G., and R.B. Le Page. *Dictionary of Jamaican English.* UWI: West Indies, 2002.

Thompson, Della. *The Pocket Oxford Dictionary of Current English.* Oxford: England, 1992.

BIBLE
CITATIONS

p. 29   1 Corinthians 7:20-22
pp. 39-40   John 5:24
p. 40   John 11:25-26
p. 40   Matthew 6:9-10
                 Ephesians 5:5
                 Mark 16:16
p. 43   Galations 5:1
p. 45   Romans 8:38-39
p. 55   Matthew 5:3
p. 62   Revelations 14:7-8
p. 64   John 3:14-14
pp. 78-9   1 Corinthians 6:9-10
p. 107   Proverbs 15:13
p. 136   Matthew 7:17-18
                 I Thessalonians 5:9-10
p. 152   Psalms 46:1-2
p. 156   Matthew 5:11-12
p. 158   Job 20:4-5;16-17
p. 171   Revelations 5:13
p. 172   Revelations 5:13
                 Revelations 2:10
                 Revelations 3:21
pp. 173-4   Exodus 3:6-10
p. 200   Psalms 32:5
                 Psalms 122:1
                 Psalms 84:10-11
p. 212   John 3:23
p. 213   Matthew3:16
p. 221   Matthew 6:24

p. 223	Joshua 8:1
p. 261	Psalms 42:11
p. 264	1 Thessalonians 5:9-10
	Isaiah 51:3
	Galations 3:28
p. 265	Galations 4:7
p. 266	Hebrews 10:36
p. 267	2 Timothy 1:7
p. 277	Matthew 6:24
	Galations 5:1
p. 279	John 8:36
p. 286	Exodus 3:7
p. 307	Deuteronomy 18:20
p. 312	2 Samuel 22:39
p. 314	Joshua 1:5
	Genesis 15:1
	Psalms 34:22
p. 316	Job 4:8
p. 321	Psalms 54:1, 3-6
p. 365	Psalms 139:23-24
	John 11:25-26
p. 370	Psalms 143:11
	Psalms 148:1-2
p. 371	Psalms 150:6

REFERENCES

The following notes aim to provide references for quotations marked by asterisks and to explain historical allusions where appropriate.

Chapter One

p. 2

Map of Island of Jamaica. Two other maps are included, 'Montego Bay' and 'Area of the 1831 Rebellion'. Data from several sources were used to design these: John Arrowsmith's Map of Jamaica, 1839; David Buisseret, *Historic Jamaica from the Air;* J. Finlayson's Island Map of Jamaica, 1827; Thomas Harrison's Estate Map of the Parish of St James, 1889 (Courtesy of the National Library of Jamaica); B.W. Higman, *Montpelier, Jamaica;* Herman Moll's Map of Island of Jamaica, 1732; Morris, Cunningham and Woolridge, Map of St James, 1832 (Courtesy of National Library of Jamaica); and James Robertson's estate maps of Parish of St James, 1804 (Courtesy of National Library of Jamaica).

p. 4

*One day, Tiger swear. . .*This Anancy story, a fable, of African Ashanti origin, is adapted from James Berry, 'Bro Tiger Goes Dead' in *Anancy Spiderman,* p. 66.

p. 4

Massa. Term used usually in an endearing way to refer to master or owner.

p. 5

Overseer. A term usually associated with the superintendent of the larger properties or plantations in Jamaica.

p. 6

*Bush*a. A word used generally to denote an overseer of any kind of estate, originally applied to White men.

p. 7

Estate. Landed property, but more specifically referring to properties where sugar, rum and molasses were produced.

p. 8

But when poor Tacky went down to the riverside that last night. . . This anecdote is based on a true slave narrative, which appears in *Remembering Slavery,* edited by Ira Berlin et al., p. 146.

p. 9

Sam Sharpe. . .too young to be my Daddy. His owner, Samuel Sharpe was born in 1791 and the slave, Sam Sharpe in 1801.

Chapter Two

p. 13

Cooper's Hill. Residence property of Samuel Sharpe Esquire, measuring 12 acres. Poetic licence has been used in the portrayal of the Sharpe's property as larger than this with 15 slaves and an overseer.

p. 13

Pen. Usually any country estate not specifically a sugar, banana, or coconut property; also known as a cattle farm or enclosure. Meaning derived from days when Spaniards caught and *penned* wild cattle.

p. 23

Mr John Lunan. A Tablet is on the wall inside of the Spanish Town Cathedral, St Catherine, Jamaica, to mark the burial place of the Honourable John Lunan, 1770–1839. Resident of the Parish of St Catherine, he at different periods filled the offices of Member of Assembly, Custos, and Assistant Judge of the Grand Court. He was known not only for his superior talents but his amiable and charitable disposition.

p. 24

I have but childhood memories of him. . . Samuel Sharpe's father died in 1800 when his son was nine years old. John Lunan would have been closer in age to his father.

Chapter Three

p. 29

If I have done wrong in that. . .for I cast myself upon the atonement. Bleby, *Death Struggles of Slavery,* p. 117, quoting Sam Sharpe's direct words when he interviewed him in prison.

p. 37

There's a brown girl in the ring. . .For she like sugar and I like plum. Olive Lewin in *Rock it Come Over: The Folk Music of Jamaica,* p. 71.

Chapter Four

p. 58

Oh me good friend, Mr Wilberforce, make me free. . . Take force by force! Matthew Lewis, *Journal of a West India Proprietor,* p. 139, quoting slave song.

Chapter Five

p. 64

A succession of terrible storms blasted Jamaica. . . Hurricanes were reported for the years 1812, 1813, 1815 and 1818.

p. 75

Tell me, Sam, Who am I? Me hab no life but me walking still. . . Anderson and Cundall, *Jamaica Proverbs and Sayings,* pp. 122–4, riddles adapted here.

p. 79

Daddy Powel will continue the prayer. . . Thomas Powel, also known as Parson Charley, was a native Baptist in the Parish of St James and later became a deacon of Thomas Burchell's church in Montego Bay.

p. 81

I hear Thy welcome voice. . .That flowed on Calvary. . . Redemption Song. Hymn # 269, p. 73.

Chapter Six

p. 88

Mr Crawford's Diary. . .Some details in this chapter, for example, 'the Clap', were inspired by the character of Thomas Thistlewood in *In Miserable Slavery* by Douglas Hall.

p. 94

Come, carry me in a room. . .*And lay me on the bed.* Moreton, *Manners and Customs in the West India Islands*, p. 126, quoting a ditty.

p. 95

Showed Bigga how to salt a hog. . .Ibid., p. 95 citing a recipe.

Chapter Seven

p. 102

They have a rude name for it. . .One of the folk names for the unopened flower of the African tulip is 'donkey piss'.

Chapter Eight

pp. 110-11

I forgot everything . . . her soul was wondering around me. . . *Royal Gazette*, vol. XLIX, 1827.

Chapter Ten

Many of the arguments put forward in this plea were widely used by campaigners for the abolition of slavery. In addition to members of the Anti-Slavery Society, which was formed in England in 1823, many ex-slaves, like Robert Wedderburn, became influential voices in the political fight for freedom, and expressed views similar to these stated here.

Chapter Eleven

p. 140

My advice to you. . . *will strike terror to your oppressors.* Robert Wedderburn, *The Horrors of Slavery and Other Writings*, p. 81.

pp. 146-7

The following quotations by William Shakespeare are cited from Wilbur L. Cross, 1993, *The Yale Shakespeare.*

Now is the winter. . .on the ocean buried. . .Shakespeare, *The Tragedy of Richard the Third*, Act First, Scene First, ll 1–4.

And therefore. . .pleasures of these days. . .Shakespeare, Act First, Scene First, ll 28–31.

A horse! A horse!. . .hazard of the die. . . Shakespeare, Act Fifth, Scene Fourth, ll 7–10.

God and your arms. . . thou acquit thee. . .Adapted from Shakespeare, Act Fifth, Scene Fourth, ll 14–16. In the original play, Henry, Earl of Richmond is victorious in the battle and says these words, not King Richard. Earl of Derby is speaking with Richmond. Cate is not present.

Let them not live to taste. . .God say amen! Words spoken by Richmond, not King Richard in the original. Act Fifth, Scene Fourth, ll 51–54.

p. 148

Jackass with the long tail. . . Bag of cocoa coming down. . . Rampini, *Letters from Jamaica: the Land of Streams and Woods*, p. 94, quoting song by two carousing slaves.

Chapter Twelve

p. 151

That Mr Burchell had said to him (Stennett). . .and they will get it. Burchell, William Fitzer, *Memoir of Thomas Burchell*, p. 195, quoting his brother, Rev. Thomas Burchell's words.

pp. 152-3

I can and do most solemnly assure you. . .as an infant child. Ibid., p. 202, quoting his brother's journal.

p. 153

The house of any person should come down. . .protected the missionaries. Ibid., p. 198, quoting his brother's journal.

p. 154

*Did not Mr Burchell tell you to rebel?. . .*Ibid., p. 201.

Chapter Thirteen

p. 164

Anancy story adapted from James Berry, 'Bro Tiger Goes Dead' in *Anancy Spiderman*. pp. 66–68.

Chapter Fifteen

p. 175

There was a time when a mighty giant. . .Many received a sentence of death according to the law. This narrative is a partial summary of Bunyan's *The Holy War,* widely read in early nineteenth-century England.

p. 177

Prince Emmanuel, the great Lord of all world. . .but we should be cast into the pit. Ibid., p. 121.

p. 178

The walking buckras. . . Derogatory. Refers to a White man who did not own or who was not using a horse. 'No disgrace being considered so great in the island as that of a white man being seen walking on foot when away from his home.' *Dictionary of Jamaican English* p. 461.

p. 180

A decree has gone forth. . .at the altar of fanaticism. F.R. Augier and S.C. Gordon in *Sources of West Indian History,* p. 130, quoting Resolutions of the House of Commons, 15 May, 1823.

Chapter Sixteen

p. 196

*As Christians, we can never condone unlawful acts to obtain freedom. . .*Reid, *Samuel Sharpe: From Slave to National Hero,*

p. 61, quoting William Knibb. Similar sentiments expressed by Thomas Burchell in his testimony to The House of Lords in the summer of 1832. BPP. . . XX 1831–2, p. 736.

p. 197

The indictment stated. . . Wright, *Knibb the 'Notorious' Slaves' Missionary, 1803–1845,* p. 108, referring to Reverend Knibb's trial.

p. 206

The one shirt I have ratta cut ahm. . .rain oh fall down and wet me up. Jekyll, *Jamaica Song and Story,* p. 164, quoting digging songs.

Chapter Seventeen

p. 217

Shall we all go on in sin. . . And open all his wounds? John Clarke, *The Voice of the Jubilee,* p. 34, quoting a hymn Moses Baker was reputed to have used in his church meetings.

p. 219

O Shout, O shout, O shout away. . .glory in my soul. Raboteau, *Slave Religion: The Invisible Institution in the Antebellum South,* p. 245, quoting verses of a Negro spiritual.

p. 219

Come in, Kind Saviour...O no man can stop me. Ibid., p. 252.

p. 226

The power of God unto salvation. . . Burchell, *Memoir of Thomas Burchell,* p. 82.

p. 226

The Chief Shepherd is always near. . . Burchell, *Memoir of Thomas Burchell,* pp. 100–103, describing an encounter and a conversation between his brother and a Parson Sam who, two to three times a week, invited hundreds of his fellow slaves to go to hear the missionary in the Bay. This is possibly a reference to Sam Sharpe.

Chapter Eighteen

p. 230

*Miss Lusty. . .*Reverend Mr Thomas Burchell's wife's name was Hester *Lusty* Burchell.

p. 230

You will observe that. . .the means and time of its accomplishment. Mathieson, *British Slavery and its Abolition: 1823–38,* p. 17, quoting *Jamaica Gazette,* May 26, 1826.

p. 231

Let it be known that the slave laws of Jamaica. . .committed to the common gaol for a month. Burchell, *Memoir of Thomas Burchell, pp.* 109–110, quoting clauses from the consolidated slave law, the House of Assembly, December 22, 1826. New clauses pertaining to the practices of missionaries were inserted. The law was to go into operation, May 1827.

p. 232

You have intruded yourselves. . . your further increase amongst us. Burchell, *Memoir of Thomas Burchell,* page 120, quoting a conversation with Grignon. On many occasions, Thomas Burchell was summoned to the courthouse in Montego Bay to account for his so-called illicit practices of collecting money from his congregation, of baptizing slaves, of training slaves to be teachers, and of holding prayer meetings after dark.

Chapter Nineteen

p. 244

*William Knibb. . .*Thomas Burchell's first main contacts with William Knibb, the Great Emancipator, occurred at the end of 1828. The following year both men agreed to purchase a property which was the start of the missions in St Ann's Bay and Ocho Rios. With the death of Reverend Mann in 1830, William Knibb, at the invitation of Burchell, became the pastor in Falmouth. It is not clear whether William Knibb knew Sam Sharpe before he visited him in prison. Brathwaite, *Nanny,*

Sam Sharpe and the Struggle for People's Liberation, p. 23, notes that Knibb explained before a Select Committee of the House of Commons in 1832 that he knew of him but had never had any conversation with him prior to the rebellion.

p. 246

*Congratulations, Thomas, to you and Lusty...*Mrs Burchell gave birth to a baby girl on October 27, 1827.

p. 247

*Are you familiar with the column by Dorcas...*See note, chapter 21, *If you would not have your blazing canefields.*

p. 251

*The Royal Gazette...*volume XLIX, from Saturday, August 18 to Saturday, August 25, 1827.

p. 251

Reports from Trinidad... Royal Gazette, vol. XLIX, August 1827, referring to a dispatch from Sir R. Woodford, paper presented to Parliament.

Chapter Twenty

p. 252

*Sam Sharpe's Sentence...*Quotations in this chapter are from a record of the actual trial of Sam Sharpe on April 19, 1832 (CO 137/185/306), cited by Brathwaite, *Nancy, Sam Sharpe and the Struggle for People's Liberation,* pp. 52–7.

p. 253

*I recall the first few Thomas Coy...*The names of the 12 jurors were reported in the Colonial Office Records, CO 137/158/307–13v: The other eight names were: Robert Scott, Joseph Osborn, James Giles, Sidney L. Levein, John Crearer, William Dewar, Thomas Excell and John Ewart.

p. 254

At a Special Slave Court...for the said parish. Ibid., Colonial Office Records.

p. 257

*Mr Grignon. . .*It is not clear from historical records whether this is, in fact, the same Mr Grignon, alias Little Breeches, whom Sam and the other slaves knew so well. C.S. Reid, *Samuel Sharpe: From Slave to National Hero,* p. 91, makes this assumption. If this was the case, then Sam Sharpe's trial was indeed a travesty.

Chapter Twenty-One

p. 261

George Reid, a slave to Cambridge Estate. . . Bleby, *Death Struggles of Slavery,* pp. 144–145, reporting this and other references in this paragraph as actual slave accounts.

p. 262

*The Lord and King have given we free but the White gentleman in Jamaica keep it back. . .*Hart, *Slaves who Abolished Slavery. vol. 2: Blacks in Rebellion,* p. 245, quoting words of a slave from 'Confessions of William Binham sentenced to Death', PP, Vol. XLVIIm, p. 212.

p. 262

Slavery! Accursed slavery!. . .which I am engaged. . . Burchell, *Memoir of Thomas Burchell,* p. 157, quoting a letter written by Thomas Burchell, Montego Bay, October 28, 1830.

p. 263

The cost of the ticket was ten pence per quarter. . . Ibid., page 165. This information is contained in letters written by Thomas Burchell to his brother in 1831. Other descriptions of tickets with details of inscriptions are given by Curtin, *Two Jamaicas,* p. 37.

p. 264

I shall be leaving soon for England. With his wife and baby girl, Reverend Burchell set sail from Jamaica for Liverpool, England, in May 1831 on board the *Nottingham,* arriving there on Friday, July 15.

p. 265

O shout, O shout, O shout away. . . glory in my soul. . . See reference in chapter 17.

p. 266

JESUS! blessed Name. . .Till we meet on heaven's shore. . . Redemption Songs, hymn # 898, p. 240.

p. 266

When the King come back. . . the gospel story . . . Ibid., adapted from Hymn # 530, p. 143.

p. 267

At Christmas, a star will fix itself. . . Senior, *Jamaica as It Was, as It Is, and as It May Be,* p. 264. Gardner, the head slave at Greenwich Estate, is reported to have said in his confessions that Burchell had assured them that before the following Christmas arrived, the slaves would be free, and if the Whites persisted in keeping them in slavery, a star would fix itself to the corner of the moon as a signal for them to cease labour. Rather than do any work beyond the specified time, they must trust 'to fire and sword'. It is highly unlikely, however, that Reverend Burchell would have directly incited the slaves to rebellion.

p. 269

Afforded the savages of Africa. . .enjoy in their own land. Bridges, *The Annals of Jamaica, Volume II,* p. 407.

p. 269

If you would not have your blazing canefields. . . attend to the warning voice of – Dorcas. . . Bleby, *Death Struggles of Slavery,* p. 135 quoting article in the *Courant,* August 15, 1831. It was commonly believed that Dorcas was the pen name of Rev. George Wilson Bridges, Rector of the Parish of St Ann.

p. 270

*It must be alarming, when whispered. . .in the event of disturbance. . .*Bleby, *Death Struggles of Slavery,* p. 135–6, quoting inflammatory statements printed in the *Courant* by

Umbratus (also believed to be Reverend Bridges), August 11, 1831. There is no historical evidence for supporting Bridges' claims.

p. 271

When we see ourselves scorned. . .human and Divine, to resist. Ibid., p. 142, quoting Resolution passed by St Ann public meeting, August 6, 1831.

p. 272

Earl Belmore's reports to England. On June 3, 1831, a proclamation was sent out to the governors from England stating that no order had been sent for the emancipation of slaves. The Governor of Jamaica thought it unwise to publish this proclamation, and instead, wrote back saying there was no discontent among the slaves. Earl Belmore's actual words are cited by Gardner, *A History of Jamaica*, p. 272.

Chapter Twenty-Two

p. 276

*My closest allies were there. . .*The names of all these slaves and freed men appear in historical records as persons who participated in the rebellion. One of Sam Sharpe's allies, Edward Hylton, provided many of the details of the meeting in Johnson's house at Retrieve in an interview he had in prison with Reverend Bleby.

p. 276

*Mr Mackintosh and his son. . .*Bleby, *Death Struggles of Slavery*, p. 120. These men actively participated in the rebellion even though they had already gained their freedom. When Bleby asked them why they would have done so, they said that it was because of their allegiance to Sam Sharpe and his religious beliefs.

p. 277

*We won't tek no flog no more. . .*Hart, *Slaves Who Abolished Slavery. Vol. 2: Blacks in Rebellion*, p. 249. Similar words were spoken by slaves prior to the rebellion when Reverend Waddell heard reactions to the Governor's proclamation that they should return to work.

pp. 288-89

Whereas it has been represented. . .obedience to their masters. Ibid., p. 246. This proclamation was originally issued in the name of King William IV on June 3, 1831. The Governor of Jamaica did not release it until December 22 of that same year. (PP, Vol. XLVII, pp. 276–7; Votes 1831, pp. 111–2).

pp. 290-1

My dear hearers, and especially those. . .he will not do you good. Hinton, *Memoir of William Knibb, Missionary in Jamaica,* pages 118–19, quoting a letter by William Knibb to Reverend Dyer from his own address at Salter's Hill.

p. 292

*Alarm filled every breast. . .*Bleby, *Death Struggles of Slavery,* p. 8.

Chapter Twenty-Three

p. 297

The family name 'Gray' has the alternative spelling 'Grey' in some of the historical records.

p. 300

Johnny Newcombe was a popular cartoon-like caricature of a West Indian planter, newly arrived in the colonies from England. The British artist and satirist was Thomas Rowlandson, 1756–1827.

Chapter Twenty-Four

p. 303

The main sequence of events, the battles, and the movements of individuals described in this chapter are reconstructed from historical accounts found in the following sources: Senior (1835); Bleby (1853); Grignon, Knibb (BPP); Waddell (1863); and *Report of the House of Assembly on the Slave Insurrection:*

confessions of T. Dove, deposition of W. Annand, confessions of R. Gardner (pp. 1831–2). The speeches and conversations have been imagined.

p. 307

Burchell, *Memoir of Thomas Burchell*, p. 184, notes that Mr Manderson, a gentleman of property, magistrate and member of House of Assembly, and Mr Roby tendered security for Messrs Knibb and Whitehorne. Reverend Mr Abbott was bailed out by James Guthrie, collecting constable.

pp. 307-8

But the prophet which should presume to speak a word. . .May this be the fate of all such as BURCHELL. Ibid., p. 208. It was reported that Mr T.J. Gray, proprietor of Croydon Estate (possibly Mrs Jane Sharpe's father) convened the meeting at the courthouse with the design of passing resolutions to influence representatives in the House of Assembly for the quick expulsion of the sectarians from the island.

p. 308

*We sey, Ma'am, black fowl can lay white egg. . .*A Jamaican proverb which has many meanings. Here it means that she should not be quick to judge.

p. 315

*Gardner looked like a real military man. . .*Senior, *Jamaica as It Was, as It Is, and as It May Be*, p. 211.

p. 317

It was not the work of man alone but that they had assistance from God. Brathwaite, 'The Slave Rebellion in the Great River Valley of St James, 1831–2' in the *Jamaica Historical Review*, Vol. XIII p. 25, quoting overseer at Ginger Hill (BPP XLVII [285]), 27.

p. 318

*I told him to swear that he would never stand between us and our rights. . .*Hart, *Slaves Who Abolished Slavery. Volume 2: Blacks in Rebellion*, pp. 284–5, quoting direct words of Sam Sharpe as reported by Annand (PP, Vol. XLVII, pp. 285–6, no. 18).

p. 318

Letters have long ago . . . for doing so. Ibid., pp. 284-85.

p. 318

Then, Haugton, the head driver at Shettlewood. . .Higman, *Montpelier Jamaica*, p. 266, citing accounts from Jamaica House of Assembly votes, 1831–32, pp. 321–22.

p. 320

It's a funny thing, me never see none of de White man shoot a gun. . .Two versions of this story are recorded. The one told here is from the confessions of Gardner and Dove and also found in Bleby, pp. 9–10. The other is told by Grignon in PP, Vol. XLVII, pp. 288–9, no. 23, cited by Hart, p. 281, in which he claimed that his regiment 'reserved their fire until the rebels had advanced within 30 or 40 yards, when they commenced a very rapid fire, which continued for about twenty minutes'.

p. 320

Two of them was from Montpelier. . .Higman, *Montpelier Jamaica*, p. 269.

Chapter Twenty-Five

p. 323

Oh, Sir, if I had had any good friend . . . I would never have been brought to this. Hart, *Slaves Who Abolished Slavery*, page 319 quoting from pp, vol xlvii, page 216.

p. 323

I thought I did hear that the Chief Justice. . .Hart, *Slaves Who Abolished Slavery. Volume 2: Blacks in Rebellion*, p. 319, quoting from *Facts and Documents* 12, pp. 11–12.

p. 323

Your friend was hurried to the gallows. . .Bleby, *Death Struggles of Slavery*, p. 110.

p. 324

Gardner indicated that the plan did not work. . .Senior, *Jamaica as It Was, as It Is, and as It May Be*, p. 263.

p. 325

*If I have done wrong in that. . .*Bleby, *Death Struggles of Slavery,* quoting Sam Sharpe's own words, p. 117.

p. 325

*It was my garden of Gethsemane. . .*Brathwaite, *Nanny, Sam Sharpe and the Struggle for People's Liberation,* p. 25, proposes this view of Sharpe as Christian martyr but does not necessarily subscribe to it. Originally suggested by Reverend Burchell's successor in Montego Bay, Reverend Cornford.

p. 325

*You must know, Sir, that destruction of property and murder formed no part of my plan. . .*Bleby, *Death Struggles of Slavery,* pp. 116–17, comments on his conversations with Sam Sharpe in prison.

p. 327

*A handful of the Montpelier slaves. . .tried to defend their Massa's buildings. . .*Higman, *Montpelier Jamaica,* p. 270, notes that it was not unusual for slaves to defend their own master's property.

p. 328

*The Gubna declare martial law. . .*On the recommendation of General Cotton, Governor Belmore declared martial law on Friday, December 30, 1831.

p. 329

*Before setting out, we prepared a big feast . .*Hart, *Slaves Who Abolished Slavery. Volume 2: Blacks in Rebellion,* p. 287, cites incident as reported in PP, Vol. XLVII pp. 283–4, no. 16.

p. 331

*That following day, the General released from gaol about a hundred prisoners. . .*Ibid., page 293, quotes in full the Proclamation from PP, Vol. XLVII, p. 288, no 21: *The Watchman,* January 4, 1832.

p. 332

When questioned by the soldiers, prisoners openly confessed. . .

Ibid., p. 295, quotes the report of Sir Willoughby Cotton to the governor, Earl of Belmore: PP, Vol. XLVII, p. 291, no. 25.

Chapter Twenty-Six

p. *337*

*Do they suppose. . .and go unpunished. . .*Ibid., p. 302, quoting from an editorial of the *Watchman*, January 7, 1832.

p. 338

They thought the only way to bring the Negroes to their senses. . . Senior, *Jamaica as It Was, as It Is, and as It May Be*, p. 238.

p. 344

*He told everybody that it was the intention of the Negroes to burn the properties. . .*Hart, *Slaves Who Abolished Slavery, Volume 2: Blacks in Rebellion*, p. 316, citing witness account of Thomas M'Neel who spoke about Dehany after his capture. PP, Vol. XLVII, pages 197–8.

pp. 344-5

And whereas there is a reason to believe. . .commands of their masters or managers. Senior, *Jamaica as It Was, as It Is, and as It May Be*, pp. 252–3.

p. 346

I am directing my observations. . .the same fate as the cane fields of your masters. Higman, *Montpelier Jamaica*, p. 274, quoting Belmore to Goderich, February 20, 1832, C.S.O., Dispatches, pp. 54–55, Jamaica Archives.

p. 346

*How d'ye, Massa, how d'ye mass buckra?. . .*Senior, *Jamaica as It Was, as It Is, and as It May Be*, p. 245.

Chapter Twenty-Seven

p. 348

The Lord forgave those. . .when his faithful will come there to enjoy them. This narrative is a summary and interpretation of the second half of Bunyan's *The Holy War*. See chapter 15.

p. 352

*Dove they committed to the hulks in England. . .*Senior, *Jamaica as It Was, as It Is, and as It May Be*, p. 266. Hulks were prison ships in England.

p. 353

The Baptist ministers are now in custody. . .carnage and slaughter, shall cease. Gardner, *A History of Jamaica*, p. 278, quoting an article printed in the *Courant*.

p. 353

The semi-savage race of beings . . .This expression is used by Senior, p. 221. Similar sentiments are expressed by Reverend George Wilson Bridges in his dissertation on 'The Original State of Negroes in their Native Land' in *The Annals of Jamaica*, Vol. 2 (1828), p. 398 ff.

p. 354

*And if word had spread to the other parishes of the capture of land and of towns, then the whole of Jamaica would have freed itself from slavery. . .*This theory is not far-fetched. There were reports of unrest in other parts of the island. Defences were strengthened at Manchioneal and a man-of-war was sent to Morant Bay because of the threat of rebellion in the northeast and in response to slaves not reporting to work (PP, Vol. XLVII pp. 290–1, no. 24; pp. 240–4, no. 7). Cited by Hart, p. 296. There were also reports of violence in Manchester. Word of the rebellion presumably had spread to other parts of the island.

Epilogue

p. 369

It was estimated that between 20,000 and 50,000 slaves and their supporters fought in the rebellion. In the slave courts of St James, Hanover, Trelawney, Westmoreland, St Elizabeth, Portland, Manchester, St Thomas in the Vale and St Thomas in the East, a total of 626 slaves were tried of whom 312 were executed. (Reckford, 1968, provides a summary of statistics by parish). These numbers do not include over a thousand slaves shot in battle.

Sam Sharpe was the last of the rebels to be executed. Several historical accounts of Sharpe's execution exist: Bleby in *Death Struggles of Slavery*, Reverend P.H. Cornford in the *Freeman*, 1855; article in the *Jamaica Watchman*, May 26, 1832. C.S. Reid in *Samuel Sharpe: From Slave to National Hero* is also a good source of information.

p. 369

*Minister Bleby's Narrative. . .*The narrative is reconstructed here from different works. Sections marked with asterisks are direct quotations drawn from sources cited. These are embedded in a narrative to retell the story of Sam's execution as if Reverend Bleby were writing it.

p. 369

His face was bright as if he had achieved some glorious victory. Description by Cornford published in the *Freeman*, 1855.

p. 370

Gentlemen, I have rebelled. . . will not be visited up by any of my fellow creatures. Reid, *Samuel Sharpe, From Slavery to National Hero,* quoting Sam Sharpe's words, pp. 92–3.

p. 371

*When he reached the top step. . .the heels of the feet about twenty inches apart. . .*Ibid., p. 93, quoting the *Watchman*, May 26, 1832.

p. 371

I have transgressed against the laws. . .the only way for you to go to salvation. Robinson, *Fight for Freedom*, pp. 161–2.

pp. 371-2

All I wished was to be free. . .but I cannot say exactly that I am going to heaven. Gordon, *God Almighty Make Me Free. . .* p. 97, quoting Sam Sharpe's own words before his execution, May 23, 1832, cited in Bleby, *Death Struggles of Slavery.*

p. 372

In a few moments the executioner. . . revolt had ceased to exist; I witnessed the execution . . . the polluted shrine of slavery. Ibid., pp. 118

p. 373

Samuel Sharpe was the most remarkable and intelligent slave I had ever known. Ibid., pp. 115.

p. 373

They buried him in the sands of the seashore ... bathed with luster his lowly place of rest. Quoted by Brathwaite, *Nanny, Sam Sharpe and the Struggle for People's Liberation*, page 25, quoting P.H. Cornford, The Freeman, 10 October, 1855, citing Mr. L. Leving.

p. 374

*My health seems perfectly restored. . .our poor murdered people in Jamaica. . .*Clarke, *The Voice of Jubilee: A Narrative of the Baptist Mission in Jamaica,* p. 69, quoting Reverend Thomas Burchell's words.

p. 374

That it is the opinion of this committee. . .with the interests of the proprietors. F.R. Augier and S.C. Gordon, *Sources of West Indian History,* pp. 139, 141–2.

BIBLIOGRAPHY

Books and Articles

Alleyne, Mervyn. *Africa: Roots of Jamaican Culture.* Chicago: Frontline Distribution International Inc., 1989.

Allsopp, Richard. *Dictionary of Caribbean English Usage.* Oxford: Oxford University Press, 1996.

Anderson, Izett, and Frank Cundall. *Jamaica Proverbs and Sayings.* Shannon, Ireland: Irish University Press, 1972.

Augier, F.R., and S.C. Gordon. *Sources of West Indian History.* London: Longman Group Ltd., 1962.

Augier, F.R., S.C. Gordon, D.G. Hall, and M. Reckford. *The Making of the West Indies.* London: Longman Group Ltd., 1960.

Austen, Jane. *Emma.* London: Longmans (1966), 1816.

Barrett, Leonard E. *The Sun and the Drum.* Kingston, Jamaica: Sangster's Book Stores Ltd., 1976.

Beckwith, Martha Warren. *Black Roadways: A Study of Jamaican Folk Life.* New York: Negro Universities Press, 1969.

Belmore, Somerset Loury-Corry, 2nd Earl. 1774–1841. Papers 1. Microfilm. UWI, Mona.

Berlin, Ira, M. Favreau, and S.F. Miller (eds.). *Remembering Slavery: African Americans Talk about their Personal Experiences of Slavery.* New York: The New Press, 1998.

Berry, James. *Anancy Spiderman.* London: Walker Books, 1988.

Bickell, Richard. *The West Indies as they are, or, A Real Picture of Slavery: But More Particularly as it Exists in the Island of Jamaica.* London: J. Hatchard and Son, 1825.

Bleby, Henry. *Death Struggles of Slavery.* London: Hamilton, Adams and Co., 1835.

Brathwaite, Edward Kamau. *The Development of Creole Society in Jamaica: 1770–1820.* Oxford: Clarendon Press, 1971.

———. 'Kumina: The Spirit of African Survival in Jamaica.' in *Jamaica Journal* # 42 (1978): 45, 1978.

———. *Nanny, Sam Sharpe and the Struggle for People's Liberation.* Published by the API for the National Heritage Week Committee, 1976.

———. 'The Slave Rebellion in the Great River Valley of St James.' 1831–2 in *The Jamaica Historical Review,* Vol. XIII, 1982. pp. 11–31.

Bridges, George Wilson. *The Annals of Jamaica. Volumes 1 and 2.* London, England: Frank Cass & Co. Ltd, 1968 (1828).

British Parliamentary Papers — House of Commons Accounts and Papers. Vol. XX, House of Lords Sessional Papers: British Museum Library, London. (Quoted by Reid).

Brown, Beverley. 'George Liele: Black Baptist and Pan-Africanist: 1750–1826.' In *Savacou* 11/12, 1975. pp. 58–67.

Buisseret, David. *Historic Jamaica from the Air.* Kingston, Jamaica: Ian Randle Publishers, 1996.

Bunyan, John. *The Holy War.* Christian Focus. 1993. Reprint, New Kensington, PA: Whitaker House, 1996.

Burchell, William Fitzer. *Memoir of Thomas Burchell.* London: Benjamin L. Green, 1849.

Carey, Bev. *The Maroon Story.* St Andrew, Jamaica: Agouti Press, Maroon Publishing House, 2001.

Cassidy, F.G., and R.B. Le Page. *Dictionary of Jamaican English.* Kingston, Jamaica: University of the West Indies Press, 2002.

Cassidy, Frederic G. *Jamaica Talk: Three Hundred Years of the English Language in Jamaica.* London: MacMillan Education Ltd., 1961.

Chevannes, Barry. 'Revival and Black Struggle.' In *Savacou,* 5 (1971): 27–39.

Clarke, John, W. Dendy, and J.M. Phillippo. *The Voice of Jubilee: A Narrative of the Baptist Mission in Jamaica.* London: J. Snow, 1865.

Craton, Michael. *Searching for the Invisible Man: Slaves and Plantation Life in Jamaica.* Cambridge, Massachusetts: Harvard University Press, 1978.

Cross, Wilbur. *The Yale Shakespeare.* New York: Barnes and Noble, 1993.

Cundall, Frank. *Chronological Outlines of Jamaica History.* Kingston, Jamaica: Government Printing Office for the Institute of Jamaica, 1927.

Curtin, Philip D. *Two Jamaicas: The Role of Ideas in a Tropical Colony: 1830–1865.* Cambridge, Massachusetts: Harvard University Press, 1955.

Dick, Devon. *From Rebellion to Riot.* Kingston, Jamaica: Ian Randle Publishers, 2003.

Edwards, Bryan. *The History Civil and Commercial of the British Colonies in the West Indies. 3 Volumes.* London: J. Stockdale, 1801.

Ephirim-Donkor, Anthony. *African Spirituality: On Becoming Ancestors.* Trenton, New Jersey: Africa World Press, Inc., 1997.

Farwell, Byron. *The Encyclopedia of Nineteenth-Century Land Warfare: An Illustrated World View.* New York: W.W. Norton & Company, 2001.

Gardner, William J. *A History of Jamaica.* London: Frank Cass and Co. 1970, (1873).

Gates, Henry Louis, ed. *Six Women's Slave Narratives.* London: Oxford University Press, 1988.

Gordon, Shirley C. *God Almighty Make Me Free: Christianity in Preemancipation Jamaica.* Bloomington and Indianapolis: Indiana University Press, 1996.

———. *Our Cause for His Glory: Christianization and Emancipation in Jamaica.* Kingston, Jamaica: University of the West Indies Press, 1998.

Goveia, E.V., and C.J. Bartlett. *The West Indian Slave Laws in the 18th Century and a New Balance of Power: The 19th Century.* London: The Whitefriars Press Ltd., 1970.

Great Britain. *Jamaica: Dispatches from Governors.* Microfilm. University of the West Indies, Mona, 1832.

Grignon, William. *Vindication of the Conduct of Colonel Grignon and of the Western Interior Regiment.* Falmouth, Jamaica, 1833.

Hall, Douglas. *In Miserable Slavery: Thomas Thistlewood in Jamaica: 1750–86.* Kingston, Jamaica. University of the West Indies Press, 1999.

Hart, Richard. *Slaves Who Abolished Slavery. Volume 2: Blacks in Rebellion.* Jamaica: Institute of Social and Economic Research, University of the West Indies, 1985.

Hawke, Harry, ed. *Complete Lyrics of Bob Marley*. New York: Omnibus Press, 2001.

Heuman, Gad J. *Between Black and White: Race, Politics, and the Free Coloureds in Jamaica, 1792-1865*. Westport, Connecticut: Greenwood Press, 1981.

Higman, B.W. *Jamaica Surveyed*. University of the West Indies Press, 1988.

———. *Montpelier Jamaica: A Plantation Community in Slavery and Freedom, 1739–1912*. Kingston, Jamaica: University of the West Indies Press, 1998.

———. *Slave Population and Economy in Jamaica: 1807–1834*. Kingston, Jamaica: University of the West Indies Press, 1995.

Hinton, J.H. *Memoir of William Knibb, Missionary in Jamaica*. London: Houlston and Stoneman, 1847.

Hodges, Graham Russell, ed. *Black Itinerants of the Gospel: The Narratives of John Jea and George White*. Madison: Madison House, 1993.

Hogg, D.W. 'The Convince Cult in Jamaica' In *Papers in Caribbean Anthropology* compiled by Sidney W. Mintz. New Haven: Yale University Press, 1970. pp. 3–23.

Holy Bible, The, containing the Old and New Testaments in the Authorized King James *Version*. North Carolina: Good Will Publishers, 1960. *Jamaica: Journals of the House of Assembly*. (#56) 1831–1832, 47.

Jekyll, Walter. *Jamaica Song and Story*. New York: Dover Publications, 1966.

Johnson, James Weldon, and J. Rosamond Johnson. *The Books of American Negro Spirituals*. New York: The Viking Press, 1925.

Lewin, Olive. *Rock It Come Over: The Folk Music of Jamaica*. Kingston, Jamaica: University of the West Indies Press, 2000.

Lewis, Matthew. *Journal of a West India Proprietor*. London: G. Routledge and Sons Ltd., 1999 (1823).

Long, Edward. *History of Jamaica*. London: Frank Cass and Co. Ltd., 1970 (1774).

McCalman, Ian, ed. *The Horrors of Slavery and Other Writings by Robert Wedderburn*. Kingston, Jamaica: Ian Randle Publishers, 1997.

Madden, R.R. *A Twelvemonth's Residence in the West Indies*. London: James Cochrane & Co., 1835.

Marly, or A Planter's Life in Jamaica. Glasgow: Richard Griffin & Co., 1828.

Mathieson, William Law. *British Slavery and its Abolition: 1823–1838*. London: Longmans, Green and Co. Ltd., 1926.

Mintz, Sidney, and Douglas Hall. 'The Origins of the Jamaican Internal Marketing System.' Reprinted in *Caribbean Slave Society and Economy: A Student Reader*. Edited by Hilary Beckles and Verene Shepherd. London: James Currey Publishers, 1991 (1970).

Moreton, J.B. *Manners and Customs in the West India Islands*. London: J. Parsons, Paternoster Row, 1793.

Nugent, Maria Lady. *Lady Nugent's Journal of her Residence in Jamaica from 1801 to 1805*. Kingston, Jamaica: Institute of Jamaica, 1966.

Patterson, Orlando. *The Sociology of Slavery*. London: Fairleigh Dickinson University Press, 1967.

Perkins, Cyrus Francis. *Busha's Mistress or Catherine the Fugitive*. Kingston, Jamaica: Ian Randle Publisher, 2003.

Phillippo, James M. *Jamaica: Its Past and Present State*. London: John Snow, 1843.

Phillips, Anghelen Arrington, and Geoffrey de Sola Pinto. *Jamaican Houses: A Vanishing Legacy*. Montego Bay, Jamaica: De Sola Pinto Publishers, 1993.

Phillips, Caryl. *Crossing the River*. Toronto: Vintage Books Canada, 1995.

Raboteau, Albert J. *Slave Religion: The Invisible Institution in the Antebellum South*. New York: Oxford University Press, 1978.

Rampini, Charles Joseph Galliari. *Letters from Jamaica: The Land of Streams and Woods*. Edinburgh: Edmonston and Douglas, 1873.

Reckford, Mary. 'The Slave Rebellion of 1831'. In *Past and Present* no. 40, 1968. pp. 108–125.

Redemption Songs: A Choice Collection of One Thousand Hymns and Choruses. London: Pickering & Inglis, 1925.

Reid, C.S. *Samuel Sharp: From Slave to National Hero*. Jamaica: The Bustamante Institute of Public and International Affairs,

1988.

Reid, Vic. *Peter of Mount Ephraim*. Kingston: Jamaica Publishing House, 1971.

Royal Gazette (Kingston, Jamaica). 1823–34.

Robinson, Carey. *Fight for Freedom*. Kingston, Jamaica: Kingston Publishers Ltd., 1987.

Schuler, Monica. 'Myalism and the African Religious Tradition in Jamaica.' In *Africa and the Caribbean: Legacies of a Link*. Edited by Margaret E. Crahan and Franklin W. Knight. Baltimore and London: The Johns Hopkins University Press, 1979.

Seaga, Edward. 'Revival Cults in Jamaica: Notes towards a Sociology of Religion.' In *Jamaica Journal* 3, no. 2: 3–13, 1969.

Senior, B.M. *Jamaica as It Was, as It Is, and as It May Be*. London: T. Hurst, 1835.

Senior, Olive. *Encyclopedia of Jamaican Heritage*. Kingston, Jamaica: Twin Guinep Publishers Ltd., 2003.

Shepherd, Verene, and Hilary McD. Beckles, eds. *Caribbean Slavery in the Atlantic World*. Oxford: James Currey Publishers, 2000.

Shepherd, Verene A., and Ahmed Reid. 'Rebel Voices: Testimonies from the 1831–32 Emancipation War in Jamaica'. In *Jamaica Journal*. 27, nos. 2–3, 2004. The Institute of Jamaica, 2000. pp. 54–63.

Sherlock, Phillip. *Shout for Freedom: A Tribute to Sam Sharpe*. London: Macmillan Education Ltd., 1976.

Sherlock, Philip, and Hazel Bennett. *The Story of the Jamaican People*. Kingston, Jamaica: Ian Randle Publishers, 1998.

Stewart, J. *View of the Past and Present State of the Island of Jamaica; with Remarks on* the Moral and Physical Condition of the Slaves and on the Abolition of Slavery in *the Colonies*. New York: Negro University Press, 1969 (1823).

Styron, William. *The Confessions of Nat Turner*. New York: Vintage International, 1966.

Taylor, Yuval. *I Was Born a Slave: An Anthology of Classic Slave Narratives*. Chicago: Lawrence Hill Books, 1999.

Turner, Mary. *Slaves and Missionaries: The Disintegration of Jamaican Slave Society, 1787–1834*. Kingston, Jamaica: University of the West Indies Press, 1998.

Viotti de Costa. *Crowns of Glory, Tears of Blood: The Demarara Slave Rebellion of 1823.* London: Oxford University Press, 1994.

Waddell, Rev. Hope Masterton. *Twenty-nine Years in the West Indies and Central Africa: A Review of Missionary Life and Adventure: 1829–1858.* London: T. Nelson & Sons, 1863.

Williams, Cynric R. *A Tour through the Island of Jamaica, from the Western to the Eastern End, in the Year 1823.* London: T. Hurst, E. Chance & Co., 1827.

Wright, Phillip. *Knibb the "Notorious" Slaves' Missionary 1803–1845.* London: Sidgwick & Jackson, 1973.